VIOLENCE

AND

THE DREAM PEOPLE

Federation of Malaya, 1948–1960

VIOLENCE

AND

THE DREAM PEOPLE

The Orang Asli in the Malayan Emergency 1948–1960

John D. Leary

OHIO UNIVERSITY CENTER FOR INTERNATIONAL STUDIES
MONOGRAPHS IN INTERNATIONAL STUDIES
SOUTHEAST ASIA SERIES NUMBER 95

Printed in the United States of America

Printed on acid-free paper ∞
02 01 00 99 98 97 96 95 5 4 3 2 1

LIBRARY OF CONGRESS CATALOGING-IN-PUBLICATION DATA
Leary, John D.
Violence and the dream people: the Orang Asli in the Malayan emergency, 1948-1960/John Leary
p. cm. – (Monographs in International Studies. Southeast Asia series; no 95)
Includes bibliographical references and index.
ISBN 0-89680-186-1 (pbk.)
1. Senoi (Malaysian people)—History. 2. Malaya—History—Malayan Emergency, 1948-1960. 3. Jakun (Malaysian people)—History. 4. Semang (Malaysian people)—History. I. Title. II. Series.
959.5'104–dc20 95-10758
CIP

This series of publications on Africa, Latin America, and Southeast Asia is designed to present significant research, translation, and opinion to area specialists and to a wide community of persons interested in world affairs. The editor seeks manuscripts of quality on any subject and can generally make a decision regarding publication within three months of receipt of the original work. Production methods generally permit a work to appear within one year of acceptance. The editor works closely with authors to produce a high quality book. The series appears in a paperback format and is distributed worldwide. For more information, contact the executive editor at Ohio University Press, Scott Quadrangle, University Terrace, Athens, Ohio 45701.

Cover and text designed by Chiquita Babb
Cover illustration: Two Young Senoi

The Monographs in International Studies series is published for the Center for International Studies by the Ohio University Press. The views expressed in individual monographs are those of the authors and should not be considered to represent the policies or beliefs of the Center for International Studies, the Ohio University Press, or Ohio University.

CONTENTS

MAPS & ILLUSTRATIONS

Maps

Plates

Illustrations

GLOSSARY AND ABBREVIATIONS

Arkib Negara	National Archives of Malaysia
ASP	Assistant Superintendent of Police
Asli	Original or source (Malay), Asal—origin
Atap or Attap	Palm thatch
Batin	Aborigine Headman
BCM	Branch Committee Member
Bren Gun	Light maching gun (WW2 and Post-war vintage)
CT	Communist Terrorist
DO	District Officer
DZ	Dropping zone for air drops or paratroops
DCM	District Committee Member (MCP)
DWEC	District War Executive Committee
FARELF	Far East Land Forces
FJC	Federal Jungle Company (Police)
Force 136	British W. W. II clandestine unit in Southeast Asia
Gunong (Gunung)	Mountain (Malay)
Gurkha	Nepalese mercenary in British Army
Ibans	Sarawak (Borneo) tribesmen used as guides by Security Forces
Jahat	Wicked (Malay)
Jelutong	Wild rubber
Kampong/Kampung	Malay village
Ladang	Aboriginal cultivated area
LZ	Landing zone for helicopters
Mentri Besar	Chief Minister (Malay)
MCP	Malayan Communist Party
MCA	Malayan Chinese Association
Merdeka	Free, Independent (Malay); in this context it means independence

Min Yuen	Ming Chong Yuen Tong, Peoples' Movement
MM	Malay Mail
MPABA	Malayan Peoples Anti-British Army
MPAJA	Malayan Peoples Anti-Japanese Army
MRLA	Malayan Races Liberation Army
OCPD	Officer commanding Police District
Orang	Classifier for Person (Malay), Orang Melayu Asli, Proto Malay
PAG	Police Aboriginal Guard
Parang	Machete
Penglulu	Malay Headman
PFF	Police Field Force
PRO	Public Record Office, Kew
RAF	Royal Air Force
RAAF	Royal Australian Air Force
RNZAF	Royal New Zealand Air Force
Sakai	General derogatory name for Aborigines
SAS	Special Air Service
SB	Straits Budget
Sel. Sec.	Selangor Secretariat
Semang (Negrito)	Small mainly nomadic Aboriginal group
Senoi	Major Aboriginal group
SF	Security Forces
Senoi Pra'ak or Pra'aq	Armed Aboriginal unit
SEP	Surrendered Enemy Personnel
SOVF	Special Operations Volunteer Force
Squadron	SAS unit of approx 50–100 men
Spitfire	World War II Fighter aircraft (British)
Squatters	Chinese living in illegal small-holdings on jungle fringe
SS	Singapore Standard
ST	Straits Times
Sten Gun	Sub-machine gun (British) WW II
Sungei/Sungai	River (Malay)
SWEC	State War Executive Committee
Troop	SAS unit approx 15 to 25 men
UMNO	United Malays National Organization
Venom	British jet fighter aircraft 1950s

PREFACE AND ACKNOWLEDGMENTS

In his paper "Achievements and Gaps in Orang Asli Studies," Geoffrey Benjamin stated, "Professional document-based historical study of the Orang Asli has barely begun. . . . and no one currently seems interested in pursuing it."[1] This book will cover some of that missing historical study in a particularly traumatic period of Orang Asli history, the Malayan Emergency. It is not intended to be a chronological account of what happened in Malaya between 1948 and 1960. Neither does it deal with great captains or generals; the armed clashes recounted are generally small skirmishes in which often no more than half a dozen combatants were involved. Many of the fighting men from both sides are not mentioned, not because their role was unimportant, but because they were not closely involved with the subject of this treatise.

This work is a positive effort to interpret the role of the Orang Asli in the Emergency and by so doing to discount the myth that for some cultural reason they were not capable of violence. It will also recount acts of violence against them which, in turn, caused them to react ferociously.

It would be overzealous to claim that this text is the definitive, scholastically pure, and fully documented narrative of events. Some documents in the *Arkib Negara* (National Archives) in Malaysia and the PRO Kew have not yet been declassified. Others are held in secret files not available to either the researcher or the general public. Although it has not been possible to obtain copies of documents from the Malayan Communist Party or to interview Chinese members of that organization, some captured documents from those sources are used. Comprehensive use has been made of archival material, but a proportion of the information has been obtained from English and Malay language newspapers. Printing and publication of newspapers required a permit from the Chief Secretary[2] and therefore writers were careful about the content. Most of their information on the daily happenings in the Emergency came from official sources or were gleaned on officially conducted tours. Some of the reports from protagonists, particularly members of the Security Force, are both anecdotal and personal views, but that does not necessarily mean they are historically incorrect or unimportant.

Orang Asli personal accounts of their involvement in the Emergency are purely oral. They are generally pre-literate and their conception of time is different from ours. They relate time to natural occurrences, or their group's misfortune or joyous occasion. Nonetheless their contributions are among the most significant gleaned during my research into the subject. I regard an interview with two former members of the MRLA controlled Asal Protection Corps[3] as one of the more important historical contributions of this work to our knowledge of the effect of the Emergency on the Orang Asli.

There are a few comments to be made on expressions used in the text. Where sources are paraphrased, the original descriptions to identify particular individuals or groups will be used. If the source material uses the words *bandit* or *Communist Terrorist* (*CT*) for a member of the Malayan Communist Party (MCP) or Malayan Races Liberation Army (MRLA) the text will also use that expression. Again, if the Orang Asli are referred to as *Sakai or Aborigine,* those terms will be included in the narrative. None of these politically or racially offensive terms reflect the personal views of the writer. The glossary will supply explanations for all abbreviations used.

Notes

1. G. Benjamin, *Achievement and Gaps in Orang Asli Studies* (Singapore, 1988), 19.

2. A. Short, *The Communist Insurrection in Malaya 1948–1960* (London, 1975), 141–42.

3. The details of the Asal Protection Corps are covered extensively in Chapter Four.

Acknowledgments

I would like to offer my grateful thanks to the following people for their assistance in putting this thesis together.

Australia

My supervisor Professor M. C. Ricklefs, for his patience, invaluable advice, and counsel in directing me during the writing of this work; Ms. Helen Hart, who helped me with my English expression and punctuation; Mrs. Doris (Billie) Russell who retyped this manuscript at least ten times and my fellow students and other members of the staff at Monash who freely gave assistance and advice.

Singapore

Professor Geoffrey Benjamin, Singapore University, for supplying me with his Working Papers and giving me good advice on how to proceed and Dr. Paul Kratoska, Singapore University, who was unsparing with his knowledge of colonial files and who gave me invaluable lists of those files to consult.

Malaysia

Anthony Williams-Hunt without whose assistance I would have found it difficult to contact the Orang Asli I met in Malaysia and obtain their versions of what happened to their people in the Emergency; Professor Lim Teck Ghee, Institute of Advanced Studies, University of Malaya, Kuala Lumpur, for helping me obtain documents from the Selangor Secretariat; and Colin Nicholas for his contribution to my awareness of present day Orang Asli problems.

And the many other people, some who asked not to be named, who helped me with my research.

Finally, my wife Ursula who put up with the mess of papers in my room and gave me every encouragement with this book.

VIOLENCE

AND

THE DREAM PEOPLE

INTRODUCTION

The Orang Asli—The Emergency

Before the onset of the Malayan Emergency in June 1948, the Orang Asli of Peninsular Malaya were generally ignored by the majority of the Malayan populace. Many urban dwellers did not know that they even existed.[1] An estimated sixty percent of the tribespeople were located in the most inaccessible areas of the country, such as the main mountain range and deep in the remoter areas of the jungle and swamps. The Emergency was to have such a traumatic effect on their lifestyle that it would force them into the public arena and make their isolation from national events no longer possible.

This study will examine the effect of that Emergency on the three major Orang Asli groups with emphasis on those who lived in the deep jungle. Particular attention will be paid to the violent acts that they committed and those that were committed against them by outsiders. Resultant internecine acts of savagery caused by their unwitting involvement in an armed conflict they neither understood nor wanted will be analyzed.

This is a historical account of those small-scale societies' efforts to come to terms with the hostile and brutal circumstance initially forced upon their people. The various endeavours used by members of these groups to deal with the violence and to preserve their own interests will be examined. It is not within the scope of this work to develop hypotheses about the anthropological and ethnographic consequences of the incursions into these societies' culture and lifestyle during the Emergency, but it is intended to be controversial and to question the myths concerning the pacifity of the Orang Asli.

Orang Asli

The Orang Asli were widespread throughout Malaya but their population numbers have always been a matter of contention. The 1947 census gave their total number as 34,737 out of a total population of 4.9 million in Malaya,[2] but this figure was disputed in 1952 by P. D. Williams-Hunt, the Federal Adviser on Aborigines, who claimed that the figures should have been nearer 100,000.[3] Later censuses, however, tend to favor a figure closer to that of the 1947 census.[4]

The Orang Asli were classified into three separate heterogeneous groups (see map 1). These groups, with approximate population percentages were:

Semang	In the north and northeast	5%
(Negrito) Senoi	In the main range area of the Peninsula	62%
Orang Melayu Asli (Proto-Malay or Jakun)	In the center and south	33%

The lifestyles of the tribespeople ranged from the subsistence existence of some wandering-hunting Semang, through semi-nomadic cultivators, to settled hamlet dwellers leading a life similar to the average rural Malay.[5]

The Senoi were the most populous of the Orang Asli groups and were located in areas that from the beginning of the Emergency in 1948 were the scenes of intense activity by both the Malayan Races Liberation Army (MRLA)—the armed force of the Malayan Communist Party (MCP)—and the Security Forces.

The two major Senoi tribes, the Semai and the Temiar, feature prominently in this study because of their involvement with the opposing forces in the Emergency and because of their geographical location. Some lived close to the main trunk road between Kuala Lumpur and Ipoh, or in the Cameron Highlands area of Perak and Pahang states and others in the remote jungle areas of Perak, Northwest Pahang, Kelantan and North Selangor. They were continually harassed by one or other of the conflicting parties. Although the Senoi, like the other Orang Asli groups, were often depicted as passive outsiders led, drawn, or coerced into the armed struggle, they knew where their interests lay and supported the most active and seemingly superior armed force in their particular area.

It is not proposed to dissect the ethnic origins, the languages, or the cultural and religious practices of the three categories of Orang Asli. Individual groups have been studied extensively by anthropologists and ethnographers since the Emergency. Skeat and Blagden, in the early part of this century, followed by Iskander Carey in the 1960s, have published descriptive accounts of the Orang Asli as a whole.[6]

It is necessary to digress and discuss the belief in the pacifity of the Orang Asli, in particular the Senoi. Although they were not the only group affected by the Emergency, the high degree of their involvement in that armed conflict made them the prime case study when dealing with Orang Asli violence. The proposition that they were a gentle, unaggressive people was based on the findings of a limited number of anthropologists who appeared to act as their apologists rather than objective observers.

Despite the historical and anecdotal evidence available concerning Orang Asli violence against both sides and against each other, there was and is a persistent belief that they are generally a timid nonviolent group of people. This belief persists about the Senoi in particular and was fuelled by non-Malays who had contact with them either as administrators or anthropologists or in one remarkable case, a psychologist. Many of these people wrote about the peacefulness of the Senoi and in the same article or book gave examples of violence committed by them for revenge, through custom, or through necessity. Richard Noone who became Adviser on

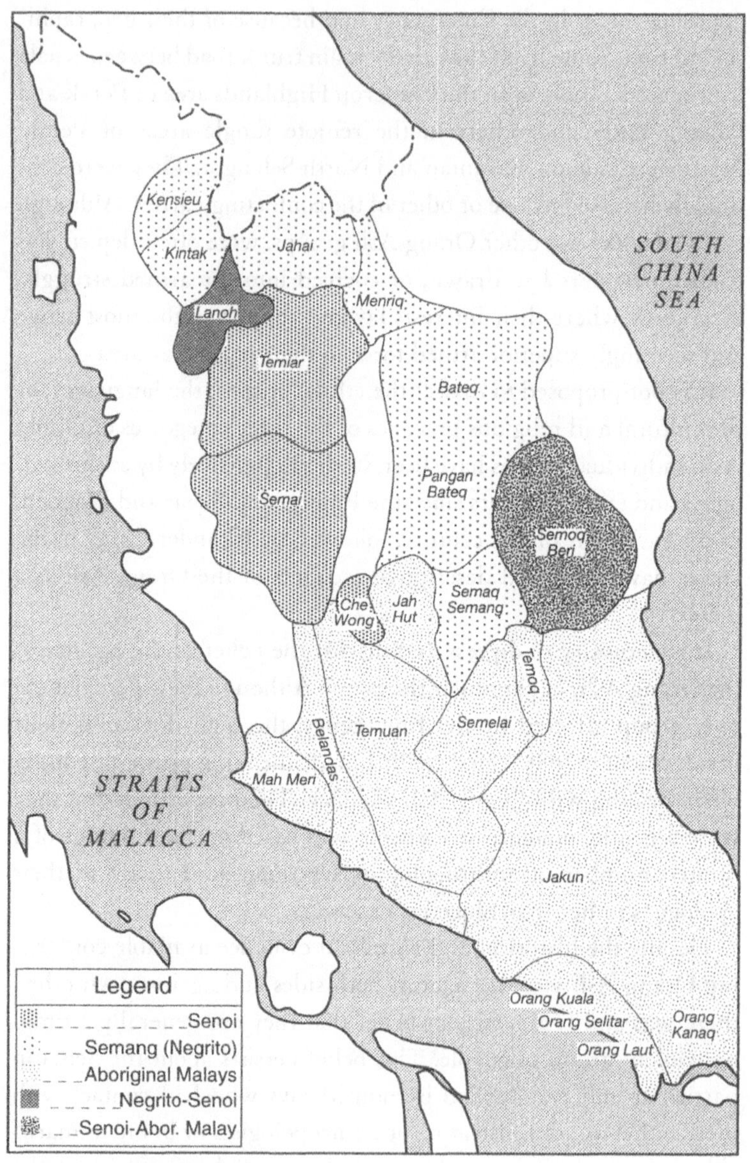

Map 1. Aboriginal Races of Malaya, 1950

Aborigines in 1953 and later commander of a Senoi fighting unit, the Senoi Pra'aq,[7] said of a major Senoi group the Temiar:

> They were a pacific people and, from what Pat [his brother] had established regarding their social psychology, emotionally too well adjusted to be capable of committing any act that was violent or resulted in violence. Crime and fighting were unknown to them: they considered selfishness the greatest sin.[8]

In the same book he wrote that toward the end of the Emergency his unit, which was composed mostly of Senoi including Temiar, eliminated a gang of eight terrorists. He went on to boast that in 1959 and 1960 that unit's record of elimination of terrorists was higher than any other unit operating in Malaya.[9]

H. D. Noone and the Temiar

In 1936 Noone's brother, H. D. [Pat], wrote that the Temiar confined crime and legal procedure basically to marriage contract quarrels. The implication was that breaches of these agreements justified violence on the part of the wronged party. If blood was shed, then through an agreed formula, the group that had lost more than the other was allowed to even the score by claiming the imbalance in casualties; this stopped the feud. Whatever the later rationalization of the occurrence, people were killed.

Noone also told of Chinese traders' huts being burned when they demanded payment of debts that the Temiar considered grossly inflated by exorbitant interest. In another case a Chinese was reported killed when he tried to seduce a Temiar woman.[10] It is ironic that Pat Noone, who wrote about and believed in the peaceful Senoi, was discovered to have been blowpiped to death by a Temiar blood brother in what amounted to a dispute over his Temiar wife, Anjang.[11]

Pat Noone's letters to his parents and brothers about the Senoi Temiar were full of hyperbole about their phenomenal emotional maturity. His brother Richard wrote that "he would uncover the strange secret by which this remarkable state was achieved—through the manipulation of dreams."[12] Apart from these letters and later conversations with his brother there is no record of Noone's researches into the Temiar dream manipulation. He does deal with the spiritual element in Temiar society but concentrates his few comments on the function of the *hulu* (medicine man) as an intermediary between man and the world of spirits, with a promise to publish a fuller account later.[13]

His record of the investigation into dream manipulation may have been with his documents that were lost during the Japanese occupation of Malaya.[14] Noone did present an outline of his Ph.D. thesis at Cambridge in 1939 entitled, "Dream Experience and Spirit Guides in the Religion of the Temiar Senoi of Malaya."[15] In reply to questions on how he was able to prove that the people whose dreams he was studying were not lying, he is reported by his brother to have answered:

> On journeys through the jungle he would get up during the night and sit listening to his Temiar porters talking in their sleep. In this way he frequently heard a dream unconsciously being related as it was happening. . . . Thus when the same dream was recounted to him in the morning he was able to check the dreamer's account.

Continuing his reply, he said that he had been told that the Temiar never lied when relating dream experience and his results were "sufficiently encouraging to bear out what he had often heard." He and the psychologist Kilton Stewart often checked dreams in this manner. An example was then quoted of where they had listened to one of the porters who was a *hulu* getting his instructions from his *gunig* (his familiar): if the porters performed a dance as directed by the *gunig* in the *hulu*'s dream, the familiar would empty the heavy boxes to be carried over a difficult pass on the slippery rain-soaked tracks the next day. The porters duly danced as directed and the boxes were handled the following day without complaint or difficulty as if they were in fact empty.[16]

Because of the loss of Pat Noone's documents during the Japanese occupation, we have no evidence that he conducted any type of controlled scientific investigation into the manipulation of dreams by the Temiars. His 1936 monograph on the Temiar is sufficient evidence of his anthropological and ethnographic capabilities and it is not this book's intention to question those skills. The contradiction between what is postulated by some of his reported observations about the link between Senoi dream manipulation and interpretation on the one hand, the debatable Senoi pacifity on the other, and the ideas which have been taken up by others, Stewart in particular, is the controversial point.[17]

Kilton Stewart

Kilton Stewart was a peripatetic psychologist and hypnotist who later in his career submitted a Ph.D. thesis in anthropology to the London School of Economics. It is said that "he had unusual talents as a speaker and storyteller."[18] He met Pat Noone in Malaya in 1934 and they proved to be compatible. He accompanied Noone on an expedition through Temiar territory from Lasah to Bertam which lasted sixteen days.[19] There is only one brief comment about Senoi dreams in this first visit by Stewart to their homelands.[20]

Stewart left Malaya in 1934 and did not go back until 1938. A young woman, Claudia Parsons, accompanied Stewart on this second visit. She describes the semi-idyllic conditions in which she, Stewart, and Noone lived in contrast to her expectations of living in the rough in the jungle. Instead they lived close to a not too remote Senoi village within sight of the group they hoped to study. She had her own house with a Malay servant who served early morning tea; hot water was available and beer with delicacies such as tongue, curries, and a gorgonzola cheese helped to sustain her. Stewart and Noone would spend their days in the village studying the inhabitants and then return at night and dictate their findings to her.[21] Parsons does not give us any idea what methods were used by the two men, how scientific were their researches, or what controls were used in attaining their results.

By 1954 Stewart was writing that "the Senoi personality is a miracle to minds built up by Western thinking. It is such an oddity that both scientific and religious prejudice prevent Westerners from believing that it exists, unless they see clearly how it comes about in terms of Western religion, philosophy and psychology."[22] The point he was espousing was that through their "dream education" the preliterate Senoi turned their children into emotionally and intellectually healthy individuals. This system, if adopted in the West, would be capable of obviating the need for corporal punishment, police, and mental institutions to stop individual and group violence.[23]

According to Stewart, the education of the Senoi child commenced at breakfast when the parent asked the child about his dream, praised him for having the dream, and discussed its significance. The questioner then queried past incidents and "(told) the child how to change his behaviour and attitude in future dreams. He (the parent) also recommended certain social activities or gestures which the dream makes necessary or advisable."[24] The child was taught to face his enemies and fears in his dreams and to kill in them if necessary. By doing so the dreamer killed what is bad even though the antagonist may have used "a good image as a disguise."[25] The Senoi adult encouraged the child to apologize on awakening for anti-social actions he initiated in his dreams. The dream figure that was offended by the dreamer was only a representation of the real person but on the other hand was closely related and could have been a spiritual fragment. Alternatively, if the child was harshly treated in a dream, the person committing the dream act was told and through his future behavior neutralized or negated the bad image generated in the dream. To do this he made a helpful, friendly gesture to the child. The crucial point made by Stewart is that "gradually, the child does do in his dreams what he is directed to do." As he achieved adolescence he regularly got to a destination and brought back a treasure for the group in the good dreams. In the bad dreams he outfaced, overcame, and destroyed his enemies.[26] Richard Noone and Denis Holman both follow Pat Noone's and Stewart's belief that the educative process in the Senoi dream culture assisted in directing the social behavior of the adult, which led to a lack of confrontation between individuals and groups and so restrained violent behaviour—what Richard Noone described as emotional maturity.[27] Noone and Stewart were intimating that the Senoi had developed a system of dream manipulation and interpretation superior to anything known to Western man.

Richard Noone and Holman did admit that dream interpretation and manipulation were not the sole reason for the emotional development of the Temiar children. A child is not scolded or punished for wrongdoing, the act itself is condemned as being antisocial and is discussed in that light. The offender is made aware that the offence is against his/her fellows and within the group lies his protection from human, animal, and spiritual destruction.[28]

Contradictory Viewpoints

G. W. Domhoff declared that Stewart had misunderstood the Senoi dream theory and practices. He went on to claim that Stewart later contradicted the claims he made in the 1950s in his account of the dreams recorded in the appendix to his Ph.D. dissertation: "in this sense he was more a romantic storyteller than the social scientist and theorist he wanted to be." There are a number of discrepancies in Stewart's account of his time among the Senoi. The most glaring is that he claimed to have spent ten months studying the Senoi on his second trip to Malaya in 1938 when in fact during the two trips he made to Malaya he spent a total of only eleven weeks there.[29] By 1962 Stewart had claimed he had "worked out a simple, easily learned system of evaluating and directing dreams," which he considered could be used not only as a "preventive or therapeutic discipline" that was potent against "psychosomatic mental and social aberrations" but also as a means through which man could increase his power to change himself through thought; ". . . the dream process represents the most basic powerful creative thinking of which the individual is capable."[30]

On a number of occasions when I had cause to stay overnight in Senoi huts, either on ambush, for the tribal groups' protection, or just for shelter, I did not see any of the after-breakfast gathering of parents and children to discuss their previous night's dreams; most Orang Asli did not seem to have any kind of formal meal in the early morning. The men got up, usually scratched, kicked the coals of the overnight fires into life if the weather was cool, then went outside and relieved themselves. Some chewed on a piece of the previous night's cooked tapioca or took some cold rice if it was there. The children, if they had overcome their shyness, would ask us for cigarettes while we either got ready to leave or settled in for another day if in ambush. The women went about their chores fetching water, tidying away sleeping mats, and clearing the fires. Later the men and youths would wander off in groups with their blowpipes or fishing nets, or set to work on cutting a new ladang while the young ones played around the hut. There was no unusual solemnity or quiet gathering in a corner as described by Stewart and others. Admittedly, although we were in the huts by invitation and without coercion of the residents, our presence was still intrusive. None of us were anthropologists looking for evidence of the dreaming highlighted by Stewart, Noones, Holman, and many others. By the same token, the presence of anthropologists in Orang Asli households, no matter how benign or welcome, was equally foreign.

The importance of dreams in Orang Asli culture and religion varies among the different groups. The Semai and Temiar place more importance on the interpretation of dreams than do other groups. Iskandar Carey claims they are in a sense an outlet for feelings of hostility and aggression and can act as a psychological safety valve.[31] Nonetheless, in the Emergency that outlet did not prevent many acts of violence by Orang Asli, particularly by the Temiar and Semai.

The Emergency

Unlike other anti-colonial insurgent movements in Southeast Asia following World War II, the Malayan Emergency was not a nationalistic movement supported by the indigenous Malay population. Primarily it was a Communist-driven armed insurrection drawn for the most part from the ethnic Chinese population joined by some radical Malay Communists[32] and nationalists, with a few Indian Communists. During the Japanese occupation of Malaya from 1942 to 1945, the Chinese controlled Malayan Communist Party (MCP) through its military arm, the Malayan Peoples Anti-Japanese Army (MPAJA), had provided the major resistance to the Japanese. When the war ended the MPAJA claimed that they were the major cause of the Japanese defeat. The lack of outside information available to the ordinary inhabitants of Malaya during the war and the presence of the armed Communists in the main centers before the return of the British in September 1945, lent credence to the MPAJA claims.[33]

The MPAJA had built up a considerable supply of arms, some of which were recovered from those abandoned by the retreating British in 1942. Others were supplied by Allied air drops in 1944–45 or captured from the Japanese after their surrender in August 1945. A quantity of those arms was surrendered to the British/Malay Security Forces when the MPAJA was disbanded in December 1945, but many were stored away in supply dumps for the inevitable armed clash between the MCP and the colonial government.[34]

Between 1945 and 1948 there was a great deal of labor unrest throughout Malaya between the Communist-dominated unions and the employers, and the government. This conflict was exacerbated by the fluctuation of wages in the mines and plantations, the two areas of major employment. The downward movement in wages was caused by decreases in the prices of tin and rubber on the world markets. During 1947 wage rates for rubber tappers were reduced by twenty percent because of the fall in world prices for rubber. In response nearly seventy percent of rubber estates were closed by a one day strike.[35]

These incidents plus a crackdown on union leaders by the Malayan and Singapore governments increased the pressure from militant members on the Communist Party Central Committee for an armed uprising. A further factor was the disappearance in 1947 under mysterious circumstances of the Party's Secretary-General, and with him a large portion of the Party's funds and valuables. Lai

Tek,[36] the former Secretary-General, who was also a British agent, had not been an enthusiastic supporter of an armed uprising, but following his disappearance a younger, more militant group gained control of the Central Committee under the new Secretary—General Chin Peng.

Declaration of Emergency

In the first six months of 1948 there were 107 murders and abductions attributed to the Communists.[37] The catalyst which caused the government to declare an Emergency was the killing of three planters in the Sungei Siput area of Perak on 16 June 1948. The State of Emergency for the whole of Malaya was declared on 18 June 1948.[38]

The MCP decided at the meetings of the Central Committee in March and May 1948, to resort to armed conflict.[39] The plan was to endeavor to drive out mining managers and rubber estate managers by a deliberate campaign of killing individuals and in doing so to terrorize others into abandoning their posts. The process of Government was to be disrupted through causing officials and civil authorities to flee the assassination and terror squads of the military army of the MCP, the Malayan Peoples Anti-British Army later renamed the Malayan Races Liberation Army (MRLA).

Many of the old MPAJA, together with new recruits, were once more to go into the jungle to fight their old ally and new enemy, the British. There are conflicting opinions about how many answered the MCP's call to arms in 1948. Estimates vary from 3,000[40] to 4,000,[41] to 12,000,[42] to 23,000.[43] Nobody really knew, not even the MCP, how many insurrectionists were mobilized in the first few months of the Emergency. The Special Branch simply did not have enough resources to cope with the task of keeping track of the MCP/MRLA. British Army Commander General Sir Charles Boucher said "I can tell you this is by far the easiest problem I have ever tackled. In spite of the appalling country the enemy is far weaker in technique and courage than either the Greek or Indian

Reds." E. D. Smith claims this assessment can be taken as the typical view of the Special Branch and Military Intelligence, both of which were badly understaffed and really did not know the actual strength of the MCP/MRLA.[44]

Against the MCP/MRLA the British mustered 9,000 police, mostly Malays, supported by ten infantry battalions consisting of two British, five Gurkha, and three Malay, a total of seven thousand men of whom four thousand were riflemen available for active operations in the jungle.[45] The British also had the Royal Air Force to support the troops. The civil authorities retained overall control of operations against the MCP/MRLA. The military's role was to act in support of the civil power. It was to take the colonial power and later the Malaysian government twelve long years to defeat a dedicated and resourceful enemy.

This conflict was not another Vietnam-style war. Total numbers killed in the twelve years were less than 12,000 of whom 2,473 were civilians. It has been described as a long haul, low cost, counter-insurgency response controlled by the civilian government.[46] The MCP did not have any significant outside assistance.[47] They had to rely on their own resources, and as those became depleted, they turned to using the Orang Asli to help them overcome their lack of supplies and in some instances, manpower.

In the political turmoil between the end of 1945 and the declaration of the Emergency the MCP kept a tenuous contact with the Orang Asli through Chinese squatters, traders, tin poachers, and buyers of jungle produce. Some of the MCP and squatters had also married or cohabited with Orang Asli women. In the early days of the Emergency the MCP/MRLA's main sources of supplies, information, manpower, and food were the Chinese squatters on the jungle fringe. A support organization of unknown numbers, the Min Yuen (Masses Organization), coordinated the supply of men and supplies and also reinforced MRLA units operating in their area. Even though old jungle courier routes and bases in Orang Asli areas were being used, most MRLA operations were on the jungle fringe until after October 1951 when the MCP directed a change of tactics and the fighting units of the MRLA moved back into the

Orang Asli homelands.[48] This in turn forced the government's Security Forces, to acknowledge the usefulness of the Orang Asli to their operations. Thus the tribespeople were drawn into an ideological struggle that was not of their making and meant nothing to them.

Notes

1. In the 1960s the Malaysian government directed that the official term for the Aborigines of West Malaysia should be Orang Asli. Asli is a Malay term meaning original. Prior to 1955 the term Sakai was used but this was officially superseded by Aborigine. Sakai, although accepted by some Aborigine groups, was regarded as an insulting term by others, having the connotation of slave or servant. The term Orang Melayu Asli (Aboriginal Malay) is also regarded as being preferable to Proto-Malay used in Colonial times.

2. M. V. Del Tufo, *A Report on the 1947 Census of Population* (London 1949), 117.

3. P. D. Williams-Hunt, *An Introduction to the Malayan Aborigines* (Kuala Lumpur, 1952), 9–13. Note where reference is made to other Williams-Hunt publications their titles will be shown in full. All other references are to this publication.

4. I. Carey, *Orang Asli, The Aboriginal Tribes of Peninsular Malaysia* (Kuala Lumpur, 1976), 9–11. A census in 1960 by the Department of Aboriginal Affairs showed the total number of Orang Asli at about 43,900.

5. Williams-Hunt, 44–63.

6. W. W. Skeat and C. O. Blagden, *Pagan Races of the Malay Peninsula* (London, 1906), Iskandar Carey, see n. 4.

7. Pra'aq is a corruption of the Malay word *Perang*, meaning war/battle.

8. R. O. D. Noone, *Rape of the Dream People* (London, 1972), 2.

9. Ibid., 201.

10. H. D. Noone, "Report on the Settlement and Welfare of the Ple-Temiar Senoi of the Perak-Kelantan Watershed." *Journal of the Federated States Museums* (Singapore 1936), 19, Part 1, 23–24, 47, and 79.

11. R. O. D, Noone, 194–95 and P. Gouldsbury, *Jungle Nurse* (London, 1960), 118–19. This killing is reputed to have occurred in 1943 during the Japanese occupation of Malaya. Pat Noone had remained behind in Malaya and at various times was a liaison officer between the Malayan Peoples Anti-Japanese Army (MPAJA) and the Orang Asli. He was reported killed while travelling between Orang Asli settlements.

12. R. O. D. Noone, 22–23.

13. H. D. Noone, 28.

14. R. O. D. Noone, 142–43.

15. G. W. Domhoff, *The Mystique of Dreams, A Search for Utopia through Senoi Dream Theory* (Berkeley, 1985), 50.

16. R. O. D. Noone, 76–77.

17. Other than the writing of Kilton Stewart much of the research into Senoi pacifity, in particular the Semai Senoi, was taken up after the Emergency. See R. K. Dentan, "Notes on Childhood in a non-violent context" in *Learning non-aggression* (New York, 1978). *The Semai: a non-violent people of Malaya.* (New York, 1968). Further references to Dentan come from the latter work.

C.A. Robarchek, "Frustration, aggression and the non violent Semai," *American Ethnologist,* 4, (1977), 762–79. *Semai nonviolence: a systems approach to understanding* (Unpublished Ph.D. dissertation, Uni. of California, 1977).

18. Domhoff, 35, 41.

19. H. D. Noone, 13.

20. Domhoff, 44 quoting from an unpublished manuscript by Stewart entitled "Journey of a Psychologist" (1936), 337. Much of this information about Stewart is from Domhoff's *The Mystique of Dreams.*

21. C. Parsons, *Vagabondage* (London, 1941), 179.

22. K. R. Stewart, "Mental Hygiene and World Peace." *Mental Hygiene,* 38 (1954), 392.

23. Ibid., 394.

24. Ibid., 396.

25. Ibid., 399.

26. Ibid., 400–401.

27. R. O. D. Noone, 23, 36–37, 53–54. D. Holman, *Noone of the Ulu* (London, 1958), 41–47

28. Noone, R. O. D., 55, Holman, 46.

29. Domhoff, 59. It is important to record that Domhoff did not do field research among the Senoi. However it should also be noted that Stewart laid claim to being an Honorary Fellow of the Royal Anthropological Society [sic] which he was not, he was a regular Fellow of the Royal Anthropological Institute by dint of paying his dues. The Royal Anthropological Institute restricted the Honorary Fellowship to a few renowned anthropologists. He also claimed to be a research fellow of "Peiping Union Medical College, Rockefeller Institute," but it does appear he was not a fellow but was paid by the Center's wealthy American director.

30. K. Stewart, "The Dream Comes of Age," *Mental Hygiene* 46 (1962), 237.

31. Carey, 201.

32. The activities Of the major Malay Communist unit, the 10th (Malay) Regiment was a cause for deep concern to the authorities. *The Straits Times* reported that there were 200 active members in the unit in December 1949. A reward of $M5,000 was posted for their leader, Wahi Annuar, and $M2,000 for his wife. In January 1950 it was reported that the 10th Malay Regiment had been smashed in its operating area along the Pahang River (*S. T.*, 19 January 1950). In March 1951 it was revived again under a Malay leader Menup Japun (*S. T.*, 7 March 1951). He was killed in May 1952. There was a reward of $M7,500 on his head (*S. T.*, 26 May 1952). There were a number of reports of this unit's destruction and survival between 1948 and 1955.

33. F. Spencer Chapman, *The Jungle is Neutral* (London, 1949); R. Stubbs, *Hearts and Minds in Guerrilla Warfare* (Singapore, 1989). E. O'Ballance, *Malaya: The Communist Insurgent War, 1948–60* (London, 1966).

34. O'Ballance, 65–66.

35. *Malayan Union Annual Report* (Kuala Lumpur, 1947), 4.

36. PRO. Kew, CO537/3752. Copy of MCP Document, *The Mr Wright Affair.* See also CO537/3757, Pagden, *Unrest,* Appendix, 1. Lai Tek (Mr. Wright) Secretary-General of the MCP since the 1930s was a suspected Japanese agent in World War II and a British agent after the war. A senior party member, Ng Yeh Loh, wrote to the Chinese Language newspaper, *Modern Daily News,* in late 1945, denouncing an unidentified important officer of the Party for betraying his comrades to the Japanese. After some initial disbelief, the party began to investigate those accusations and the investigators began to close in on Lai Tek who fled.

37. R. Thompson, *Defeating Communist Insurgency* (London, 1966), 27.

38. *Annual Report on the Federation of Malaya, 1948* (Kuala Lumpur, 1949), 13. The British planters and miners had been pressuring a reluctant High Commissioner to declare a State of Emergency for months beforehand.

39. Short, 43–49 and 52–53. Lawrence Sharkey, an Australian Communist is reputed to have advised the MCP of the results of the Communist organized South East Asia Youth Conference in Calcutta in February 1948. That conference supported the "two camp" policy which accepted the need to use force of arms to resist Imperialism if required.

40. O'Ballance, 80.

41. R. Clutterbuck, *The Long Long War* (London, 1967), 43.

42. R. W. Komer, *The Malayan Emergency in Retrospect: Organization of a Successful Counter Insurgency Effort* (Santa Monica, 1972), 8.

43. E. D. Smith, *Counter-Insurgency Operations: Malaya and Borneo* (London, 1985), 111.

44. Ibid., 10.

45. Clutterbuck, 42–43.

46. Komer, preface, v and vi.

47. *Straits Times,* 27 May 1954, General Templer to *S. T.* reporter "There is no evidence at all of any outside source of arms or ammunition, except for a few in Kedah and Perak from over the Siamese border." Col. Young, the Commissioner of Police was censured in 1953 for saying that the MCP was getting resources and instructions from Moscow or Peking (PRO. Kew, CO1022/SEA 75/01 12 August 1953).

48. The significance of these tactics will be explained in later chapters.

CHAPTER 1

Historical Background

THE ORANG ASLI were no strangers to violence and into the early years of this century they were the greatest source of slave labor for the Malays. "The supply of Orang Asli slaves has constantly been augmented by slaves raiders up to the time slavery was officially abolished [in Malaya]."[1] Although slave labor was officially abolished in Perak in 1880 it was unofficially practiced in some states up to 1915 when it was finally abolished under strong British pressure. Following the treaty of Pangkor in 1874, when a British Resident was accepted in Perak, the *Laksamana*[2] remarked, "The one good point about the treaty was that the Resident could not interfere with Malay custom and they could continue to capture and enslave as many aborigines as they liked."[3] Another commentator claimed that "prior to the English occupation of Perak, the Malays used to hunt the Sakais like wild beasts and endeavour to capture and enslave them."[4] In the C[h]endering area of Perak, the Semai still show visitors the *Batu Musuh* (enemy stones), which are large rocks with deep scars where over many years the Rawa Malays had sharpened their swords before assaulting Semai encampments. Normally it was the children and young women who were enslaved; the adults were killed or put to flight because they were considered untameable.

In the collection of slaves the Orang Asli were not always the victims. Intertribal rivalries were exploited by the Malays and, it is suspected, provided an excuse for one group to inflict damage on another for its own purposes, as well as for reward. In 1824 John Anderson, of the Honourable East Indian Company's Civil Service, Pinang (Penang) reported,

> At Perak, the principal tin country of the Peninsula, there are two distinct races of wild people in the interior, the one called Semang, resembling those of Quedah [Kedah] in personal appearance, but speaking a different dialect . . . the other race are called Sakei by some and Orang Bukit or Hill People by others. They are much darker complexioned than the Malays but fairer than the Semangs and their hair is str[a]ight like the Malay. . . . Both tribes are reported to be pretty numerous on the hills which divide Perak from the Patani States, and they are often engaged in hostilities with each other.[5]

For as little as "two rolls of coarse cloth, a hatchet, a chopper and an iron cooking pot," some Malay-controlled Temiar would kidnap children from other non-Temiar groups and sell them into slavery.[6] Some lowland Temiar also slave-hunted under duress to "preserve their own women folk from captivity."[7]

In the 1960's an elderly Temiar man, Udah Pioh (Jamah), related stories of Temiar aggressiveness to Geoffrey Benjamin: "As if to belie their present day extraordinary peacefulness the Temiar seem occasionally to have taken the initiative and laid military attacks against their oppressors [usually Malay slave traders and Chinese women stealers]." His informant also claimed that there were frequent fights before his father's time (possibly before 1900) between Aboriginal groups, other Temiar, Semai, and other tribesmen under Malay control.[8]

K. Endicott suggests that the Temiar's preference for living in long houses may have been partly for defensive reasons. The long houses were raised above ground, some fortified, with the land around them cleared. Packs of dogs living under the houses acted as both scavengers and guard dogs.[9] There were of course other reasons for raising the houses, such as a precaution against wild animals and to benefit from prevailing breezes. I believe the Temiar in the remoter areas were spared the violence of frequent slave trading attacks because of the difficulty in getting to their settlements over very rugged terrain. Long before a hostile party could have arrived at these dwellings the Temiar would have detected their approach and either fled or organized ambushes against the intruders. I can attest to the virtual impossibility of approaching an isolated Temiar settlement undetected, having been in many patrols that tried to do so but failed.

The Semai, some of whom lived in the lowland valleys, were most often attacked by the slavers. They learned not to live by navigable rivers and to plant mantraps along the paths to their settlements. Anthony (Tony) Williams-Hunt, whose mother is a Semai, and Dr. Alberto Gomes who lived and worked with them, related anecdotes to me that the old Semai men recounted of slave wars with the Malays, tales which the Semai narrators had heard from their fathers.[10] Most Orang Asli were illiterate and they had no written history of happenings before the 1960's.

It was not only the Senoi who suffered, and the slave traders were not always Malay. Paul Schebesta describes how an old Semang (Negrito) man, Pa Loa, "remembered very well this terrible time when the Siamese descended upon them from the North East driving the Semang like wild game before them and carrying off their children. . . . they were [at that time] all wandering in the inhospitable areas up the smaller rivers, where they were safe from pursuit.[11] The Semang who were the poorest and most primitive of the major groups often placed themselves in servitude to the local rural Malays for protection, or just fled from danger. Some were completely nomadic and difficult to locate. These people also had been known to turn on their oppressors and despite their attackers' overwhelming fire power advantage, had used blowpipes with poisoned darts, or bows and arrows to defend themselves.[12] The Orang Melayu Asli (Aboriginal Malay) were equally subject to these iniquitous raids. Skeat and Blagden, quoting Le Tessier, describe slave raids on these tribal groups of Orang Asli in Selangor:

> The Malays would then fire several rifle shots, spreading terror and confusion in every family, whose breaking up made them an easy prey to these assailants, who would promptly make a rush for the spot when they heard the shrieks of the women and children. The girls were, as a rule, at once knocked on the head, and the boys were carried off and sold as slaves.[13]

Social Relations between Orang Asli and the Malays

Marie-Andree Couillard suggests that "the question of the relations between the Malays and the aborigines in the Malay Peninsula is a sensitive one. In my opinion the emphasis which has been placed on the tension between these two groups hides the complexities of the historical process which has generated these tensions."[14] Couillard goes on to suggest that the relationship between the Sakai (Orang Asli) and the Malays deteriorated from that of equal trading partners to one of voluntary dependency, and as the Malays began to settle the more remote regions of the Peninsula, to that of antagonism and rivalry for land. "As long as the population from the interior of the Peninsula remained scanty and mobile while constituting the only qualified labour force to collect jungle produce, it is probable that the oppression of the Orang Asli by Malays would not go beyond certain limits."[15] Upheavals following the fall of Malacca to the Portuguese in 1511 together with internal conflicts in differing parts of the Indonesian Archipelago that were exacerbated by European interventions (from the Dutch to the British, beginning in the sixteenth century onwards) caused migrations of the Bugis, Minangkabau, and Javanese into the Malay Peninsula. The migrants' need for land caused conflicts with the Orang Asli, "Some of them imposed themselves violently, others opted for alliances, especially matrimonial, legitimizing in the process their moving into Orang Asli territories."[16] The discovery of and demand for tin compounded the rivalry with the migrants occupying more and more land belonging to the indigenous inhabitants. The internecine wars between the Malay Chieftains for land and areas with tin mines drove the Orang Asli further inland away from the warring parties who tried to involve them. Cant quotes W. Linehan's description of the Orang Asli's plight in Pahang in 1857 which stated, "Harried by both sides, impressed, forced to provide food for conflicting forces, deprived of what little property they possessed, subjected to great cruelties . . . their villages overrun by foreign fighting men, their lot was unenviable. Many of those who could fled to adjoining States."[17]

The increased British trading interests in the Peninsula in the latter half of the nineteenth century caused a rapid development of demand for produce and minerals. The advent of thousands of single Chinese laborers and miners "created a permanent demand for women as concubines, prostitutes, servants and even wives."[18] Orang Asli women were seen as an easy target to satisfy this need. Couillard postulates that it was possible that the Malays protected their own women by supplying captured Orang Asli women to meet that insatiable appetite.[19] Land titles were introduced under the British administration and shifting cultivation by Malays and Orang Asli alike was discouraged. The State also appropriated all non-cultivated land and formed forest and game reserves, all of which prevented free access to the Orang Asli who moved further away from the settled areas, causing them to be further isolated and to rely more and more on middlemen to sell their produce.[20] The religious distinctions between the Muslim Malay and the animist Orang Asli were a further cause of friction. As the Orang Asli were infidels, not Muslims, they had no legal rights, and in Perak in the nineteenth and early twentieth century "not the slightest notice was taken of the murder of a Sakai."[21]

Despite the antagonism between the Malays and the Orang Asli, it is important to stress that in areas where the two races lived in close juxtaposition there were trading contracts between them. Certain intermediaries such as the Mikongs of the Nenggiri and the To'Pangku of the Plus and Korbu who were feared and respected by both Malays and Orang Asli were able to foster those trading links. H. D. Noone refers to both these Malay chieftains/headmen in the 1930s as does a former Malay policeman and Administrator of Aborigines in Perak, Marcel Dawson, from personal experience in the 1950s. The former stated that

> These Mekongs are the hereditary liaison between the Temiar hill people and the Malay Kampongs [villages] towards the Ulu (jungle). There are now only two of them left, one at Kampong Temengor in Perak and one at Kuala Betis in Kelantan. These two are related being cousins. They were originally Siamese and are relics of the Siamese domination of the north of the Peninsula. Their ancestors married hill women and thereby, according to the story told by the Malays, got to understand the lore and magic of the hill people. . . . The To' Pangku at Lasah, serves the same function for the Temiar on the Plus and Korbu, a considerable area.[22]

Geoffrey Benjamin, in interviews with Panglima Dalam, the Temiar chief of the Betis area and others, was able to expand on Noone's and Dawson's accounts. The Mikong were originally from a group of supporters of the losing side in the Kelantan Civil War which followed the death of the Sultan Muhammad who died without an heir in 1835. "Some of whom fled out of reach up river to Ulu Kelantan and others over the watershed to Temengor." There were continuing links of kinship between the Mikongs through intermarriage with Temiar wives from their hill tribe "subjects." Benjamin's informant described how "the Mikong acted as economic middlemen at a time when the Temiar were not sophisticated enough to do their own trading." He points out that the relationship between the Temiar and the Mikong was a convenient one for the Temiar in their external relations with outside traders. It is Benjamin's contention that the same situation must have held true between the To'Pangku of Lasah and the Temiar of the Plus area in Perak.[13]

I met the To' Pangku in Lasah in early 1951 at the Perak Aborigines Area Constabulary (PAAC) encampment. He looked like a very dignified Orang Asli dressed as a Malay but was treated with a great deal of respect by the Aborigine and Malay constables. Despite the influence of these intermediaries, the Orang Asli frequently got into debt to the Chinese and Malay middlemen; this also added to the friction between the groups when the debts were called in. P. D. Williams-Hunt complained that the Aborigines, through a system of advance payments by Malayan and Chinese traders trying to make a quick profit, were kept permanently in debt. So much was due that in Kelantan and Perak some Negrito (Semang) and Ple (Temiar) communities were kept in a state of semi-slavery near Malay kampongs

> undertaking all sorts of tasks—pounding, planting and reaping padi, providing firewood and roofing, having their jungle produce stolen and so on for a mere pittance—two or three bananas or half a cigarette tin full of rice for a day's work . . .

A similar situation also prevailed in Pahang. He blamed the Malays for being harsher than the Chinese in dealing with their Orang Asli debtors.[24]

There were successful efforts to assist various groups of Orang Asli before World War II. A number of administrators and anthropologists did attempt not only to study the Orang Asli but to assist them positively in retaining their homelands and preventing further encroachment into their tribal areas by outside interests of Malays, Chinese and Europeans. They were sometimes aided in their efforts by the Malay rulers of various States under whose direct control the Orang Asli were administered. Despite the hostile attitude of some of his people to the Orang Asli, the Sultan of Perak showed interest in and gave cooperation to these friends of the tribal people including the appointment of G. B. Cerruti as Superintendent of Aborigines in Perak during the early 1900s.[25]

One of the best-known of the anthropologists was H. D. "Pat" Noone, a young Cambridge anthropologist who became field ethnographer to the Perak Museum in Taiping in 1931. He grew enamoured of the Orang Asli, particularly the Temiar, and in 1934 married Anjang, a young Temiar.[26] Through the lobbying of Noone, supported by the British Administration, and with the concurrence of the Sultan of Perak, the *Aboriginal Tribes Enactment—Perak: No.3 of 1939* was promulgated. Although it could not be considered a full granting of land rights (the occupancy of any land was strictly on a tenancy basis only), it gave certain protection to the

Orang Asli in Perak against exploitation and alienation of their existing tribal regions against possible interlopers. It is also worth noting that at various times during this century certain rights were reserved for Orang Asli in specific Forest Reserves in Perak subject to the approval of the Deputy Conservator of Forests in that State. (See Plate 1).[27]

During the Second World War Orang Asli were used as couriers, guides and cultivators by the mainly communist Chinese guerrillas of the Malayan Peoples Anti-Japanese Army (MPAJA). These anti-Japanese dissidents moved into the jungle in 1942 and formed the major armed resistance units to harass the occupiers. Advised by H. D. Pat Noone, the British anthropologist and ethnographer who had been the Protector of Aborigines in Perak at the outbreak of World War II, the MPAJA wooed the Orang Asli to support their activities in the jungle. Their involvement with the guerrillas resulted in reprisals by the Japanese who killed numbers of Orang Asli in their forays into the jungle.[28] It is not recorded if Orang Asli took any active part in attacks on the Japanese but their help to the MPAJA was invaluable and in this indirect way they contributed to the violence. During a visit to Malaysia in June-July 1990, Tony Williams-Hunt told me an unsubstantiated story about the MPAJA. In the Cameron Highlands area they gathered all their Orang Asli allies together after the Japanese surrender in 1945 and trucked them in captured Japanese vehicles to Tapah, Bidor, and Kampar to give them the freedom of those towns for a week. They were allowed to enter any shop whose owners had not actively supported the MPAJA and take whatever goods they fancied. After the week they were trucked back to the road head nearest their settlement and allowed to take their loot back with them.

The British Return

Following the surrender of the Japanese in August 1945 the British returned to Malaya in September of that year. The establishment of the British Military Administration (BMA) did little to resolve the

2.

Rights in the Forest Reserves of Sakais. (continued).

Papulut Forest Reserve. Gaz.Notn.No: 2423 published on 4 May, 1923.

No:	Particulars of holders.	Particulars of rights & privileges.
x	x x x	x x x x
2.	The two Sakai tribes owning allegiance to the chiefs Changa and Sapi, and their descandants to the number in all of not more than 200 persons.	(i) The right to live in the reserve at such places as may be approved by the Dy.Conservator of Forests. (ii) The privilege of utilising their old clearings for the purpose of shifting cultivation. (iii) The right to take water from the streams for their own domestic purposes. (iv) The right to timber, bark, atap, canes, bamboos, honey, wax, woodoil, jungle-fruits, roots, vegetables, leaves and fibres, as if the reserve were State land subject to section 27 of the Forest Enactment, 1918. (v) The privilege of hunting, shooting, trapping and fishing to provide food for themselves and their families subject to such restrictions as may be in force generally or in reserved forests. (vi) The right of way through the reserve for the purpose of exercising any or all of the above rights and privileges.
3.	The Sakai tribe owning allegiance to the chief Sapi and their descandants.	The right to maintain and take the fruit from dusun Ganda.
x	x x x x	x x x x x

Korbu Forest Reserve. Gaz.Notn. No: 772 published on 31 January, 1930.

No:	Particulars of holders.	Particulars of rights and privileges.
	The Sakais living within the reserve - (i) K.Kerbau, about 26 persons (ii) K.Dak, about 105 persons (iii) Barau, about 51 persons (iv) K.Jalong, about 203 persons (v) K.Plias, about 42 persons (vi) K.Chabong, about 125 persons (vii) Landap, about 53 persons (viii) Krot, about 47 persons (ix) Lek, about 42 persons (x) Kuan, about 50 persons (xi) Panchor, about 138 persons (xii Cherak, abour 27 persons.	A. The privilege of sultivating old clearings, & the right to live on such clearings or in such other places as may from time to time be approved by the Dy.Con: of Forests, Perak North. B. The privilege of taking or receiving forest produce, other than timber of Class I, for their own domestic use within the reserve. C. The right of way to and from dwellings and clearings within the reserve for themselves and their dependents. D. The right to durian fruit from the following dusuns: K.Kerbau, Chengkai, Langkor, K.Larik, Kelmoching & K.Lek. E. The privileges of hunting & fishing to provide food for themselves & families subject to such restrictions as may be generally enforced on State land or within reserved forests.

Plate 1. Rights in Forest Reserves

problems facing the inhabitants of the Peninsula and nothing for the most neglected section, the Orang Asli.[29] In May 1946 a Mr. T. A. Kendall of Sungei Buloh wrote to the Economics Adviser, Malayan Union Government (civil administration had been restored in April 1946), concerning the state of the Orang Asli.

> The Sakais are badly in need of assistance both with regard to food and clothing and, since the death of Mr. Noone who so ably looked after their welfare, have no one to plead their cause. As the original inhabitants of the country, they are entitled to some consideration. Except for a few near Tanah Rata and in contact with Europeans, the Sakais are near the borderline of starvation and practically without clothes. . . . Their staple of food is tapioca and there is a severe shortage of this food stuff in the Highlands, while there is a considerable surplus in the plains. Lack of transport is the great difficulty in rectifying this position. Their demands are not great, but they do want cigarettes [local price 60 cents for a packet of 10], dried fish, tinned fish and, most of all, salt. Sakais are an intelligent people and quick to learn.[30]

No action appears to have been taken to alleviate the suffering of the Orang Asli until April 1948 when the Protector of Aborigines sent a memorandum to the District Officer Kajang in Selangor,

> I am shortly to be supplied with salt, medicines, seed and tools, for distribution to Aborigines in need of the same, and I shall be grateful if you will undertake to do the distribution for urgent cases in your District; the quantities will not be large and very little storage room will be needed. In the case of medicines, great care must be taken to ensure that the Aborigines concerned fully understand what the dose is, as not infrequently if a supply is given to them, a party will sit around a camp fire in the evening and forthwith proceed to eat the entire supply. The supplies should only be given to Headmen, and the recipient made to repeat the instructions not immediately, but say after 10 or 15 minutes conversation.[31]

In August 1946 Captain Edney-Hayter, formerly Food Controller, Pahang, was appointed Protector of Aborigines, Federation of Malaya.[32] The new appointee then left on demobilization leave for England in October 1946 and did not assume his duties until early in 1947. In the two years he was in his position Edney-Hayter

DUTIES OF CAPT. E.G. EDNEY HAYTER - PROTECTOR OF ABORIGINES

The primary object of this appointment is to ensure that the welfare and interests of the nomadic tribes of aborigines are given proper attention and this should be your main duty. You are however to give, in consultation with the administrative officers concerned, attention when necessary to the semi-settled groups of aborigines. You are not required to preform the duties of an anthropologist or ethnographer or any duties of a scientific nature.

In particular your duties will be:-

(a) to supervise the 1947 Census of all aboriginal tribes which continue to lead a nomadic life and who have not adopted a settled abode and for this purpose you will be appointed a Deputy Superintendent of Census. The general lines on which this Census will be taken have been already communicated to you by the Superintendent of Census.

(b) to keep in close contact as Protector, with the tribes of nomadic aborigines and bring their difficulties to the notice of Government and to make suggestions as to the new forms of welfare work which might be carried out amongst them.

(c) to study the contacts made by the nomadic aborigines with other races and to bring to the notice of Government any cases where, in your opinion, their economic interests require protection, to assist them in disposing of their produce at fair prices by some form of barter or co-operative arrangement and to introduce new industries and new foodstuffs where such action appears desirable.

(d) to give relief where this is necessary. In giving relief you will bear in mind the desirability of confining relief to really necessitous cases so as not to undermine the morale and independence of these peoples.

(e) to carry out the duty assigned to the Protector of Aborigines under the Aboriginal Tribes Enactment, Perak, as if that law applied to the whole area of the Malayan Union. Such duties will include the delineation of aboriginal settlements, areas or reserves, the administration of any Common Fund set up and the payment of compensation to dispossessed aborigines: the provision of the written information necessary for any exclusion order, the arrest without warrant of any person found within the aboriginal area or reserve mentioned therein in defiance of an order, and control of the felling of jungle within any aboriginal area or reserve.

(f) to make yourself fully acquinted with all laws affecting the daily life of the aborigines and to bring to the notice of the aborigines the provisions of laws such as the Forest or Game Departments which affect them and endeavour to see that these laws are known, understood, and obeyed.

(g) to safeguard the health of the aborigines by establishing medical service points and to see that medical supplies are made available whereever and whenever they may be needed.

(h) in the event of disputes amongst the tribes to act as mediator.

(i) to compile a register of aborigines living within an aboriginal settlement and to establish schools within them.

Plate 2. Duties of Protector of Aborigines

seems to have done very little for his charges. There are very few accounts of his activities available; his role was mainly that of a census taker and welfare officer and he appears to have had very little authority. The control and administration of Orang Asli remained under the aegis of the State Rulers. This appointment was not without controversy and it is worth noting that his duties (see Plate 2) did not include those of an anthropologist or ethnographer or any duties of a scientific nature.

The Director of Museums, Malayan Union, H.D. Pagden remarked,

> "The present Director of Aborigines comes under welfare. He has no scientific qualifications and I feel that some remarkable observations might ensue if work of this nature was attempted by an untrained man."[33]

This point was made to the Assistant Secretary (C), a Mr. P .O. Wickens, in a comment about a submission from Collings, the Assistant Curator, Raffles Museum, for a grant to carry out an anthropological survey of the aborigines of Malaya.[34]

In 1947 the United Malays National Organization's (UMNO) Acting General Secretary, wrote to the Deputy Chief Secretary expressing this body's dissatisfaction at the appointment of a non-Malay as Protector of Aborigines. UMNO had passed a resolution at a meeting of its General Assembly on 2 May 1947, that suitable Malays be appointed as Protectors of Aborigines.[35] UMNO, under the leadership of the charismatic Dato Onn bin Jajafar, the Mentri Besar (Chief Minister) of Johore, had waged and was still waging a virulent campaign against the unpopular British post-war policy to alter the constitutional framework of the Malay States and the Straits Settlements.[36] Any opportunity to embarrass the Colonial Administration and bolster the cause of Malayan nationalism was taken and this was one such occasion. Pagden commented in another letter to Wickens:

> I understand this matter was discussed between the late Messrs Pendlebury and Noone before the war, and Mr. Noone expressed

the view that Malays would not generally make good Protectors of Aborigines. Doubtless Mr. Noone had reason for this view . . .

As Protector of Aborigines one of his duties is to see that the Aborigines are in no way exploited in their contacts with the outside world and for this purpose I believe that it would be better to have a European rather than an Asiatic Protector of Aborigines. He must prevent, as far as possible, the introduction of such things as top hats (no figment of the imagination) which the Batak Mission on the Boh Road, Cameron Highlands, at one time, persuaded their converts to wear on Sundays and may still do so for all I know.

The majority of the Malays do not care to spend long periods in the jungle and this itself would be a drawback.[37]

The Secretary-General of UMNO again wrote to the Deputy Chief Secretary, at the instigation of the *Persatuan Kaum Darat*[38] requesting that:

1. All Sakai reserves in the Federation to be surveyed and gazetted under the appropriate land law;
2. All Sakai Headmen
   (a) in Selangor to be appointed after consultation with the *Persatuan Kaum Darat* in Selangor;
   (b) In other states to be appointed after consultation with the *Batin* and *Anak Buah* of the area concerned.[39]

He went on to claim that strong representation had been made to UMNO by the *Persatuan Kaum Darat,* Selangor, in which it stressed the need for the above procedures. His working committee had instructed him that they considered these requests to be reasonable. The *Persatuan Kaum Darat,* Selangor, here expressed its dissatisfaction at the current system of designating areas as Sakai reserves. This was done without surveys and publication in the Government Gazette as intended by law. This left the Sakai community without sufficient security. They were aware of cases where land they considered to be in the boundaries of a Sakai reserve was alienated to non-Sakais. They considered this type of action to be an injustice (*Inaya* [sic]) to their people.[40]

A circular was sent by the Deputy Chief Secretary to States, soliciting their views on this approach from UMNO. In one of the few pieces of correspondence emanating from him, Edney-Hayter replied on 20 May 1948 to the Economic Secretary of the Federation supporting the Secretary-General of UMNO. He also stated that no headman had been appointed by him without the approval of the *Batins* and the *Anak Buah*. He did not consider it impracticable to define boundaries for reservations and he had done so in Pahang and Kelantan. He was now working on several areas in Perak and would send his proposals for approval by States Councils to the State Secretaries concerned. The replies, set out below, from the states with the largest populations of Orang Asli were enlightening and showed the lack of interest by most. Some were so tardy in sending answers that the Emergency had already overtaken them and was used as a reason for either doing nothing or may have changed their original ideas.

> *Johore.* Reply dated 18 August 1948. His Highness the Sultan in council does not consider that any survey is required in Johore for Sakai reserves as the Aborigines here are of the nomadic type. Under Secretary, Johore.
>
> *Pahang.* Reply dated 23 November 1948. Impracticable to create reserves for the small group of Sakai who are nomadic and will not remain permanently in one place. Where large groups exist, the State Government was not yet in a position to create reserves. The interests of the Sakai were being carefully watched wherever land alienation takes place. State Secretary.
>
> *Perak.* No reply located but it did have a State Protector of Aborigines and the 1939 Aboriginal Peoples Ordinance to protect Orang Asli in that state.
>
> *Kelantan.* No reply located but it did have a State Protector of Aborigines.
>
> *Selangor.* Reply dated 12 September 1950. Request noted. State Secretary.

(This reply from Selangor was puzzling as a full review was carried out in Selangor and completed on 10 August 1948. These detailed comments from the various districts in that state are in Sel. Sec., 675/1948 p.12 [see Appendix B]. It can only be assumed that because of the exigencies of the Emergency, the State Secretary may have had second thoughts about sending them to the Federal Secretary.)

Kedah. Reply 9 September 1950. No Aboriginal problems in state. State Secretary.

Trennganu. Reply 26 September 1950. The Aborigines were like children, it was easy to exploit or spoil them. It was easy to fritter away a great deal of time in their company accomplishing very little except a shaggy beard and perhaps a self-boosting article or two in the *Straits Times.* [This was a personal reference to P. D. Williams-Hunt who now had succeeded Edney-Hayter as the Adviser on Aborigines for the Federation. He had grown a beard and written several articles for the *Straits Times*]. District Officers and Forestry Officers and others were encouraged to take an interest in Aborigines. An officer of the Games Department could possibly carry out the duties of Protector of Aborigines in addition to his normal duties. Commissioner of Lands and Mines, Trennganu.[41]

What Policy ?

As previously stated, Aboriginal administration was the responsibility of the local state and settlement governments prior to, and immediately following, World War II. There was no federal policy as such and even after the appointment of a Federal Protector of Aborigines in late 1946 his role was not clearly defined. The fact that he was chosen for his lack of scientific qualifications and that he was in essence a welfare officer and census taker did not allow for any in-depth research into the culture and social order of the Orang Asli. However well-meaning Protector Edney-Hayter may have been, he did not have the background or the authority to set a federal policy and an agenda to which rulers and administrators of the various states and settlements would acquiesce.

There were individuals such as Pat Noone before the Second

World War and the Kelantan planter Anker Rentse before and after the war who tried to help the tribespeople in their particular states, but their attempts were circumscribed by the lack of a federal authority. Rentse, a Dane, wrote to Pat Noone when the latter was Protector of Aborigines in Perak in the late 1930s. In his letter Rentse praised the Temiar for what he considered their advanced outlook. He intimated that they were "keen on settling down as agriculturists and hunters, doing a little barter as well with jungle produce." He assisted them to obtain some goats they had asked for and he helped them acquire some hill padi. He noted with pleasure their request for fruit trees and flowers to decorate their gardens with in the future. He believed that a Temiar reserve was necessary "to preserve the race for the future," but it should be open to mineral exploration and development if minerals were found on it. The Chinese jelutong (wild rubber) tappers, in the jungle were, he declared, overtapping and spoiling the trees which could kill that industry. In contrast, the Temiar would not over-exploit the rubber trees if they were allowed sole access on the reserve. Wildlife would also be better preserved because the Temiar restricted their hunting to small game and birds to meet their needs and did not hunt big game. He concluded:

> If the Temiar can be guarded and guided, there is reason to believe that they will develop further into a useful primitive community, living according to their own laws and traditions. I think they should be guarded against outside influence and civilization, which may have the opposite effect of what is desired, and turn them into a lazy, almost degenerate community, going to cinemas in motor cars with cowboy hats and blue sunglasses.[42]

During World War II, Rentse was dropped behind Japanese lines by parachute in June 1944 and spent some time trying to find the then missing Pat Noone.[43] He later became Development Officer in Kelantan and his responsibilities included the Aborigines in that state. He was friendly with Williams-Hunt who wrote of him:

> In Kelantan the late Anker Rentse, unhappily killed in an air crash

> in 1950, had considerable influence with the Aborigines, and both before and after the War undertook a considerable amount of welfare work.[44]

Whatever Rentse's good intentions, he could not implement them on a federal basis but his influence in Kelantan may have led to that state's stated intention to adopt Pat Noone's *Aboriginal Tribes Enactment—Perak: No.3 of 1939,* in the early 1950s. This enactment in turn was one of the catalysts which led the federal administration to submit the *1954 Aboriginal Peoples Ordinance* to the Legislative Council rather than having a proliferation of separate state ordinances.[45]

The Noone-inspired *Aboriginal Tribes Enactment—Perak: No.3 of 1939* was the most coherent statement of policy on Orang Asli by any of the states or settlements in Malaya before World War II. This provided for the recognition of the Senoi as subjects of the Sultan of Perak to whom the benefits enjoyed by the Sultan's other subjects should be extended. Further, it required that the land occupied by the Senoi be set aside as controlled Aborigine reservations and not as Malay reservations for which purpose much of the unsurveyed land on the state map of Perak had been formerly designated. These reservations would be properly protected against exploitation by non-Senoi; in addition the introduction of drugs, liquor, and the "sale of useless gewgaws should also be controlled." Tribal customs should be preserved and in each river valley a Temiar chief should represent the interest of his group to the district officer in the locality directly and not through the Malay *Penghulu* (headman). The people of the Reservations should be encouraged to increase their incomes by washing for tin (which some already did) and selling jungle produce and handicrafts. If work was available clearing the jungle, or portering, or cutting paths, they should get it. Other work to be considered was that of elephant mahouts, at which occupation, some Temiar around Kampong Jalong were very proficient. Applications for mining exploration and mining leases and licences in the reservation for non-Orang Asli would be approved on a temporary basis with proper regard to the welfare of the local inhabitants. The leased land was to be returned to aboriginal care after the mining had ceased. There is no mention of mining royalties for Orang Asli.

Noone was very keen that a system of Pattern Settlements be extended throughout these reservations, initially on what he called the border settlement and then extended to the remotest areas. These he thought would prevent indiscriminate destruction of valuable timber areas. The idea, based on similar cultivation he had seen among the Toradjas of Central Celebes, involved the local group remaining in permanent settlements. They would then clear and plant ladangs in rotation on the surrounding hills. Each ladang would be allowed in turn to lie fallow for five years to give the soil time to regenerate after the first harvest; the secondary jungle growth which would spring up on the fallow land was rich in nutrients which would help the soil. This would prevent the wholesale encroachment into the heavily timbered areas and the destruction of commercially valuable timber. The reserves would also be accessible for district officers and agricultural officers who could keep a watching brief on them.[46]

Although the *Perak Aboriginal Tribes Enactment* was adopted in 1939, World War II intervened before it was put into practical effect. While the Perak authorities did endeavour to implement their Enactment, the political and economic confusion after World War II and the declaration of the Emergency prevented them from fully doing so. Whatever the shortcomings of the Perak decree, it was an effort to formalize the state administrators' dealings with its Aborigines. As Noone stated, the previous situation was full of anomalies. No land tenure was available to the Senoi and there were examples where they had been ejected to make way for Chinese squatters. Some Senoi were given compensation for land alienated for a European estate, but in another case in the Cameron Highlands the European interlopers did not pay any. In hindsight Noone's ideas may have been paternalistic and old-fashioned but they were improvements on the laissez-faire system that had existed. As Williams-Hunt wrote: "In other States less work was undertaken but here and there a headman received letters of appointment and Aboriginal reserves were created,"[47] (See comments on plate 1).

Apart from the district officers responsible for Orang Asli in their districts, most administrators had little knowledge of and less interest in the affairs of those indigenous jungle people of the Peninsula. H. D. Collings, a Cambridge educated anthropologist and ethnologist who was the Assistant Curator of Raffes Museum in Singapore,wrote in 1946 that

> It is only a matter of time, perhaps a few years, before these primitives cease to exist. In the meanwhile, modern conditions make the lot of the Aborigines increasingly hard and the administrator is faced with a number of problems in trying to fit them into present day life, problems which are hard to solve through lack of accurate information about the numbers, customs and ways of life of these jungle folk.[48]

This lack of policy and neglect of the Orang Asli would allow the MCP/MRLA after 1951 to obtain a psychological and tactical advantage over the Security Forces when dealing with the indigenous people of the jungle. Because of this lack of coherent direction by the federal administration, the Orang Asli would be submitted to violence by both sides through the ignorance of those who inflicted that violence.

MCP/MRLA: Policy Toward Orang Asli Before 1951

Up until late 1951, when the Politbureau of the MCP issued directives on how the MCP/MRLA should deal with the Orang Asli, there was no apparent centralized policy by the insurrectionists toward the jungle peoples. Individual MRLA units dealt with the Orang Asli as they saw fit which resulted in situations of close association between some of those units and the tribesmen. In other cases units brutally mistreated and killed those they viewed as uncooperative or hostile.

There was a belief by the anti-MCP forces that the World War II association between the MPAJA and the Orang Asli was continued in the years between the end of the war and the Emergency.[49] There is no evidence to support this premise. As previously stated, many of the members of the MPAJA had dealings with the Orang Asli in civilian life as *jelutong* (wild rubber) tappers, tin poachers, village shop keepers, jungle produce traders, and squatters, who lived close to tribal homelands. Some of these were married to Aborigine women or cohabited with them and could speak their dialect. In turn, many Orang Asli remembered that the MPAJA had promised to protect them from the Japanese and their Malay and Indian auxiliaries during the latter's forays into the jungle fringe in search of guerrillas or British officers (such as H. D. Noone, Spencer Chapman and others) who had remained behind Japanese lines during the occupation. The MPAJA had engaged Japanese–Malay–Sikh combined army/police units in Orang Asli areas and had killed some of them. Even though many of the engagements were purely for self-defense they were the major armed resistance group to the Japanese and the only force which could give any protection to the Orang Asli during World War II. From Spencer Chapman's account the Chinese Communist guerrillas' behavior towards their Aborigine allies was impeccable. They were very careful to pay for any assistance received.[50] Certainly MRLA camps were built in Orang Asli areas in preparation for the armed insurrection in 1948 and generally the guerrillas were able to live there without fear of betrayal.

Most of the Communist units learned to rely more on the Chinese squatters for food and other supplies in the early days of the Emergency so there was no requirement to use the services of the Orang Asli. One important exception was among the Semalai in the Tasik Bera area on the Negri Sembilan-Pahang border where the Communist Party Central Committee was located from 1948 to 1951 before it moved to North West Pahang.[51] Strong contacts seem to have been retained with these tribesmen; they acted as an early warning screen for the MCP Headquarters. My informant also claimed that this area was the headquarters of the Negri Sembilan State Committee.[52] A number of strong expeditions were mounted by the Security Forces during the Emergency to take control of the area and the tribesmen.

The MPAJA/Orang Asli nexus was to become useful to the MCP/MRLA as the security forces gradually forced them on the defensive in the 1950s. Despite a number of horrendous killings of Orang Asli by the MRLA prior to 1951, the tribespeople supported the guerrillas until the Security Forces finally moved into the jungle and set up permanent locations in tribal areas.

As demonstrated, the Orang Asli were a people who had been subject to direct and indirect violence by their Malay and Chinese neighbours in addition to old bloody internecine conflicts between groups. They had been exploited by venal merchants and middlemen, and in World War II subjected to reprisals by the Japanese. The British, after their return in 1945, treated them with a benign neglect and some of the Chinese guerrillas of the MPAJA appear to be the only people to have shown them respect and protection. This unfortunate minority were about to have further indignities and hardships heaped upon them as the Emergency progressed. What was to happen to the Orang Asli during this armed conflict would surpass all the traumas and violence they had previously encountered. These pressures and tensions forced on them by the warring factions would lead them to react violently in some cases, in others to flee the torment, and, in extreme cases, to give up fatalistically and slowly die.

Notes

1. K. Endicott, "The effects of slave raiding on the Aborigines of the Malay Peninsula," *Slavery Bondage and Dependency in South East Asia,* (St. Lucia, 1983), 218.

2. *Laksamana*, Malay for admiral or officer in command of a fleet of ships.

3. R. Winstedt, and R. J. Wilkinson, *A History of Perak*. Reprint Number 3, (Kuala Lumpur: *MBRAS,* 1974), 99.

4. N. Annandale, *Fasciculi Malayenses: Anthropological and Zoological results of an expedition into Perak and Siamese Malay States, 1901–1902 by N. Annandale and H. C. Robinson* (New York, 1903), 180.

5. J. Anderson, *Facsimile reprint of Political and Commercial Considerations relative to the Malayan Peninsula and the British Settlements of the Straits of Malacca,* with an introduction by Dr. J. S. Bastin (Singapore 1965), xxxiv–xxxv.

6. R. J. Wilkinson, *Papers on Malay Subjects: Supplement: The Aboriginal Tribes* (Kuala Lumpur, 1910), 49.

7. H. Clifford, *In Court and Kampong* (London 1897), 178.

8. G. Benjamin, "Temiar Social Groupings," *Federation Museums Journal,* 11, New Series (Kuala Lumpur, 1966), 8.

9. Endicott, 230.

10. Anthony P. Williams-Hunt, Bah Toneh, is the son of P .D. .R. Williams-Hunt, Adviser on Aborigines 1949–1953. His father who was married to a Semai, Wah Dramin, was killed in an accident when Tony was an infant. He was brought up with his mother's people and is now a prominent activist in the Orang Aslis' battle for recognition in Malaysia. Dr. A. Gomes is the author of a number of works on the Semai and other Orang Asli groups. See Justin J. Corfield's "A comprehensive Bibliography of Literature relating to the Orang Asli of West Malaysia," *Working paper 61, CSEAS* (Monash University, 1990), 27–28.

11. P. Schebesta, *Among the Forest Dwarfs of Malaya* (Kuala Lumpur , 1928; reprint, 1973), 148.

12. Endicott. 224–29, 239.

13. Skeat, and Blagden, 532–33.

14. Marie-Andree Couillard, "The Malays and the Sakai: Some comments on their social relations in the Malay Peninsula," *Kajian Malaysia: Journal of Malaysian Studies,* 2 (1984), 81–108.

15. Ibid., 98.

16. Ibid., 99.

17. R. G. Cant, *An Historical Geography of Pahang* (Singapore, 1973), 25.

18. P. F. S. Loh, *The Malay States 1877–1895. Political Change and Social Policy* (Kuala Lumpur, 1969), 186.

19. Couillard, 101. n.

20. In February 1951 I recall a party of Temiar arriving in bamboo rafts at Lasah on the Sungei Plus in Perak. They sold the rafts and the jungle produce they brought such as *rotan* (rattan), *jelutong* (wild rubber) as well as blowpipes, mats, and baskets to the Malay and Chinese middlemen. They bought parang blades (machete), salt, tinned fish, meat, and trinkets. After a few day's stay in Lasah, I and some police from the Perak Aboriginal Areas Constabulary (PAAC) joined the chattering group on their way home. We parted from them after an overnight stop at the PAAC's Fort Luckam about a day's march from Lasah. They still had a two day walk ahead of them to get home.

21. Winstedt and Wilkinson, 1974, 91.

22. H. D. Noone, "Report on the Settlement and Welfare," 23, also J. M. A. Dawson, "Aborigines of Malay and the Problem of their Administration" (Unpublished manuscript, 1956), 26–27.

23. G. Benjamin, "Headmanship and Leadership in Temiar Society," Reprint from *Federation Museums Journal, 13,* New Series (Kuala Lumpur, 1968), 9, 10, 11.

24. Williams-Hunt, 46–47.

25. G. B. Cerruti, *My Friends the Savages amongst the Sakais in the Malay Peninsula: Notes and Observations of a Perak Settler (Malay Peninsula) richly illustrated with original photographs taken by the author,* (Comense, 1908).

26. R. O. D. Noone, 62 and Holman, xvi–xvii.

27. *Arkib Negara,* DF 787/54.

28. Spencer Chapman, 276. Noone's brother Richard claimed that Pat Noone had shown the 5th Corps of the MPAJA how to make successful contact and woo the Orang Asli to assist them. R. O. D. Noone, 124–25.

29. Stubbs, 10–41.

30. The letter in Selangor Secretariat, R.C. SEL 677/46–lA dated 18.5.1946 is unsigned but is referred to in a memo from the Deputy Chief Secretary, undated, to all resident commissioners and others. See R. O. D. Noone, *Rape of the Dream People,* about his brother's disappearance in the Malayan jungle in World War II.

31. Sel. Sec. R. C. SEL 677/46–5A et al. Letter to District Officer, Kajang from the Protector of Aborigines.

32. *Arkib Negara,* MUS 24/47–1. Duties of Captain Edney-Hayter, Protector of Aborigines. Note: the Protector is variously referred to as Adviser or Director by different correspondents.

33. Ibid., MUS 63/46–12.12.46–24.5.47 minute dated 20.12.46 from H. D. Pagden to A.S.(C), P. O. Wickens.

34. *Arkib Negara,* MUS 63/46–15 November 1946.

35. Ibid., UMNO/SG 48/47–No.68 letter to Deputy Chief Secretary, dated 5.5.47.

36. Stubbs, 22–32.

37. *Arkib Negara,* MUS 24/47–23, May 1947. H. T. Pagden, to P. A. S. (C). P. O. Wickens.

38. Malay, literally: Association of the people of the interior. The term Orang Darat for some Orang Asli, meaning people of the interior, was used by some Malay speaking Orang Asli. There is not much information available on the "*Persatuan Kaum Darat.*" UMNO, at that time, would have welcomed any complaint from whatever source for its own political purposes to embarrass the Colonial Administration.

39. Batin is a chief of a group of Orang Asli villages. Anak Buah means

people (normally crew or personnel); in this context it means tribal group. Batin was a term used by the Orang Melayu Asli.

40. Sel. Sec., 675/1948.

41. *Arkib Negara,* FS 2203/48.

42. H. D. Noone, Appendix II, 78–79.

43. R. O. D. Noone, 104–105.

44. Williams-Hunt, 76.

45. *Federal Legislative Council Proceedings, March 1953–January 1954. The Aboriginal Peoples' Ordinance* is produced in full in Appendix C.

46. H. D. Noone, Appendix II, to report on the *Settlement and Welfare of the Ple-Temiar Senoi.*

47. Williams-Hunt, 76.

48. *Arkib Negara,* MUS 63/46, 15 November 1946. Request to government to apply for a grant from the Social Science Research Council to carry out an anthropological survey of the Aborigines of Malaya.

49. Refer to Spencer Chapman for information on the MPAJA/Orang Asli association.

50. Spencer Chapman, 170 passim and 200, 207.

51. Letter from former ASP Lim Cheng Teng KMN AMN Malay Police Special Branch, 19 August 1990, and discussion with him during my visit to Kuala Lumpur June-July 1990.

52. Tasik Bera was a large lake surrounded by jungle and swamp. Spencer Chapman wrote that the journey to Tasik Bera was "extremely hazardous" for the Chinese and "quite impossible for a European," 187.

CHAPTER 2

Resettlement

WHATEVER THE MOTIVES of the authorities responsible for the involuntary resettlement of many thousands of Orang Asli in the early years of the Emergency, their action in the displacement of a confused and traumatized people was one of the less savory deeds of the hard-pressed colonial administration trying to combat the communist insurrection.

Unlike the federally planned resettlement of the Chinese squatters under the Briggs Plan,[1] the movement of Orang Asli from their tribal territories to "safe" areas where they could be isolated from MCP contacts was uncoordinated, chaotic, and misguided. In 1950 the Adviser on Aborigines sent a circular to state secretaries stating his views on the ad-hoc resettlement of Orang Asli by the Security Forces, district officers and other administrative authorities.

> The administration of these resettlement areas is frequently neglected usually from shortage of trained personnel but the results are often such that were these communities Malay, Indian or Chinese there would be a public outcry. Indeed, many evacuated aborigine communities claim that they would be better off in the jungle under Communist influence than under Government control.[2]

The relocation of these unfortunate people was to cause misery, disease, and death to many of them. They were arbitrarily moved in the often mistaken belief by the colonial authorities that, because they were living in particular areas, they were a potential risk to Security Forces and were voluntary allies of the MRLA. These peremptory actions of the Security Forces and administrators in forcibly moving tribespeople presented the MCP with a propaganda weapon. Later they were able to exploit this to the full among the frightened Orang Asli when the communists changed tactics in 1951 and moved their main military forces back into the deep jungle.

The lack of priority given to the properly administered resettlement of Orang Asli in the early days of the Emergency is reflected in the amounts spent on these operations. In 1949 the following sums were allocated for Orang Asli resettlement (in Malay dollars):

Perak	$42,000
Selangor	$45,350
On the Perak-Pahang border-	$ 7,500[3]

These were paltry sums even in those days for administration, food, clothing, and accommodation for thousands of displaced people. As a comparison, a reward of $15,000 was offered in Selangor for the killing or capture of Hither, a Malay member of the MRLA.[4] In 1950–51 a total of $41,154,900 was provided for the resettlement of some 350,000 to 500,000 Chinese squatters under the Briggs Plan and $715,000 for the Orang Asli (the latter sum as a matter of urgency "because of their contacts with the MRLA").[5] A further $30 million was allocated for the rehabilitation of squatters in 1952.[6] Even with such large sums allocated for the movement of the Chinese evacuees, there was still hardship and maladministration. It was even more so for the unfortunate Orang Asli whose needs were just as great. The tribal groups did not have the political and social strength that the Chinese could muster through the Malay Chinese Association (MCA) and other clubs and organizations who lobbied on their behalf. The MCA gave not only physical assistance to their compatriots but were able to raise $2.5 million through lotteries, to be used to improve their lot.[7]

The numbers of Orang Asli who died as a result of the panicky and uncoordinated actions of the various individuals and authorities who chose to move the Orang Asli from their normal habitat may never be known. John Cloake quoted a figure of eight thousand.[8] Haji Ahmad bin Khamis, Director of Planning and Operations, *Jabatan Hal Ehwal Orang Asli* (Department of Aboriginal Affairs), Kuala Lumpur, told me he had seen a figure of between five and seven thousand mentioned somewhere in official files. Against that, Hood Salleh stated that hundreds of Orang Asli perished from the severe physical and psychological trauma.[9] Tony Williams-Hunt said that many Orang Asli died in that period but his people, the Semai, have no memory of thousands dying. Dawson claimed that no official figures had been published of the number of evacuees, but he estimated three thousand were resettled or regrouped in Pahang, fifteen hundred each in Perak and Kelantan up to the middle of 1952.[10] This omits Johore, Selangor, and Kedah where there were other large movements of Orang Asli.

Iskandar Carey, like other commentators, wrote on the resettlement of the Orang Asli as if it coincided with the resettlement of the Chinese squatters, when in fact many forced removals of these unfortunate people preceded the Briggs Plan. Carey states that some areas set aside for the tribespeople resembled miniature concentration camps surrounded by barbed wire and patrolled by armed guards. Often these locations were without proper shelter and the food supplied was inadequate or not compatible with the tribespeoples'normal diet. "There was no overt cruelty—just ignorance and stupidity."[11]

Administration and Health

The maladministration and piecemeal nature of the resettlement programs for the Orang Asli were compounded by the lack of control by a central federal agency and the fact that each state was responsible for the care and welfare of its Orang Asli population. An early example of the casual manner in which the movements were carried out, was a report in August 1948 by Doctor Ramsay of the Social Welfare Department that without warning his department had been placed in charge of one hundred eighty Sakai in Perak. These people had been moved to the Social Welfare Camp for the Destitute at Morib for their own protection.[12] The move had the ad-hoc nature that was to be the hallmark of most Aborigine resettlements during that undeclared war. As Williams-Hunt stated in 1952, "Aboriginal administration is the responsibility of the local, State and Settlement Governments but there is a Federal Adviser on Aborigines to conduct technical research and advise on difficult problems."[13] There were Protectors of Aborigines in Perak, Kelantan, and Pahang, but it was only in the last named state that the Protector was full-time. In Perak the State Game Warden acted as Protector and in Kelantan the Development Officer was the part-time Protector.[14] As previously pointed out in Chapter One, it was a deliberate policy decision in 1946 to appoint a Federal Protector without any professional qualifications and to restrict his duties to that of a census taker and welfare officer. Not until the full-time appointment of P. D. Williams-Hunt in November 1949 was a professional anthropologist to become the Federal Protector. In 1950 a Department of Aborigines was formed, as a branch of the Federal Secretariat, unconnected with the Welfare Department. Williams-Hunt continued with the new title of Adviser on Aborigines and head of the department. Even though he was Federal Adviser, his duties only allowed him to advise states and settlements on measures for aboriginal advancement, welfare and administration, and to assist local authorities in the coordination of such measures.[15] These rather vague and ambiguous instructions placed Williams-Hunt in an unenviable position of responsibility without authority.

Resettlement Conditions

The Orang Asli were given land for cultivation in some resettlement areas but there were problems of sanitation and water supply which caused diseases. The tribespeople were not used to living in close settlements so they continued their old practices of using adjacent streams for all their effluent and toilet purposes while groups close downstream drank and washed in water already contaminated. In a paper written by Williams-Hunt on the evacuation of Aborigines he stressed that "it is essential that they settle along approximately the same contour level—i.e., one community is not placed on a slope overlooking another." He warned of the possible outbreaks of dysentery due to the fouling of the water.[16]

The most notorious of the resettlement camps was at Bukit Betong, Kuala Lipis, in Pahang state. It came under stringent criticism from the newly appointed Adviser on Aborigines in late 1949 and early 1950.[17] In an undated letter to Chief Secretary M.V. Del Tufo he wrote that the resettled aborigines, on the weekly figures he had received, "were dying off like flies."[18] Of fifteen hundred Semai in the settlement there had been forty deaths and two births between October 1949 and January 1950. He accused the Medical Department of being unhelpful and went on to say that officers of that department felt it was incumbent on sick Aborigines to make their own way to a hospital rather than be serviced by staff in the field. He substantiated his accusations with detailed figures on 17 January 1950 and claimed that the deaths were caused by an intestinal disorder due to the change of environment and food[19] (See Plate 3).

A letter from the Medical Officer at the General Hospital at Kuala Lipis in December 1949 proved to be less emotive than Williams-Hunt's claims. Clerkin, the Medical Officer, claimed that the mortality rate for the inhabitants since the founding of the camp in October 1949 was fourteen, not the forty claimed. He described in detail the illnesses and treatment given by his assistants and wrote that "recently a Hospital Assistant from Kuala Lipis Hospital has accompanied the [ration] truck weekly to attend the sick and to distribute medical supplies." The Medical Officer visited the settlement on 15 December 1949 and contacted the more seriously ill people in their ladangs, while the hospital assistant held clinic in the village for the sick who could walk. A list of patients seen by both is as set out below:

Seen by the Hospital Assistant:

Neuralgia	6
Diarrhea	3
Malaria	6
Scabies	4
Tinea	12
Ulcers	1
Wounds	1
Bronchitis	2
Septic Wound	1
Constipation	2
Subtotal	38

Seen by the Medical Officer:

Chronic Otitis Media Suppurative	1
Chronic Malaria (with Splenomegaly)	5
Chronic Bronchitis	10
Dysentery	2
Purulent Conjunctivitis	1
Active Yaws	1
Subtotal	20
Total cases	58

He summed up his report by declaring that "the condition of the remaining Sakai seen [those who were not ill] did not appear to be worse than that of the inhabitants of any normal Malay kampong."[20] Unlike Williams-Hunt he did not supply any detail about how the fourteen Orang Asli died. The Adviser on Aborigines in 1952 quoted figures based on data supplied by the Pahang state government, that 217 of the Bukit Betong evacuees had died in the first fourteen months of resettlement (see Appendix). Only twenty-four were thought to be over fifty years of age, the implication being that there was an unnatural death rate among the younger adults and children. These figures support his contention on the excessive mortality rate although they do not correspond with his original

(6A)

Semai Senoi from Ulu Jelai Kechil, Pahang resettled at Bt. Betong, Lipis District.

Total number at 4 December, 1949.

Adult Males	564
Adult Females	469
Male Children	230
Female Children	222
Total	1,485.

October.

Deaths	2.	
Births	nil.	

(Note, Most groups arrived in October and complete figures are not available.

November.

Deaths	18	All "Fever"
Births	1	

December.

Deaths	14	One "Birak Darah" One "Sakit Tua". Rest Fever
Births	1	

January.

Deaths	6	Four "Fever" One "Sakit Tua" One "Sakit Bengkak"
Births	2	

All children born are females.

January figures up to 11.1.50 only.

P.D. Rider Williams-Hunt

Adviser on Aborigines,
Federation of Malaya,
(P.D.Rider Williams-Hunt).

Plate 3. Sickness rates at Bukit Betong

findings.[21] (Williams-Hunt seemed to be continually at odds with other authorities regarding Orang Asli numbers. It is probable that this was not done from any intention to deceive, but was inspired by a sense of altruism to further the cause of the people he regarded as his charges, whose problems he obviously believed were being overlooked by all the colonial authorities.)

A Malay viewpoint on the resettlement of Orang Asli was provided by the Mentri Besar (Chief Minister) of Pahang, Dato Mohamad bin Mat, when he claimed on 9 December 1949 that the resettlement of the fifteen hundred Orang Asli at Bukit Betong was proving to be an interesting experiment; he did not clarify why he thought it was interesting. They were moved from their homes, he claimed, partly for their own security and partly to deny a source of food to Chinese bandits. Those bandits had been threatening the Sakai. He expressed his doubts whether these Sakai would remain in the settlement once it was considered safe for them to return to their normal habitat.[22]

A particularly brutal and stupid forced evacuation was that of an Orang Melayu Asli group from Dusan Eileign in Ulu Langat, Selangor in February 1950. In an affidavit (see Plate 4) signed by thumbprint by the headman of the group, he stated that the twenty-eight Malay speaking people under his control had been directed to evacuate their homes and ladangs by two European police sergeants accompanied by a small party of Malay police. He claimed, "In the hurry we only managed to remove half our belongings." The police then burnt the houses. The headman gave a list of items lost, which were later assessed at $162.10 in value. In an investigation of the incident the officer in charge, Police District Ulu Langat, claimed that the police "gave the Sakais ample time to remove their belongings." They inspected the houses before destroying them and saw nothing of importance left in them except a few pots. He blamed the Orang Asli for forgetting to remove their goods from the houses or nearby caches. Williams-Hunt, in a report on the incident submitted to the State Secretary Selangor, said, "It appears that this particular group was evacuated in error." He then asked what compensation should be paid to the group and which

Penghulu ATIN, headman of an aboriginal group evacuated by the Police and resettled at Semenyih states:-

I am the headman of twenty eight Orang Kanar or Belanas (Note by Adviser, Malay speaking, Proto Malay aborigines) living at DUSUN EILEIGn, Sg. Ternang in Ulu Langat District. We had our own ladang and some of my people had their own rubber small holdings. We had lived in this area since the time of my great-grandfather. We always stayed in the same area and did not move about like some aborigines.

Eight or nine days ago two Police Sergeants - Europeans - wāch came to my house early in the morning. They had a small party of Malay Police with them. As soon as they arrived they told us to evacuate the place. In the hurry we only managed to remove half our belongings. The Police burnt our houses and we estimate the following was lost.

Padi	about 20 gantangs
Cooking pots	9
Frying pans	5
Plates and cups,	21
Blowpipes	10
Chicken	4
Parangs	6
Beliongs	1
Fishnets	2
Spear (Malay iron spear)	1

Right Thumb Print
Penghulu Atin.

Before me,

Advisor on Aborigines.

Witness. CHIN PENG LEONG.
Chinese Interpreter, A on A.

Witness. MOHD. Yusoff,
Field Staff, A on A.

Plate 4. Orang Asli Affidavit

department should pay. It took until 28 November 1950 for the Federal Secretariat to decide that the Chief Social Welfare Officer of the Federation should recompense the evacuees.[23]

Most resettlement areas were as close as possible to tribal lands and usually consisted of groups of fifty Orang Asli or less. Contrary to this general situation there was another large encampment of some twelve hundred Temiar in Kelantan. "By aboriginal standards most resettlement areas were grossly overcrowded, especially the larger ones in Kelantan and Pahang."[24] Even though the resettled tribespeople were allowed to cultivate land around the area where they were settled, the land was often unsuitable for ladang cultivation. It was common practice for the authorities to supply rations, some clothing, and medical attention to evacuees. The Adviser on Aborigines set down a standard scale of rations for evacuees.[25] In addition a disturbance grant of up to one hundred dollars was supposed to be given to each family to compensate for the loss of property left behind in their old settlements. This was a windfall to many of the Orang Asli who had never seen that much money before in their lives. Invariably it was quickly spent on food and useless, colourful, cheap jewelery or other fancy items that caught their unsophisticated fancy.[26]

Perak Aboriginal Areas Constabulary

The Perak state government in 1950 did try to bring some order into the chaotic resettlement situation in that state. At the instigation of Mentri Besar of Perak Dato Panglima Bukit Gantang, an organisation called the Perak Aboriginal Areas Constabulary (PAAC) was established in March of that year. It was under the control of the State Protector of Aborigines Mr. M. H. Woods, commanded by J.A. Hyslop, and officered by three former State Assistant Protectors of Aborigines and four other locally recruited Europeans.[27] It had a complement of some one hundred and fifty Orang Asli, Malay, and Indians based on Ipoh. The Perak government met the costs of the training, equipment, and payment of the force. Its main duty was the resettlement of Aborigines in the state, and its European officers performed the duties of Assistant Protectors of Aborigines to a great extent. It was intended to patrol remote areas in the jungle, contacting Aborigines and establishing whether or not they were in contact with the MRLA. The unit built two strong police posts on the Sungei Plus, one at Lasah and the other at Fort Luckam, some nine miles east of the roadhead at Lasah. They also established friendly relations with the Senoi and Semang groups in the area and were on good terms with the To'Pangkau at Lasah.[28]

Overall the unit was unsuccessful due to the poor discipline exercised by its European officers, who, though well experienced in the jungle, were too cavalier to administer a paramilitary unit such as the PAAC. They were careless of their personal safety, often advising their proposed visits to Orang Asli ladangs well in advance of the date they were to arrive. They regularly rafted down the Sungei Plus on Fridays to get back to base on weekends, a bit of information of which the MRLA soon became aware. In addition, the operations by the unit were opposed by the federal police who saw it as a freelance operation outside their control and competing in their area of responsibility.[29] It was eventually incorporated in the Police Federal Jungle Companies (PFJC) as 20 Jungle Company in 1952 after three of its European officers were killed by the MRLA as they rafted down the Plus from Fort Luckam to Lasah.[30] Despite its shortcomings it was an interesting example of a multi-racial unit. When it was amalgamated with the PFJC it consisted of twelve Aborigines, fifteen Indians with the balance being Malays, and was officered by Europeans. Dawson, who was second in command of 20 PFJC, claimed that the Malays "were usually sympathetic towards the Aborigines whom they treated with consideration."[31] Fort Luckam was closed although it was a forerunner of what was to come later, when the Security Forces moved into Orang Asli areas and established forts.[32]

Williams-Hunt, in an effort to minimize the trauma of evacuation and resettlement to the Orang Asli, wrote a series of suggestions for Security Forces which were published in an article in the *Malayan Police Magazine* in March 1950.[33] It was a curious article ranging from a sympathetic summation of the tribespeople's plight, to recommendations on how to destroy their possessions and burn their houses (see Appendix E). The Adviser called the Aborigines "useful members of the Malayan Community" who added to the economy by not only being self supporting in most cases, but also positively contributing materially to the welfare of the country by harvesting jungle produce such as rotan (rattan), jelutong (wild rubber), bamboos, and various gums. He then went on to recommend that they be put in a position where they asked to be evacuated rather than be coerced.

This could be achieved by patrols visiting and staying in ladangs on a regular basis, which would allow them to get to know the inhabitants, and by distributing gifts of tobacco and other desirable items to establish friendly contact. This friendly approach would be reciprocated by the tribespeople. Williams-Hunt expected this friendliness to lead to threats by the MRLA against the by then compromised Orang Asli who would ask to be taken out of their local habitat to escape reprisals. He also advocated bombing or shelling close to inhabited ladangs to scare the local tribespeople to flee out of the jungle to safety. Of the actual evacuations themselves, he strongly advised that the local authorities at the receiving locality be told of the arrival of the evacuees to minimise hardship which previous lack of communication had caused. The actual evacuation should be done in a series of steps. He emphasised that even when an escorting party arrives at a settlement to be evacuated they do not advise the residents of their plans until the very last moment to ensure that none leave. After sentries were positioned to prevent escapes, the people were to be told that they were to be moved, but that the move was only a temporary one for their safety. The Malay headman (*Mukim Penghulu*) of the area to where they were to be evacuated, should be invited to meet the evacuees to reassure them that preparations had been made for their reception. They must be directed to take all moveable possessions including live stock. Finally their houses were to be destroyed, usually by burning, or, if they were close to a road or river any useable material in the houses should be saved and trucked or rafted to the new destination. One of the more callous suggestions he makes is that the Orang Asli be encouraged to destroy or burn their own homes; "They might as well get some fun out of the evacuation." Regrettably it has not been possible to find an Orang Asli who suffered these indignities to talk about them and find out if they considered the burning of their homes a matter for merriment.

These instructions highlight the ambivalence of Williams-Hunt's position. As a faithful servant of the administration it was incumbent upon him to carry out administration policy and assist the Security Forces in literally rounding up his charges. At the same time, his appointment as Federal Adviser on Aborigines required him to do everything necessary for the welfare of the people for whom he was responsible. His training as an anthropologist must have made him question the wisdom of his and the Security Forces' actions in herding the tribesmen from their homes into localities that were manifestly unsuitable for a people used to moving freely over a large area in which there were often no other humans. His letters of protest to Del Tufo and the State Secretaries, and his book in which he points out the many problems besetting the Orang Asli are a reflection of his real feelings on how to deal with the tribespeople.

Added to the Adviser on Aborigines' problems, his department's budget for 1950–51 was minuscule, as the figures below indicate:

Subhead 1—Personal Emoluments			
Item (90)	Adviser on Aborigines		$6,300
	Other salaries		$10,571
Subhead 7—Welfare of Aborigines			
(1)	General Welfare	4,000	

(2)	Incidental Expenses	300	
(3)	Photography	1,000	
(4)	Periodicals and Publications	750	
(5)	Transport and Travelling	10,000	
(6)	Telephone	300	
(7)	Uniforms	300	16,650

and (b) additional provision as follows:

Subhead 11—Books and Works of Reference		1,000	
Subhead 12—Equipment			
(1)	Equipment of Field Staff	500	
(2)	Anthropometrical Instruments	400	
(3)	Draughtsman's materials	500	
(4)	Filing Cabinets	333	
(5)	Cabinet Guides	85	
(6)	Card Index Cabinets	77	
(7)	Index Cards	33	1,928
			$36,449

It is difficult to understand how some of the items under Subhead 7 could add to the welfare of the resettled Orang Asli.[34]

Williams-Hunt was married to a Semai woman. Through her and her family connections he must have been aware of how her people regarded the resettlement process. While taking every action within his limitations to stop it, he also tried to ameliorate the hardships involved in the mass evacuations. That the Orang Asli appreciated his position is shown in the respect they display towards his son Tony, who today is their spokesperson in dealing with the government. I did not hear any critical comments about Williams-Hunt in visits to the Semai near Tapah in June-July 1990.

A mass evacuation which followed guidelines set by Williams-Hunt took place in the Jelai Kecil area of Pahang in April-May 1952. Many MRLA cultivated areas and camps had been located in

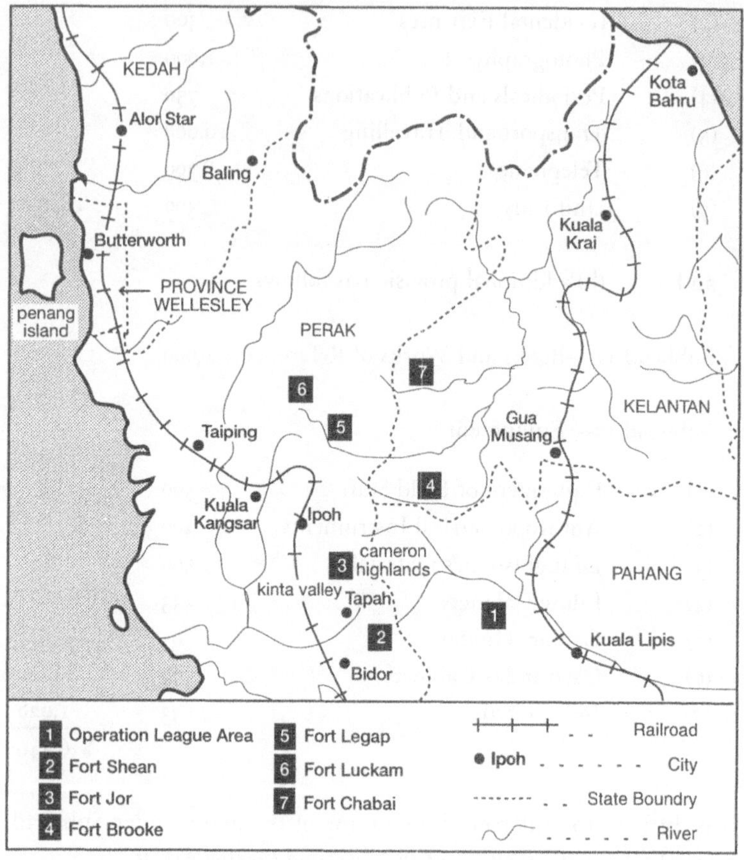

Map 2. Major operational area Perak/Kelantan, 1948–1960

this region so it was decided to evacuate the local inhabitants.[35] Designated "Operation League," it involved three squadrons of the 22 SAS Regiment (some 130 to 150 troops), supported by two companies of the 5th Malay Regiment and police from the Police Federal Jungle companies.[36] The Malay regiment units and the police acted as stops to prevent the escape of Orang Asli to be resettled, and to guard against any attack on the evacuating force by the MRLA. The SAS was accompanied by Donald MacPherson, an anthropologist and member of the Department of Aboriginal Affairs, who spoke the local Orang Asli dialect. He was assisted by some Malay-speaking Civil Liaison Officers attached to the SAS squadrons. It took weeks of patient negotiations to gather in the relevant tribes. The SAS escorted MacPherson and the Malay Liaison Officers to Orang Asli ladangs to discuss the evacuation with the Semai Senoi elders. Medical treatment was given freely to the sick and some were evacuated by helicopter to the Orang Asli hospital at Selayang outside Kuala Lumpur. An experimental voice aircraft (one of the first used for this purpose) circled the area continuously, broadcasting both in Malay and the local language, calling the people to come to safety at the base camp. Suspected targets within hearing distance of the displaced were bombed and rocketed to display the Security Forces' power and to show what was in store for those who did not willingly leave their homes.[37] Great play was made by the liaison groups of the power of the Security Forces. Here they were in force and these were their aircraft and weapons.

This was reasonable counter-propaganda to the MRLA claim to the Aborigines that the aircraft flying over the jungle were theirs and that they (the MRLA) were the pursuers of the soldiers. A better life was promised to the Orang Asli who allowed themselves to be evacuated and veiled threats were made about the possible lethal results that could occur to those who remained. From their ladangs they could see the activity at the SAS base camps. Aircraft were seen dropping rations and helicopters came and went, often with some of their sick kin. Included in the airdrops were rations for the tribespeople who came in to the base camps. They were given liberal handouts of rice, ikan bilis (dried whitebait), tinned fish, camp pie, chillies, salt, sugar, coffee, condensed milk, tobacco, and cigarette papers. As groups trickled in they were fed and their clothing was replaced with new garments. Welfare staff from the Department of Aborigines looked after their other needs. A medical clinic was available for the sick.

The object of the operation was to gather in all neutral or friendly Semai in the area. Once this had been accomplished the whole region would be declared a prohibited zone where any remaining Orang Asli would be classified as hostile and shot on sight. It was believed that by clearing the ladangs the MRLA would be deprived of intelligence about the Security Forces' movements. They would also lose a source of information, supply, and willing labor. The

RAF would be given a free hand to bomb any cultivated areas or settlements.

Finally, the last of the sick Aborigines were evacuated by helicopter. The healthy men, women, and children were assembled in a base camp and escorted on a five-day march over the main range into Perak and along the Sungei Sungkai Valley to the town of Sungkai.[38] On arrival in Sungkai the evacuees were met by senior representatives of the Department of Aboriginal Affairs, loaded on trucks, and taken to a resettlement camp at the 19th mile, Cameron Highlands Road near Tapah in Perak. Their new home was a bare hillside surrounded by barbed wire, ostensibly for their protection, but in reality to keep them from returning to their homeland.

Dawson's version of this evacuation differs in some aspects from the reported version and the SAS account. He claims the Semai in the Jelai Kecil area "were given the option of resettlement at Bukit Betong, which was quite close, or at Jor Camp situated at the 19th milestone on the road to the Cameron Highlands." After inspecting both sites, headmen from the locality to be cleared chose the Cameron Highlands.[39] It seems the use of such a large force to move an allegedly willing group was superfluous if Dawson's account is correct. Dawson's unit 20 Field Jungle Company (FJC) was detailed by the State War Executive Committee Perak (SWEC) to set up a police post at Jor to protect these Jelai Kecil Semai. Despite the alleged choice of the Jor area by the tribesmen's representatives it proved to be a failure. Huts were built in the exposed hillside which got the full heat of the day. Most of the adult males found themselves with little to do now that their normal occupations of fishing and hunting were no longer available to them. Sitting around in idleness all day, they lost the will to exert themselves and pined away in desperation at their plight while others escaped back to the jungle, sometimes to join the MRLA-supported ASAL organization.[40] Some of the SAS passing the area in which the Aborigines were resettled saw the changes in health and general manner of the people and this caused some of the soldiers to question their role in this type of operation. This mass movement was to be the last of its type during the Emergency.

Orang Asli Resistance

Rather than tamely submit to resettlement, some Orang Asli fled at the first opportunity. They were, on occasions, actively supported by the MRLA in their efforts to escape back to their homes. The *Straits Times* reported on 20 October 1949:

> Eighty-two Sakai who were living on the compound of the Tanjong Rambutan Police Station, 9 miles north east of Ipoh, went away with the bandits who attacked the station for an half hour this morning. They took away all their belongings, leaving behind only three of their number—a woman and two of her children.[41]

The report went on to say that these Sakai were from a settlement seven miles into the jungle in the Tonggang area. They had been rounded up the previous February and kept in the Police compound for "security reasons" and had escaped through a hole cut in the wire. A follow-up operation by the police found a large "bandit" camp in the area with signs that the Sakai had also been there. The *Straits Times* again reported on 28 October that the husband of the woman who had stayed in the compound returned and asked permission to stay with her. Permission was granted but later in the day the family disappeared with all their belongings.[42]

Even the Orang Asli who asked for voluntary resettlement to escape pressure from the MRLA needed to be handled with sensitivity and understanding. In early 1950 a group of Senoi came down from the hills around Tanjong Malim on the Selangor-Perak boundary seeking protection.

> They were given I. D. cards and rice cards [for rations], and money was found for new ladangs or huts. The Senoi began to move into the new campsite, when a dysentery epidemic [dysentery has always taken a heavy toll of the Sakais] broke out, causing them to disappear again in the jungle.
>
> Superstitious over the alarming increase in the number of deaths, they were anxious to escape from the ghosts of the dead. Several efforts since to find them in the jungle have failed.[43]

That incident was typical of the haphazard, thoughtless uprooting of a people, an estimated seventy-five percent of whom had practiced some form of shifting agriculture for centuries. Even though some of them also cultivated fixed rubber and fruit plantations they were free to come and go as they pleased, hunting and fishing in their homeland. Individual groups had different customs connected with death and burial which in some instances varied enormously.[44] These factors were not taken into account by the authorities who organized the individual resettlement areas and the experts like Williams-Hunt were generally ignored. R. O. D. Noone, who succeeded Williams-Hunt, wrote:

> Used to living at a higher altitude, these unfortunates could not stand the heat of the plains. Their stomachs could not get used to the abrupt and complete changes from their staple diet of cassava and fresh meat and vegetables to rice and salt-fish. After living a naturally energetic life, the men fishing and hunting, and the women planting and collecting wild fruits and tubers, they could not adapt themselves to a life of idleness.[45]

The MCP were slow in taking advantage of this propaganda coup presented to them by the British-Malay administration. Some MRLA units continued to harass the Orang Asli to obtain food, intelligence, and labor. Others were wise enough to point out how cooperative they were with the tribesmen—unlike the Security Forces who bombed their ladangs and dragged them from their homes. The Politbureau of the Malayan Communist Party issued a directive on 25 September 1951,[46] laying down instruction for dealing with the Orang Asli whom they referred to as "the masses of the nationality in the jungle." The directive stated that:

> In certain areas, the masses of this nationality have already been driven away and concentrated by British Imperialists beyond the jungle areas. Similarly one should strengthen our links with them, propagandise and agitate among them and call upon them to flee and return to the jungles to cultivate. But one should see that this is done in a prepared and planned manner.[47]

The instructions go on to say that before calling on the Orang Asli in the resettlement camps to return to the jungle, "tools, ploughing utensils, and planting sites etc., should first be prepared beforehand." This was in addition to providing enough food and salt to help them over the initial period before they were able to hunt and fish again. The results of this directive will be discussed in later chapters.

So far the effects of the resettlement on the most numerous of the Orang Asli, the Senoi, and the two major subgroups, the Semai and the Temiar, have been highlighted. The Semang and Orang Melayu Asli were also drawn into these actions which disrupted the lives of many of them. The smallest group, the Semang, often moved in close to Malay kampongs for protection from both the MRLA and the Security Forces. There they tended to be exploited by their protectors who looked upon them as a source of cheap labor. Before condemning the rural Malay too harshly for his penurious treatment of his Orang Asli neighbour, it should be remembered that the average Malay peasant existed just on the poverty line and could ill afford to be over generous to those he employed.

The Orang Melayu Asli were subject to resettlement where the authorities considered them to be at risk from the MRLA or they suspected them of helping the insurgents. This was despite the fact that some were Muslims. There was a resettlement camp at Mersing in Johore where Jakuns from the upper reaches of the Rompin and Endau Rivers were sent to prevent them from consorting, willingly or unwillingly, with the MRLA.[48] The smallest group of Orang Melayu Asli, the Orang Kanaq, consisting of thirty-five people, was evacuated en masse for safety from Mawai, near Kota Tinggi, Johore, to a settlement outside Kuala Lumpur. They were held there until the Emergency ended in 1960.[49]

Voluntary Resettlement

It should be understood that not all the Orang Asli who were resettled were forced to do so. Many voluntarily asked for protection because of pressure from the MRLA. At Kerdau in Pahang a group of Orang Asli fled from pressure from the MRLA in the jungle and built a camp for themselves in comparative safety near the Kerdau settlement. This group had lost their leader when he was murdered by the "bandits" and so they had fled to safety of their own accord.[50]

This contrasts with the care taken to evacuate twenty-five Sakai families comprising one hundred and fourteen people from an area outside Kuang in a remote part of Selangor in June 1951. The District Officer (DO), Ulu Selangor, earmarked a piece of state land close to the town board limit of Kuang to which the evacuees stated their willingness to move and build their own houses at their own expense. They did ask for the provision of rations which had been provided for other evacuees in this district. When asked for his comments, Williams-Hunt wrote, "These people are Aboriginal Malays—not Sakai—and should be treated in the same way as if a Malay Kampong is being moved."[51] He supported the DO's proposal and promised to visit the group. The sum requested for rationing the Orang Asli, estimated at three thousand dollars for the balance of 1951, was duly approved. The same DO applied for a total of sixty-seven thousand dollars for four resettlement areas in his district, at Kuala Kubu Bharu, Batang Kali, Ulu Yam Bharu, and Kuang.

The sum was to cover food, water supply, and accommodation but the number of evacuees is not stated. The District Officer finally received a total amount of $69,860 from the Secretary of Defense's vote for 1952.[52] Hand-written notes on this matter, from Williams-Hunt, the State Secretary Selangor, and the District Officer Ulu Selangor, taken from the minute papers, are on file 2597/51-9 at the *Arkib Negara*. They show that official attitudes toward the Orang Asli were varied, from Williams-Hunt's concern that the evacuees would become dependent on handouts, with which the State Secretary concurred, to the practical attitude of the DO whose worry was to win them away from the MCP. When the Emergency was over they could return to their previous settlements in the jungle as far as he was concerned.

A number of factors helped to obviate the distress of resettlement for the Selangor Orang Melayu Asli. Many spoke Malay which gave them empathy with Malay and European District Officers. They were close to the federal capital, Kuala Lumpur, so their plight was more obvious and immediate to federal officials than the more remote tribal groups. In addition, UMNO was not loathe to prod the State Secretariat into action. In a letter dated llth October 1950, UMNO inquired from the Selangor State Secretariat what that state government's policy was toward the Aborigines. The State's District Officers and the Federal Adviser on Aborigines were canvassed for their views. The DO's supported Williams-Hunt's recommendation for a federal establishment for detailed research into the Orang Asli supported by a parallel organization in each State or Settlement. This would be strengthened by a Federal Enactment for Aborigines.[53] However, all these were recommendations, not policies. The reaction of UMNO is not recorded.

One of the more unusual cases of voluntary resettlement involved a group of eighty-one Jakun (Orang Melayu Asli) located in the jungles of Johore in late June 1948. They had gone into hiding in 1942 to get away from the invading Japanese and were found by a forest ranger on the right bank of the Sungei Linggui, a tributary of the Johore River. While hiding there in comparative safety, they lived off tapioca, sweet yams, bananas, vegetables, and a few acres of rice especially planted for the old people and children. The noisy cocks among their poultry had been killed to prevent detection by passing patrols. So terrified were they of aircraft passing overhead, that even after the Japanese defeat they were still too timid to come out of hiding; this was despite seeing Europeans in their locality. After being located they were medically examined and found to be in good health. They received some aid from airdrops which included supplies and tools but later it was decided to move them because of "bandit" activity in their area. This move took place in July 1950 under military escort to a settlement three miles north of Kota Tinggi. In this new location they were allowed to spread out into family units, building their own dwellings, and cultivating plots of land. "According to a Government official who has recently visited them, they seem to be quite happy in their safer surroundings and are very industrious."[54]

Activities of Adviser on Aborigines

Williams-Hunt's monthly reports in 1950 give some idea of the scope of his duties in dealing with the resettlement problems.[55] With a staff of four in January 1950, consisting of the Adviser, a Chinese assistant, a draughtsman, and one Malay field staff member, he was responsible for the administration of Aborigines throughout the Federation. In covering his duties the adviser came upon unusual situations. In January 1950 the Officer Commanding Police District (OCPD) at Tanjong Malim in Perak, requested that Williams-Hunt contact a group of Mai Sengei (Senoi) to see if he could take some action regarding their welfare; they had been wandering in the jungle for nine months after fleeing from an air strike. In April he reported that Dr. I. V. Polunin (B.A., B.Sc., M.B., B.Ch.) from the University of Malaya was carrying out research on the incidence of disease among Aboriginal groups. "His discoveries have been of a somewhat disquieting nature and, in some cases, point to a faulty administration of these evacuated groups." In the same report the Adviser stated that local authorities had not been able to comply with suggestions from his department. "In at least [number not on the original paper] cases this has led to serious illness and avoidable deaths amongst evacuated groups." He was of the impression that the local authorities lacked facilities to meet requirements, although, there was a marked improvement in one area where the District Officer was changed. During the month he visited evacuated aboriginal groups at Semanyih in Selangor, and Bukit Betong in Pahang. He also visited various Semai encampments with "Rajah Tom, overall headman of the Semai who was thus enabled to contact many of his headmen whom he had not seen since before the war."[56]

In August Williams-Hunt reported that considerable progress had been made by the PAAC in evacuating Aborigines in the Sungei Plus area of Perak. This was a Perak state operation. He also went to Raub in Pahang to discuss with the DO and OCPD the evacuation of a group near Bentong, and then evacuated a group from Bentong to Benta Estate. Again at Kuala Lipis in Pahang, he had a conference with the SWEC on a proposed move of Aborigines. Among his visits to Aboriginal communities he visited some resettled groups at Tanjong Rambutan and Gunong Tasek.[57]

In the meantime some of the Orang Asli, particularly the Semai and Temiar, who had been either voluntarily or involuntarily resettled, were beginning to come to terms with their new lifestyle. They began to cultivate as best they could the new lands in which they were resettled, or to sell their labor. Some found work with the Security Forces as guides, porters, or informants on their brethren still in the jungle. Others became rubber tappers. It was reported on 12 November 1949 that "Sakai and Malays are being recruited as labourers by the Public Works Department when there is a shortage of Tamil (Indian) labour." The report went on to say that more Sakais who had been driven from the jungle by the Emergency were moving on to rubber estates. A manager of an estate at Sungei Choh in Perak claimed that although the fifty Sakai employed on the estate were of limited intelligence and simple, they were good workers. Before being employed as field labourers they had to be shown how to use a *cungkil* (a hoe). "The manager hopes to train one or two of the more forward ones to tap."[58]

The *Straits Times* again carried a report on 24 November 1949 that "Sakai labourers are returning to live in accommodation provided by the estates and insist on putting up their own huts."[59] A few of the resettled Orang Asli joined the Special Constabulary.[60] Some resettled Orang Asli showed more enterprise than most. In an editorial in the *Straits Times* in March 1951, it reported on the resettlement area at Karak, fifteen miles west of Bentong in Pahang. "About eighty Sakai have their new ladangs along a steep hill slope within a stone's throw of the Police Post at Karak." They had been moved from their homelands around "the once notorious Christa Mani granite hills four miles from Karak." The writers of the article found three generations of Orang Asli living in one house in the center of the settlement. One of the inhabitants, Utan bin Jahat, had a Chinese wife, Ling Ching, daughter of a timber worker. (It was unusual for an Orang Asli to have a Chinese wife; it was more common for Chinese men to be married to aboriginal women.) Utan and his seven brothers all worked on rubber estates as tappers. The reporter concludes that the general health of the evacuees was very poor "but they are a happy lot despite sores or rickets."[61]

By 1952 the colonial and state governments were beginning to question the policy of clearing Orang Asli from their homelands, even temporarily, because not only did it cause health problems for the evacuees but it proved counter productive, causing hostility among the indigenous jungle people. The disruption to their lifestyle and abandonment of their homes and crops was driving them to support the MRLA. In July 1952 the Perak SWEC proposed two new policies on the resettlement of Orang Asli designated "Influenced Migration" and "Protected Attraction." The first meant that "aboriginal communities would be induced to accept resettlement in a new area that would be inspected and approved of by themselves [and] where protection would be offered them."[62] Although the new area may not necessarily have been close to their normal habitat, it would be in territory which resembled their homeland as much as possible and they would be able to follow their normal daily pursuits. The second proposal was that of "Protected Attraction" which would require a police post (designated a fort) to be built in an Orang Asli area; the inhabitants would move close to the fort for protection and welfare facilities.[63] The second proposal was the one to be adopted on a federal basis and will be covered in full in a later chapter.

Despite the discontinuation of the resettlement policy in 1952-1953, there would still be more disruptions to the lives of the Orang Asli. Attempts would be made to relocate them (a euphemism for resettle) close to forts or clear them from their tribal lands for operational requirements. Despite these moves the bad days of the 1948–1952 mass resettlements were over. The Orang Asli would not be left in peace but they would face their problems on familiar ground.

Notes

1. Lieutenant-General Sir Harold Briggs was the Director of Operations in Malaya from 1950 to 1951. He organized the movement of some five hundred thousand Chinese squatters from their homes at the fringes of the jungle into fortified "new villages" where they could be separated from immediate contact with the MRLA and Min Yuen. In 1949 Emergency Regulations 17D, 17E, and 17F were promulgated to try and deal with the Chinese squatters but they were mainly used as an instrument to either detain or deport Chinese under suspicion. See Department of Public Relations, Federation of Malaya, *Communist Banditry in Malaya* (Kuala Lumpur, 1950), also Stubbs, 100–27 and Short, 231–53.

2. Sel. Sec., 1411/50.

3. S. T., 30 September 1949.

4. Ibid., 17 March 1950.

5. Ibid., 12 July 1951 and CO 537/7270, High Commissioner to Secretary of State for the Colonies, 26 May 1951.

6. Dawson, 134.

7. V. Purcell, *Malaya: Communist or Free* (Stanford, 1954), 107; also see Short, 346 fn. This avenue of assistance was closed by legislation, supported by the High Commissioner General Sir G. Templer, in 1953. The MCA was considered to have access to too much money and also the Muslim Malays objected to the gambling aspect.

8. J. Cloake, *Templer Tiger of Malaya* (London, 1985), 256.

9. Hood Salleh, Ilmu Masyarakat: 6, "Orang Asli Perceptions of the Malay World: A Historical Perspective," *Malaysian Social Science Association*, KDN 1263/84.

10. Dawson, 148.

11. Carey, 307.

12. *S. T.*, 26 August 1948. This is the first record I have been able to locate of the resettlement of Orang Asli in the Emergency.

13. Williams-Hunt, 3.

14. Dawson, 128. Two European planters and an Indian schoolmaster were recruited in Perak and appointed Assistant Protectors of Aborigines.

15. P. D. Williams-Hunt, *Notes on the Administration and Recording of Technical Data Relating to the Malayan Aborigines*. Compiled by the Department of the Adviser on Aborigines, Federation of Malaya (Kuala Lumpur, 1951). Williams-Hunt's professional titles were F.S.A., F.R.A.I., F.R.A.S., R.R.P.S., and A.M.A.

16. Sel. Sec., 1411/50–15B.

17. Williams-Hunt's title was changed from Protector to Adviser on

Aborigines in March 1950, the title Adviser to be shown with an asterisk to show it had not been gazetted. *Arkib Negara*, FS 1220/1950–22 March 1950, letter from Acting Malayan Establishment Officer—Williams-Hunt had been using that title unofficially for some time.

18. *Arkib Negara*, FS 12072/50–1.

19. Ibid., FS 12072/50–6 and 6A.

20. Ibid., FS 12072/50–8A.

21. Williams-Hunt, 32–33. I place some emphasis on the matter of different figures relating to Orang Asli to point out the difficulty in establishing an accurate total for the number who died in the resettlement phase. It is suggested that Williams-Hunt's figures for Bukit Betong may at some time have been extrapolated to include like figures from other settlements to arrive at a total of all who died in the resettlement camps and possibly from this calculation the figures of seven and eight thousand may have come.

22. *S. T.*, 9 December 1949.

23. Sel. Sec., 481/50–1–11.

24. Dawson, 148–49.

25. Sel. Sec., 1411/50–17.

26. Dawson, 158. As a comparison, the ordinary Malay police constable was paid $60 per month and an Iban tracker $62. Both amounts are in Malay dollars.

27. Dawson, 146. *S. T,* 8 March 1960. Short, 442. Williams-Hunt, 78.

28. Dawson, 154.

29. Short, 442 fn. I was a witness to their insensible attitude to their personal safety during visits to Lasah and Fort Luckham between February and March 1951.

30. *S. T.*, 5 September 1951. The former O.C. 20 PFJC, ASP John West confirmed much of this information during interviews in October 1990 and April 1991.

31. Dawson, 168.

32. Luckam was not the first permanent strong point to be set up in a potentially hostile Orang Asli area. In early 1949 a company of Seaforth Highlanders was sent into then relatively unknown Tasik Bera (Tasik is Malay for Lake) country on the borders of South Pahang, Negri Sembilan, to contact the Semalai in the area who were believed to be under MRLA control. After establishing friendly relations with that group, they handed out food, tobacco, sarongs, and axe heads which had been dropped by air. The Semalai were the only Orang Asli group to brew alcohol which the Scottish soldiers were not loathe to share; this helped to cement good relations between the two groups. The Seaforths withdrew leaving the area to a large police contingent, which constructed a police post and an airstrip.

The post remained until 1951 when it was abandoned, but in 1953 Fort Iskandar was established on the same spot as part of the new policy of meeting the Orang Asli on their own ground. See H. Miller, *Menace in Malaya* (London 1954), 124–32.

33. P. D. R. Williams-Hunt, "Evacuating Aboriginal Communities," *Malayan Police Magazine,* Vol. 2, No. 3 (Kuala Lumpur, March 1950), 61–62.

34. *Arkib Negara*, FS 12121/50–7.

35. Dawson, 177.

36. *Federation of Malaya, Annual Report 1952* (Kuala Lumpur 1953), 11, and SAS eye-witnesses who were interviewed by me. Also see Map 4.

37. In 1952 the RAF attacked seven hundred targets in Malaya in four thousand offensive sorties. They dropped four thousand tons of bombs, fired ten thousand rockets and used two million rounds of ammunition. Ibid, 11.

38. *S. T.,* 27 May 1952.

39. Dawson, 178.

40. The MCP/MRLA used the term Asal or Asli from 1951 when referring to the Orang Asli rather than the less acceptable Sakai commonly used by the-SF and most Malays. The formation and functions of the MRLA organized and controlled Asal Clubs or Protection Corps will be discussed in a later chapter.

41. *S. T.* 20 October 1949.

42. Ibid., 28 October 1949. "Bandit"-terminology used by the Security Forces and media before 1951 to describe any armed member of the MCP.

43. Ibid., 13 March 1951.

44. Williams-Hunt, 44.

45. Noone, 154.

46. This directive is not to be confused with the later (31 October 1951) directive which details new military tactics and political actions by the MCP.

47. PRO. Kew, CO 1022/187.

48. *S. T.,* 16 July 1952. *Masuk Melayu* (to enter the Malay community) was the terrminology for Orang Asli converts to Islam.

49. Although classified as Orang Melayu Asli, the Orang Kanaq, according to their own tradition, had arrived in Johore from the Rhio Islands off Singapore about two hundred years ago. See Carey, 219.

50. *S. T.,* 25 May 1949.

51. Sel. Sec., 1519/51–1–12 and attached minute papers.

52. Ibid., 2597/51–9.

53. Ibid., 1988/50–1A–2–3.

54. *S. T.,* 28 June 1948, 26 September 1950.

55. *Arkib Negara*, FS 12198/50–1A.

56. Ibid., FS 12198/50–4A. See also Dr. I.V. Polunin, "The medical natural history of Malayan Aborigines," *The Medical Journal of Malaya* 8 (1 and 2) 1953, 55–174.

57. Ibid., FS 12198/50–8A.

58. *S. T.*, 12 November 1949.

59. Ibid., 24 November 1949.

60. Dawson, 149.

61. *S. T.*, 16 March 1951.

62. Dawson, 178.

63. Ibid., 179.

CHAPTER 3

Violence 1948–1953

It is not proposed to give a blow by blow account of the abductions, killings, or the indignities heaped on the Orang Asli in the years following the declaration of the Emergency. Instead this chapter will illustrate particular happenings in which the tribespeople suffered questionable, extraordinary, or heinous actions at the hands of either the MCP/MRLA, the Government Forces, or their fellow tribal groups or individuals. Some incidents involved all three parties. Some eyewitness accounts will be given, supported by other evidence where it is available.

The ad hoc resettlement of the Orang Asli was, unintentionally, the most cumulatively lethal cause of indirect violence against the peoples of the jungle in the Emergency. There were also numerous other acts of direct brutality by the protagonists in the struggle against the tribespeople. As a result many of them were killed, wounded, or just disappeared. Orang Asli also were guilty of such barbaric internecine atrocities that they helped to discount the myth of their peoples' timidity and pacifity. Some direct and indirect acts of violence by individual tribesmen against their fellows were so murderously cold-blooded that the sanity of the perpetrators was questionable. Many tribesmen were involved as willing allies with the MRLA or the Security Forces in armed clashes, supporting one or other of the combatants. Some were coerced into killing under threat of punishment if they did not comply with the directions they received.

The Fear Factor

Fear was a common factor shared by both the protagonists in dealing with the Orang Asli. Some of the random killing of those people could be attributed to this dread of the strange and unknown in the jungle environment with which many of them were not familiar. The Security Forces generally regarded the Orang Asli in the jungle with wary hostility. The semi-literate urban and rural Malays who were hastily recruited into the Special and Auxiliary Police had either never seen the jungle dwellers before or were used to dealing with them on an exploiter/exploitee basis. The latter were aware of the Orang Asli's prowess with the blowpipe and the fatal effect of that weapon's poisoned darts.[1] They were not loathe to pass on this information to their fearful, inexperienced, urban comrades. Rural Malays believed that the Negritos and Senoi had magical powers which added to their apprehensions, and conversely, the tribespeople regarded the Malays as "malicious sorcerers."[2]

To the British conscripts, Malaya, and particularly the jungle, were completely alien environments. They viewed all the inhabitants with an unjustified sense of racial superiority combined with a wary suspicion; their attitude to the Orang Asli was tinged with the fear of the unknown. The other major force up to the early 1950s who had contact with the jungle peoples was the Nepalese Gurkhas who treated the tribespeople as they were directed to do by their officers, but they too shared this dread of the unfamiliar.

To the MCP/MRLA the Orang Asli were useful as a source of labor, intelligence, and food, when the MRLA's normal sources were hard- pressed. This did not prevent certain units and individuals behaving with a paranoiac, homicidal panic towards the tribespeople when they felt their security had been compromised.

The Non-violent Semai

Before examining specific details about violence, it is worth commenting on a conclusion about Semai behavior during that conflict, drawn by the American anthropologist, R.K. Dentan, some years after the Emergency. He recorded that one Senoi/Semai veteran, in what he referred to as the counter insurgency troops, boasted,

> We killed, killed, killed. The Malays would stop and go through people's pockets and take their watches and money. We did not think of watches or money. We thought only of killing. Wah, truly we were drunk with blood.

Dentan continued, "One man even told how he had drunk the blood of a man he had killed." He goes on to rationalize the story by declaring that "the Semai seem bemused." They were quite pleased that they were good soldiers but could not explain their actions. They regarded this homicidal outburst as a separate experience outside the routine of their normal existence. The action quoted, he claimed, was an exception to their usual behavior and after the Emergency the Semai returned to their habitual non-aggressive life-style.[3]

Why this boastful account by the Semai of their violent actions and their later reactions should be regarded by him as extraordinary is difficult to understand. Many other soldiers of other races committed brutal actions in combat situations. The Scots Guards, in December 1949 at Batang Kali in Selangor[4] shot dead twenty-four unarmed Chinese prisoners under very dubious circumstances. There is no indication that the soldiers involved were homicidal maniacs. What they did was a murderous act and without justification, but it happened in a war situation where the troops panicked and began shooting. There is no evidence that these soldiers behaved aggressively when they returned to civilian life or that they acted other than as normal peaceful citizens. Like the Semai and many others who had been in military or paramilitary units, they would have regarded their service in the Emergency as something out of the ordinary. Again, like the Semai, some would exaggerate their experiences and boast of their prowess as killers. Some others who served in the Emergency, such as former Police Lieutenant Roy Follows, who was not at Batang Kali, would matter of factly recount their experiences and conclude their reminiscences in somewhat the same manner as he had in his book.

> In England I got married, and with Doris went back to Malaya and the Marine Police for a further three years. But I never went back into the jungle; that part of my life ended, as I had anticipated it would, when I plodded, more dead than alive, out of the Pengerang Swamp for the last time.

Follows had killed men he regarded as his enemies but that did not prevent him from returning to a normal existence.[5] Most people know of kind and unaggressive former servicemen who lived extraordinary lives while in the military but have, just like the Semai, returned to gentle behavior and avoidance of violence in peacetime. There was nothing exceptional in the reversal of the Semai to a peaceful existence.

Incidents

Most Orang Asli were involved in the Emergency against their will. Before they were able to go about their normal peaceful pursuits again, the violence of the jungle war would cause ferment and trouble amongst them and in their homelands.

Reports of their entanglement with the armed forces of both sides commenced soon after the Emergency was declared in June 1948. Police ambushed a Sakai village in the Batu Gajah area of Perak in August 1948, killing two Chinese terrorists suspected of supplying arms to its inhabitants. In October, three Orang Asli were arrested in Bidor, Perak, and a further two in Tapah in December, all for allegedly helping the Communists.[6] Among the 267 civilians killed between June and October 1948, three Sakai civilians were listed. Who killed them and why was not stated. By a coincidence three Sakai "bandits" were killed by 23 February 1949.[7]

RAF Beaufighters (World War II vintage fighter bombers) in December 1948 rocketed and fired cannon into the jungle twenty miles west of Kuantan in East Pahang, with the aim of what was called flushing the jungle "in areas bandits were known to be heading."[8] That was Orang Melayu Asli territory. A headman and his son-in-law were reported missing in the Cameron Highlands from 1 February 1949 after taking a party of thirty followers to Ringlet for registration. It was known that the MCP opposed the registration of civilians which would enable the government to identify and keep track of the population by issuing registration cards to those registered.[9] No further information on the two missing Orang Asli came to light in later reports.

In 1949 a series of running battles ensued between Senoi/Semai, MRLA, and Chinese civilians in the Tapah, Kampar area of Perak from 13 to 15 July. Press reports based on official Security Forces' press releases indicated that a party of armed Communists attacked two Semai villages, in the aforementioned area. In the attack two Sakai women were killed, three Sakai men wounded, and three men and five women abducted. "Following the attacks, Sakai from Kampong Kerikai, [Kikit], south of Kampar went to Bukit Pekan with four shotguns and parangs [machetes] and killed four Chinese, three women and a man. About a dozen women and children were wounded. Police later rounded up the Sakai and brought them into Kampar." The attack on the Orang Asli at Kampong Kerikai was made by ten men with sten guns (sub-machine guns) and other weapons. The report gave the casualties in the unnamed second village but does not give an account of the number of attackers involved. Police going to the scene were fired on by the attackers who retreated when their fire was returned.[10] The running battles continued. It was further reported that in a revenge attack by the Semai, again on Bukit Pekan, fourteen Chinese were killed and thirteen wounded on 14 July. "Police have arrested twenty-three Sakai in connection with the incident. More Sakai have been abducted in the Tapah area."[11]

During a visit to Perak Special Branch Headquarters in Ipoh in July, 1990, I interviewed a Semai, Udah Mat bin Long Sohr, from the Kampar area, who described an incident which occurred when he lived in Kampong Changkat Pinggin, west of Kampar, in 1949 when he was about ten years old. The location is very close to the villages in which the incidents previously related occurred. The Orang Asli in that area were, he stated, uniformed Special Constables armed with shotguns and employed by the Anglo-Oriental Tin Dredging Company to protect their tin mine. The MRLA continually harassed the Orang Asli villagers in an attempt to get them to help with food supplies and information, and tried to get the armed men to defect. The pressure was so strong that the whole Semai group left their village and moved to the Sungei Garah (possibly should be Sungei Groh) area. He thought his group moved back to their old village in July 1950 where they were surrounded and attacked by the MRLA. Udah was wounded in the neck by a sten gun bullet and two Orang Asli women were killed. They beat off the attackers and next day launched an assault on a nearby Chinese village to avenge their losses. Many Chinese, he was not sure how many, were killed in the attack.[12]

Udah subsequently became a teacher and claimed that he had heard a number of reports about other killing of the Orang Asli while located at Bidor, near Tapah in 1958. I was able to substantiate only one of these which will be related in this chapter. He joined the Senoi Pra'aq in 1959 and took part in a number of operations with that unit. He is currently employed by the Special Branch in Perak.

It was reported in the local press that on 13 July 1949 troops were investigating the reported abduction of thirty-five Orang Asli in the Cameron Highlands area earlier in July. They had been taken into the jungle by twenty armed bandits.[13] Following this report, Chinese squatters in the Bertam Valley in the Cameron Highlands were evacuated on 21 August 1949. "The operation follows a series of bandit outrages culminating in the mass murder of thirty-four Sakai on July 4." There were three hundred and fifty people moved, mostly Kwangsi Chinese. An MRLA camp was discovered two hundred yards from the nearest squatter's hut. The report then went on to tell about the killing of Sakai who were on their way up the Bertam Valley to work on the Boh tea plantation.

> They were stopped by two armed bandits and made to go back down the valley. Subsequently thirty-four out of thirty-five Sakai were seized by a party of forty bandits, strangled to death, and all buried in communal graves. One man escaped and reported to the Police.
>
> Squatters in the area helped the bandits to dig the graves of the Sakai and also to fell the trees with which they covered the graves.[14]

The following day thirteen Chinese were among thirty men and two women detained for questioning during the evacuation of the Chinese settlement in the Bertam Valley. The thirteen were held in connection with the strangling of the thirty-four Orang Asli.[15] In October, 3,252 people were screened by the police in the Cameron Highlands settlements of Ringlet, Lubok, Temang, and Tanah Rata. "Of the fifteen detained following the screening, one has been identified as a grave digger for the bandits when they strangled a number of Sakai and buried them in Bertam valley."[16]

During a visit to Malaysia in September–October 1988, I contacted the Royal Malaysian Police and Tony Williams-Hunt regarding the possibility of locating the reported survivor to the massacre described above. The police were unable to help but Williams-Hunt advised he would follow up my request. On returning to Malaysia in June–July 1990, I received a message that Williams-Hunt had contacted the survivor, Bah Hoi anak Pengsa, who would speak to me about the massacre.

The story that Bah Hoi anak Pengsa told of the massacre of his people was made more horrifying by the apparently senseless, random slaughter of a group of harmless tribespeople attempting to seek work away from their homeland. Williams-Hunt's stepfather, Bah Akeh,[17] made his house outside Tapah available for the interview. The narrator related the account of the killing in a matter of fact tone while the occupants of the house in which he was interviewed carried on with their normal routine. We drank sweet, weak, milky coffee with Bah Hoi as he quietly spoke of the violent deaths of the relatives and friends of some forty years ago. He was not clear about the exact date but he was aware it was in 1949 or early 1950. He was a young boy of about ten at the time.

He said that a party of thirty-five people consisting of ten women, five children, and twenty adult males had started on the way to the Boh tea estate in the Cameron Highlands to get money for work they had done and to receive identification cards. They had worked at the tea estate for a time and had returned to their village, Kampong Lemus,[18] on the Sungei Jelai Kecil, near the Pahang, Perak border and had gone home to notify people in their kampong that they intended to look for permanent work on the tea estate. The party was returning to the estate along the Bertam Valley and were about one mile clear of the jungle edge when they were stopped by three armed Chinese. The armed men told them not to go to Ringlet, a hamlet in the Cameron Highlands, which they would have passed through on their way, because there were many soldiers there. The group followed the instructions they were given but then met another four or five armed men a short distance from the jungle edge. These told the now confused Senoi to change direction and led them in the direction of some adjacent Chinese vegetable plots. Before reaching these gardens, the guerrillas ordered the Orang Asli to change direction again and sit down near some bushes. Then a much larger party of Chinese, Bah Hoi estimated seventy strong, also armed, arrived and repeated the order to go back to their home because there were a large number of soldiers in the Ringlet area.

In what appeared to be a change of mind by their captors, the now thoroughly frightened tribespeople were then directed into an empty hut near the market gardens. They were told to wait there until a well-known Semai supporter of the MCP, Bah Pelankin, arrived. "Bah Pelankin will decide your fate, he is your leader," the senior guerrilla told them. Sometime later Pelankin arrived escorted by five armed MRLA. He asked where they came from and when told they had come over from the Sungei Jelai Kecil, the narrator claimed Pelankin said, "You people will die at five p.m." None of the Orang Asli party had any idea why he made that decision.

They were then commanded to pack up and move back in the direction from which they had just come and guided to a patch of jungle between the path leading to the hut. In the meantime Bah

Pelankin had disappeared. It was then that the young Bah Hoi had a stroke of luck. A dog with the party broke away and ran off. He was told to run after it and bring it back. Two of the armed guards followed him. It must have taken him some time to chase the dog which was not found. When he returned to the hut, some Orang Asli men had been taken outside and tied, in pairs, back to back, to poles. He saw large freshly dug holes near the scene, but did not know who had dug them or when. More men were being led out of the hut at gun point and tied up. He was directed to follow but he ran away when the armed men turned to tie him. His escorts then fired at him, but because he was small and ducked and weaved as he quickly ran, they missed him.

The frightened boy hid in the jungle edge and as daylight faded he heard shots and cries for help. He claimed that he heard automatic weapons firing. Exhausted and nearly fainting, he managed to climb a tree and slept there until just before daylight. The terrified boy then wandered aimlessly in the half dark but finally set out for the Jelai Kecil and in three days reached his home ladang. He told relatives and kinsmen what had occurred and they then took him back to Ringlet. There he told the manager of the tea estate what had happened. The manager took him to the OCPD Tanah Rata in the Cameron Highlands. The OCPD, who he referred to as Ted Morrow, did not seem to believe him but the estate manager said they would go to see the Chief Police Officer (CPO) at Ipoh. He spent four days in Tanah Rata and a week in Ipoh before any action was taken.

Bah Hoi was then taken in a large army convoy back to the Cameron Highlands. In the early morning he led the army party to where the killings took place. He had some difficulty in finding the spot which he knew was at the source of a stream. The troops were sceptical about his story as he scouted around trying to find the graves of his relatives. He then saw some partially covered limbs showing up through the ground. As the army started to dig, the smell of the bodies was sickening. They had great difficulty in uncovering the graves which were covered by large felled trees; Bah Hoi had heard the sound of saws when he had hidden originally from his pursuers. Some female bodies, with clothing removed, were disinterred and one child's body was found in a sack. He did not think the army was able to recover all the bodies because of the heavy trees covering the graves. Two of Bah Hoi's brothers and a sister were among the dead.

The survivor of the massacre, forty years on, was still mystified about why his people had been killed. He could only surmise that the MRLA had suspected that they were spies. From his experiences he thought most Orang Asli were killed by the guerrillas because they failed to supply food. Bah Pelankin, he claimed, was notorious for directing that his fellow Semai be killed. Bah Pelankin used the MRLA to do his killing. In answer to questions about Orang Asli deaths by the Security Forces, he said *beribu* (many) were killed by stray bullets when caught in fire fights between the Security Forces and the MRLA. He also claimed that some of his people were killed by aerial bombing in the early days of the Emergency.

Bah Hoi later joined the Police Field Force as a special constable. He was ambushed in the Telok Anson area of Perak, but although some Malay constables were killed, he escaped. He was also stationed in Tanah Rata near the scene of the massacre and was then sent to the Orang Asli research center at Selayang outside Kuala Lumpur. He now lives in the Cameron Highlands.

As mentioned previously, Udah Mat was aware of an alleged killing of Orang Asli in the Bidor area of Perak in 1950. I followed up this matter but due to lack of time I was not able to contact any survivors personally. Williams-Hunt very kindly undertook to investigate the allegation for me and I have transcribed, verbatim, his account of an interview with Yok Serungkop[19] who was present at the killings. It has been deliberately not edited or paraphrased to show the contrast between a non-Semai recording of an incident—as set down in the previous paragraphs—and a Semai account of their fellow tribespeoples' ordeals. The first paragraph, although not recording the actual incident, demonstrates how the Semai look back on that time of terror for their people.

Massacre at Ulu Kenyor Bidor

The Emergency was unquestionably one event which brought a lot of traumatic experiences to the Orang Asli. Drawn forceably [sic] into it, mainly because the war was also fought in their territories, the Orang Asli were subjected to much sufferings at the hands of the two opposing sides, the British Colonial Government and the communist terrorists. Many of them perished in the not uncommon massacres carried out by the communists throughout the peninsula, most of which went unreported and were not known to the public. One such massacre occurred early during the insurrection, possibly in 1950, near a Semai village in Ulu Kenyor Bidor in southern Perak. Yok Serungkop, an eyewitness, then about ten years old, related the incident as follows:

One morning, about ten o'clock, my father (Yok Nieley), his elder brother (Yok Terhool) and I were collecting perah [also known as perah in Malay] and wall [known as bua pentalin in Malay] nuts in the forest close to our village, Kampong Poh, when three Chinese communists and a Semai headman, Penghulu Gemok approached us. They were on their way back to Penghulu Gemok's village in Ulu Kenyor from another Semai village called Rantau Panjang in Ulu Bikam. Sensing trouble, my father had thought of running away, but when he realised that the communists had already seen us and moreover since my uncle had a bad sore on one of his legs which would prevent him from moving fast, he aborted the intention. When the communists were close enough to us they sat down and almost immediately offered us some tobacco which were [sic] accepted by my father and my uncle. Then the communist with the shotgun asked my uncle to go with him for a meeting at Penghulu Gemok's village. My uncle however refused, giving the excuse that if he went for the meeting there would be no one to look after his two young daughters at home, as his wife had left them to follow her lover to another village. The communists then became furious, and instantly grabbed him and tied his hands with a parachute string. They then, pointing their guns at us, forced us to follow them.

After travelling for several hours, mostly walking uphill, we met with scores of communists put on guard along the path leading to Penghulu Gemok's village. These communists, who were fully armed, then walked with us to the village, which was made up of only one longhouse. We got into the house, and in it we saw several communists were tying the hands of the villagers. The children and women were tied together with the men individually. I do not know how many people were there in the house, but in those days a Semai longhouse would contain about ten families made up of about fifty people. Several other communists were also confiscating belongings, like machetes and sarung [sarong] of the villagers. When the villagers protested and asked the communists why they were doing that to them, the communists asked the villagers not to talk and also threatened to beat them up.

Subsequently, the villagers and the three of us, hands all tied except for mine, were taken to a place not far from the longhouse. There, again except for me, all the captives were tied standing up to trees around the place, the children and women were tied together, the men individually. Then one by one the men were taken to a spot not far away for interrogation which however took only a short while, and after which they were brought back and tied to the trees again. The question asked by the communists was, I was later informed, whether the villagers supported them or the Government.

While the interrogation was being carried out, we suddenly heard cries of pain from the longhouse. We learned later from the other survivors that the cries came from an old lady who was hanged upside down from a high beam in the house and beaten with gun-butts by the communists to death.

Not long after this there were sounds of gunshots again coming from the direction of the longhouse. On hearing this, the communists who were with us, untied the villagers and almost immediately at point blank fired shots at them. What followed were cries of pain and for help, and within seconds bodies covered with blood were lying all over the place. The sight was horrifying and a strong smell of blood filled up the air. My father was hit in the thighs, and as I approached him he asked me to look for my uncle. I looked around and saw my uncle some distance away, his body covered with blood, lying down face towards the ground. He was hit in the stomach and was in great pain, judging from the groanings he was making. I asked him to stand up and run away, but he refused to do it, and instead asked me to leave him there as he said faintly that he felt he was going to die. I then ran back to my father, told him about my uncle, and next with my father struggling, we ran away. The communists saw us and fired a few shots but fortunately none hit us.

We ran, my father falling down several times along the way, towards the Malay village of Kampong Poh. It was six in the evening when we reached this village, and immediately we were given help by the villagers. My father was treated for his wound which was still bleeding and after that we were taken to the army stationed at the village. Later the army sent us to the hospital in Tapah where we remained until my father recovered from his wound.

We later learned that the gunshots which we heard while the villagers were being interrogated were shootings when the security forces made contact with the communists positioned at the longhouse. When the communists came to the longhouse the day before, two men who suspected the bad intention of the communists especially after knowing that these same communists had killed a Semai village headman in Sungkai, sneaked out at night and went down to Bidor to report to the army of the communists presence in the village.

Besides Yok Serungkop and his father, the other survivors of the massacre were an old man and his wife, and another man who was hiding under a heap of rattan placed under the longhouse. All these three other survivors escaped unhurt.

As stated in the document above, many killings of the Orang Asli went unreported. In the early years of the Emergency the Security Forces were only able to react to MRLA attacks. They did not have the resources to investigate every report or rumour about killings of Orang Asli in remote areas and which involved people who, in their eyes at the time, were not important. Only the survivors or relatives remembered those victims caught up in a war they did not understand.

Security Forces Violence

The Security Forces were not blameless in their dealings with the Orang Asli. Some of the minor incidents early in the Emergency are mentioned at the beginning of this chapter. An unusual and questionable report of an Orang Asli killing on 29 March 1949, cast some doubt on the veracity of the unit involved. It claimed, "Seven letters found on a Sakai shot dead by a patrol of the 1/10 Gurkhas in Johore yesterday when crawling toward their camp, proved him to be a bandit messenger."[20] On 10 November it was reported that "two Sakai bandits who are said to have attacked a Gurkha patrol were shot dead in the Segamat area of Johore, but no further details were available."[21] The Orang Asli were not noted for suicidal attacks on heavily armed military patrols. At Mancis police station in the Bentong area, in February 1950, one of two Sakai held in custody who tried to escape was shot dead, the other escaped.[22]

From the beginning of the Emergency[23] to March 1950, forty-three Sakai civilians and seven Sakai bandits had been killed. These were the known and reported casualties and did not include people who died in the resettlement process. Two Sakai women were convicted by the Sessions Court, Segamat, on a charge of consorting with an armed person. Saidah, aged fifty-three years, was sentenced to four years imprisonment and Selamah, who was fifteen years old, received a two year sentence.[24]

Orang Asli were not mentioned in official Colonial or War Office despatches until 1952. That first report claimed that "a party of 3 PJC contacted two Sakai terrorists in Rompin District. Both terrorists were killed but only one body was recovered as the other fell in a river and did not surface again."[25] In a situation report from Far East Land Forces to the War Office on 29 August 1953, it was reported that "near Tapah in Perak an unknown number of Sakai with blowpipes, fired darts at a Security Forces patrol. No casualties were reported. This isolated incident illustrates the worst type of CT control over some Sakai."[26] In February 1953 a police patrol, together with some armed Semai from Fort Jor who had been allowed to return home to the Jelai Kecil area, attacked a hut in a ladang where the Semai had seen MRLA. In the resulting melee two Chinese were killed, as were six Aborigines who were in the hut with them, three more were wounded. It is not reported whether the killed and wounded Orang Asli were armed. Dawson said, "These Semai had come without permission from Bukit Betong resettlement area and this was the unfortunate result." The wounded tribesmen were evacuated by helicopter and recovered in hospital.[27] As the Security Forces concentrated on winning over the Orang Asli from 1953 onwards, reports of random hostile actions against them became less prevalent.

Aerial Attacks

The aerial bombing of jungle areas and clearings was one of the ongoing acts of intended or unintended violence against the Orang Asli. Clutterbuck wrote:

> Except for occasional successes with pinpoint bombing, offensive air strikes were almost wholly unsuccessful in Malaya; they probably did more harm than good. Hundreds of tons of bombs were dropped on the jungle every month, particularly in 1951–1952; they probably killed fewer than half a dozen guerrillas a year—more by accident than design.

He continued on to claim that the enemy was contemptuous of this massive expenditure of force for such a little result. The MRLA used this contempt to belittle the Security Forces to the Orang Asli. It also whipped up feelings of fear and hate among the Aborigines if one of their number was accidentally killed by an air strike.[28] It is not known how many Orang Asli were killed by what was indiscriminate bombing in many instances.[29] Press reports announced bombing of clearings supposed to be bandit cultivation areas, others were announced as rest camps or assembly areas. A Police Lieutenant described indiscriminate jungle bombings as "like dropping bombs in the sea in the hope of hitting a passing submarine."[30]

In 1953 Australian Air Vice Marshal Scherger took over as air officer commanding Malaya. He gave directions to concentrate more on accurate bombing rather than the hitherto hit-and-miss saturation bombing by both the Royal Air Force and the Royal Australian Air Force. Following Scherger's appointment the bombing of targets where MRLA may possibly have been located was abandoned. The air force had realized that this former practice was causing the alienation of those villagers who were caught in the bombing without knowing why they were targeted. They had not even been aware of the presence of terrorists. They blamed the Security Forces for what they saw as random violence against them.[31] Scherger could not resist playing with his big toys. Twenty thousand pound bombs left over from World War II were used at his direction to try and clear helicopter landing pads in the jungle for future jungle operations. "But all the big bomb did was to scare the devil out of everybody within about ten miles of where it was dropped. It blew a great hole in the jungle, but left the tree trunks standing, stripped of their vegetation, like so many telegraph poles." It also left the area impassable for ground troops.[32] What it did to Orang Asli in the area is not recorded.

Chemical Spraying

There is confusion as to whether or not the Orang Asli were submitted to the great obscenity of the Vietnam war, poisoning and defoliation of crops and the jungle by aerial sprays. Short reported that in 1951 the Chairman of the Kelantan SWEC requested that the RAF concentrate on bombing food cultivation areas because the Air Force "considered the aerial spraying of sodium arsenite to kill cultivation to be too dangerous to its own personnel."[33] Scherger claimed that helicopters were used to spray suspected CT food growing areas in the jungle with 2-4-D to kill the crops. He also claimed the CT fired on the helicopters.[34] This is the only time in the Emergency that a helicopter was reported to have been fired at by the enemy. Henniker reported that a helicopter was used to spray weed-killer on enemy cultivations.[35] He then claimed that the "bandits" picked off all the leaves on which the drops of spray had fallen. This left the roots intact and healthy. Because of the failure of the aerial spraying, troops were sent in to pull up and burn the plants in about sixty gardens. Harry Miller confirmed that chemical sprays were used by aircraft to destroy vegetable plots planted by the MRLA in the deep jungle after their change of tactics following the MCP's 1951 directive.[36]

Roadside areas such as blind corners which were susceptible to ambush, were sprayed manually or by tanker trucks to clear vegetation, but the accounts of wholesale crop spraying in the jungle are questionable. In the Belum Valley during Operation Helsby in February 1952, after its Malay inhabitants were evacuated, the SAS began to poison the coconut trees in the area with manually applied chemicals. This was stopped almost immediately by the senior civilian authority who had accompanied the police into the valley. He was fearful of the effects the chemicals could have on Malay and Orang Asli settlements down river and their long term effects on the Belum area.[37] The troops had to chop down the trees to prevent the MRLA from using the coconuts. On another occasion, during Operation Galway-Valiant in October– November 1953, a field of hill padi, some one point five hectares in area, was discovered close to a MRLA camp and vegetable patch. This would have been an ideal size to have been destroyed by aerial chemical spraying, but instead an SAS Troop of some twelve men spent two days cutting it down with machetes.[38]

There was some correspondence from 1952 to 1954 between Malaya Command, the War Office and Imperial Chemical Industries [ICI], concerning the use of chemicals. Mr. E. K. Woodford of the Unit of Experimental Agronomy, Oxford, and Mr. H. G. H. Kearnes of the University of Bristol Research Station, Long Aston, visited Malaya between 4 and 23 December 1952 to investigate the use of spray chemicals. They estimated that it would take one month of spraying by 2-4-Dichlorophenoxy Acetic Acid and 2-4-5-Trichlorophenoryacetic, to cover twenty-three and a half miles of road. Chemicals alone, they concluded, could not be expected to provide adequate destruction of ambush sites. It would be cheaper and quicker to use manual labour to cut back the vegetation.

A letter from the Defence Department in Malaya to J. D. Higham at the Colonial Office claimed that they believed that ICI was only using Malaya for its own experiments at government expense. Some experiments were carried out using a helicopter to spray the chemical CMU (Monuron) on crops.[39] In April 1952 *The Times* wrote an article on the poisoning of the crops by chemicals from the air in Malaya.[40] A very irate Mr. B. Scott of Leeds wrote to Mr. C. Pannel, his local MP on 20 April 1952,

> I have heard on the BBC news this evening that our troops have been using chemicals to destroy crops in Malaya. I protest most vigorously at this shocking and inhuman form of warfare and I am writing to ask you to join with other MPs to make a protest in Parliament. . . . It is urgent that in the defense of the good name of Britain throughout the world, to end this chemical warfare, bring General Templer back to Britain and end the war in Malaya.[41]

A question was asked in Parliament on 30 April 1952 and elicited a negative reply.[42]

In January 1953 a Mr. T. C. Jerrom of the Malayan Civil Service wrote to Mr. Piper in the Colonial Office saying that he did not think that the question of political repercussions from the use of CMU to destroy terrorist food crops needed to be raised. Professor Blackman of the Department of Agriculture at Oxford University, who had been requested to evaluate the situation, wrote also to Piper that there was no prospect of the use of large quantities of 2-4-5-T in Malaya. Templer had the final word when a letter was sent to the Colonial Office on 9 February 1953 stating that the High Commissioner had decided that experiments in the use of Trioxone and STCA (Sodiumtrichloroacetate) would cease in Malaya. He had intimated that he too believed ICI were only using Government money for their own experimental purposes.[43]

The Orang Asli were thereby spared what would have been an act of horrendous if unintended violence against them. By 1953 the MRLA had begun to disguise their cultivation plots to be indistinguishable from those of the tribespeople and it was very likely that the latter's plots would also have been sprayed. Even if the chemicals had not been dropped directly on the jungle people or their crops, the results of chemical spraying in the Vietnam war are sufficiently documented to allow conjecture on what would have happened in Malaya if the use of chemicals had been allowed to continue. There may have been some minor experimental spraying of crops as described by Henniker and Scherger but there was no general long term use.

Orang Asli Aggression

Aggressive actions by Orang Asli against both Security Forces and MRLA continued to be reported during the 1950s. These belie the alleged timidity and pacifity of the tribespeople. Many were spontaneous actions when the Orang Asli acted without instigation from either of the protagonists. These actions followed on from particular groups deciding to take a stance supporting one or the other of the opposing parties and proceeding to act to confirm that support. An exceptionally brave and aggressive incident by the adherents to Security Forces was the killing of three armed guerrillas in November 1953 by four tribesmen armed only with parangs (machetes). One of the dead men was Sit Way, a Branch Committee member for part of the Bentong area in Pahang. Another was Mong Fai, a District Committee member, and the third was a woman. The MRLA were armed with a sten gun, a pistol, and a grenade which were recovered by a patrol of the King's African Rifles led to the scene by two of the Orang Asli.[44] In the same month in the Cameron Highlands area one of three Orang Asli fired his shotgun at a Security Forces patrol; one of the tribesmen was killed and another wounded.[45] Direct acts of violence by the jungle dwellers increased as the opposing forces moved further into tribal homelands.

Indirect violence by the jungle dwellers was also a feature of the conflict in their homelands. As they began to accept that the Security Forces were better equipped than the MRLA and had much more to offer them with medical care, paid work, rations, and cash rewards for leading patrols to guerrilla locations, they began to betray their erstwhile allies or controllers. They understood that by guiding police or military patrols to cultivation areas or hidden camps the occupants of those locations would often be killed. For these killings, in which they often took no active part, they expected to be rewarded. In two instances involving SAS patrols where they failed to kill all the targeted enemy, the Orang Asli guides roundly abused the patrol commander.[46] In one of these incidents where two of three MRLA were killed and the third one wounded and captured, the headman who had guided the patrol demanded that the wounded prisoner be summarily killed. He saw the injured man as a future threat even though he (the headman) had not been seen by him.[47] The fact that the guides often stayed at the rear away from the firing line did not mean that they were any less involved in the killing of the people on whom they had willingly informed. They were fully aware that their actions could result in the deaths of those whom they had betrayed.

Social and Cultural Violence

The Orang Asli were also victims of indirect violence against their culture and social order by well-meaning helpers. Pamela Gouldsbury insisted that the young women who were normally bare breasted, wear *bajus* (blouses in this context) in the vicinity of Fort Shean "to conform to Western ways." Ostensibly this was done to protect them from, what she prudishly considered, the lascivious gaze of the members of the fort garrison. It was also intended to stop visitors pestering them for photographs. In theory the young women were to put on the blouses on coming into the fort and take them off when they returned home.[48] In practice the youngsters were delighted to wear them all the time and did not take them off as long as they were serviceable. This caused skin rashes from which the Orang Asli in the Highlands areas were generally free.

Ray Walker, the first Asian policeman to command a fort, when interviewed by me in 1988, told of a lightning visit by Gouldsbury to a fort where he was stationed. He was in a schoolroom he had constructed in the fort, where the Aborigine Liaison Officer was teaching Orang Asli women basic hygiene, when Gouldsbury arrived. She was shocked when she saw this virile young man in the presence of all the young bare breasted women and said she did not want to see this type of situation the next time she visited. In his next air-supply drop he received two boxes more than he expected. On opening them he found they contained brassieres and a terse note from his visitor directing him to issue them to the young women visiting the fort. He did as he was ordered with the consequence that they rarely took them off and got skin rashes. These women allowed others to wear their clothes and eventually all the women ended up with these rashes.

On 17 February 1953, a letter from the Acting Secretary to the Member for Home Affairs, to all State Secretaries suggested that where possible yearly or half-yearly jamborees should be held for Orang Asli. These were to assist in maintaining good relations between the Government and the Aborigines.

> His Excellency the High Commissioner is interested in this proposal and has asked that your government should give consideration to reviving such jamborees where they have been held before and to initiating them in other districts where there are a large number of aborigines in the neighbourhood. [49]

It is worth noting that his Excellency was also the Commissioner of Boy Scouts in Malaya, and in that official capacity was familiar with that body's practice of holding regular jamborees. It is unclear what exactly these jamborees were supposed to achieve unless the High Commissioner equated the Orang Asli with the Boy Scouts. The letter suggested that the Adviser on Aborigines could be contacted for advice.

Not everybody shared the High Commissioner's enthusiasm for exposing the Orang Asli in jamborees. In a letter of 23 May to the editor of the *Straits Times,* headed "Jungle Folk Insulted," the writer was scathing about Orang Asli being exhibited as some kind of freak spectacle. He had seen a group in a fun fair at Kuala Lipis huddled together and feeling out of place. He was advised that they had been especially brought down "to create a funny situation." He went on, "If this is so, it is surely an outrage to human dignity. It was," he continued, "an insulting exploitation of an illiterate section of Malayan people." The letter was signed Viva Malayans.[50] Whatever the intentions were of the Government concerning the purpose of the jamborees, most Orang Asli involved were used to performing at agricultural shows. At the Kuala Langat district agricultural show in Selangor, three hundred Orang Asli took part in a special jamboree. This included tribal dancing, beauty contests, *ronggeng* (Malay dance), blow pipe contests, tug of war, and fortune telling, while some took part in wedding ceremonies for the edification of the onlookers. The Sultan of Selangor saw part of the wedding ceremony.[51] His comments were not reported, nor were the comments of the Orang Asli who were transported to the show and supplied with food and prizes for the duration of their visit. Their presence at those functions was for their entertainment value, not to try and integrate them into the surrounding society. They performed their "party piece," then were transported home. Exhibiting them in this manner did very little for their advancement and reduced them to the category of circus exhibits.

The Orang Asli's reputation for pacifity did not stand up to scrutiny as the Emergency continued. They were not always timid, peaceful victims of others' violence as will be demonstrated. They too could be as bloodthirsty as the interlopers who forced their way into their homelands to pursue their armed struggle, and involved the inhabitants in that conflict.

Notes

1. Del Tufo, 94 in his review of the 1947 Census, showed that general literacy for Malayan males between 15–19 was 60.2%. The test of literacy was an ability to read and write simple letters in Malay.

2. Carey, 78, 197.

3. Dentan, 58–59.

4. *S. T.,* 14 December 1949, *Hansard,* 4 February 1970.

5. R. Follows, with H. Popham, *The Jungle Beat: Fighting Terrorists in Malaya, 1952–1961* (London, 1990), 144.

6. *S. T.*, 26 August 1948, 16 October 1948, 1 December 1948.

7. *Malay Mail*, 27 October 1948, *S. T.*, 24 February 1949.

8. *S. T.*, 1 December 1948.

9. Ibid., 11 February 1949.

10. Ibid., 14 July 1949. There were problems in pronunciation of names and location of remote settlements among the Security Forces in the early days of the Emergency. I have been unable to locate Kampong Kerikai on a map, but Kampong Kikit (adjacent to the Tronoh mines), is close to where these incidents were reported. See also R. O. D. Noone, 175–76 who refers to a Chinese-Semai battle at Changkat Pingan in the early days of the Emergency. Note Noone's spelling of Pinggan.

11. *S. T.*, 15 July 1949.

12. This account does bear some resemblance to the newspaper reports. As stated previously, actual calendar dates were not a strong point of the Orang Asli. In addition, most peoples' memories of what happened to them when they were ten years old would be shaky. His age would also be only approximate, the Orang Asli did not have records of births.

13. *S. T.*, 14 July 1949.

14. Ibid., 22 August, 1949.

15. Ibid., 23 August, 1949.

16. Ibid., 28 October 1949.

17. Williams-Hunt's mother re-married a Semai, Bah Akeh, after her first husband's death.

18. I have been unable to locate Kampong Lemus on a 1950 ordinance map or a 1957 RAF aeronautical chart. It could have had another name and may have been just one ladang in a series of ladangs known by the name of the largest one.

19. Bah and Yok are interchangeable titles which are roughly equivalent to Mr. in English. It may seem to be a remarkable coincidence that all the narrators of the stories of the massacres were ten years old. The men I met were generally somewhere between fifty and sixty years old as far as I could judge. They really did not know their exact calendar age but had an idea about what it was in our terms. Ten was a nice round number which was close to their age at the time the occurrences they related had happened.

This story has since been published by A. Williams-Hunt in the "Center for Orang Asli Concerns" (COAC) magazine *Pernloi Gah (Orang Asli News)*, 1, December 1990, 11. Pernloi Gah is the Semai for disseminating a message.

20. *S. T.*, 29 March 1949.

21. Ibid., 10 November 1949.

22. *M. M.*, 20 February 1950.

23. Ibid., 18 March 1950.

24. *M. M.*, 28 November 1950 and *S. T.*, 21 December 1950.

25. PRO. Kew, CO 1022 Summary, 134 for week ending 27 November 1952.

26. Ibid., GO/1380, Sit rep.280, 7 September 1953, FARELF to W. O., Part 3, Para. 5.

27. Dawson, 194.

28. Clutterbuck, 160–61.

29. Short, 444–45.

30. Follows, with Popham, 110. It should be recorded that in April 1953 Chin Peng's camp in the Cameron Highlands was bombed and one of his body guards killed. Ref. CO 1033, 7 January 1954.

31. H. Rayner, *Scherger: A Biography of Air Chief Marshal Sir Frederick Scherger,* ACT, 1984, 104.

32. Sir Frederick Scherger interviewed by M. Platt, transcript Tape 2, track 2:2/1 Canberra, 1975.

33. Short, 444.

34. Platt, 4.

35. Brig. M. C. A. Henniker, CBE, DSO, MC, *Red Shadow over Malaya* (London, 1955), 180. Clutterbuck also quotes this source in *The Long Long War,* 160.

36. Miller, 226.

37. Discussion with former members of "B" Squadron, 22 SAS, and personal experience.

38. Ibid.

39. PRO. Kew, CO1022–26, 1951–53, Chemicals, 10/60/03.

40. *The Times,* 9 April 1952.

41. PRO. Kew, CO1022, 10/60/03.

42. *Hansard,* 30 April 1952, Question 38.

43. PRO. Kew, CO1022, 10/60/03. It was reported in 1959 that arsenic spraying by farmers was causing wildlife deaths. Nine elephants and many cattle had been killed in Selangor by this spraying and game wardens were keeping a look out for excessive damage from this source. *S. T.,* 11 April 1959.

44. PRO. Kew, DEFE, Intelligence Summary 183, 5 November 1953, and *S. T.,* 15 November 1953.

45. Ibid., DEFE, Intelligence Summary 186–26 November 1953.

46. Letter from Mr. Roger Levett, BEM, 15 September 1987 to me. He was the patrol commander. His version is supported by another eyewitness who does not wish to be named.

47. *S. T.*, 25 November 1953, also eyewitness accounts personally interviewed. The prisoner was patched up, taken out by helicopter for interrogation, tried and hanged.

48. Gouldsbury, 147.

49. Sel. Sec., 1726/1948 (4) H.A. 414/53/6.

50. *S. T.*, 23 May 1953.

51. *M. M.*, 29 October 1953, *S. T.*, 13 November 1953, *Singapore Standard* (pictures of the weddings), 16 November 1953.

CHAPTER 4

1953 The Fateful Year

Changes of Tactics

THE DECISION IN late 1952 by the Colonial Administration of Malaya to discontinue the counter-productive policy of resettling the Orang Asli outside their normal habitat was not prompted by purely altruistic motives. The MCP/MRLA had begun to capitalize on the animosity of the resettled tribespeople and the transitory, sometimes hostile, incursions by the Security Forces into tribal lands. They began an attempt to establish a permanent alliance with the people they referred to as "nationalities of the masses in the jungle." In contrast, the Government's forces in many areas had tried to regroup or resettle the local people resulting in negative and sometimes fatal consequences for the resettled. Those they could not reach, they bombed close to or on their ladangs, causing both panic and hostility among the inhabitants. With some exceptions the Security Forces had denied themselves the most productive sources of intelligence about their antagonists' operations in the jungle by their cavalier attitude to the presence and welfare of the indigenous tribespeople of the remote hinterland.

The changes in the government and command structure resulting from the killing of High Commissioner Sir Henry Gurney in an

MRLA ambush in October 1951, was to have a major impact on the course of the Emergency and eventually on the overall tactics used in combating the MRLA. In turn, the MCP, at what appeared to be the time of their greatest triumph, the killing of Gurney, were already planning major changes to their military and political strategies. From late October 1951, the Politbureau's instructions on these alterations were being distributed to political and fighting units through a series of directives. Neither sides' plans were able to be put into operation immediately and it was not until 1953 that the effects of those amendments began to take effect. These changes were to involve closely many of the Orang Asli, particularly the Senoi.

The accidental death of Peter Williams-Hunt in June 1953, when he fell during a walk in the jungle and was impaled on a bamboo stump,[1] resulted in a change in direction of the Department of Aborigines. This came under new Adviser R. O. D. Noone who was appointed in October 1953. This appointment was not made until the dismissal, in dramatic circumstances, of another short-lived Adviser. This will be elaborated upon later in this Chapter. *The Aboriginal Peoples' Ordinance* was tabled in the Legislative Council in 1953. This ordinance was passed into legislation by that body in early 1954.[2] Although it did not have any immediate effect on the Orang Asli it did give their problems prominence at the highest level of government. It also obtained more responsible public exposure in the media for their plight, rather than the previous practice of trivializing most news relating to them.

General Sir Gerald Templer was appointed the new High Commissioner in January 1952 to replace Gurney. His other role as Director of Operations gave him complete executive authority over all civil and military staff and functions. This was to have a particular influence on the future involvement of the Orang Asli in the Emergency. Thus the two sides were gearing up for a new phase in the battle in which both hoped to win the allegiance of the indigenous peoples of the jungle.

The strategic series of directives issued by the Politbureau of the MCP in September–October 1951 changed both the military and

Bah Dek (*left*) and Bah Sepidi, Cameron Highlands 1990.

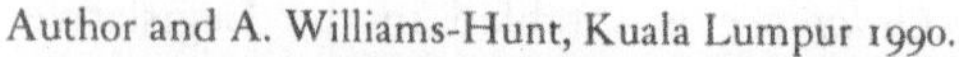

Author and A. Williams-Hunt, Kuala Lumpur 1990.

political tactics of the party in dealing with the armed struggle.[3] This study is primarily concerned with the military implications of the new policy which led to the withdrawal of the MRLA into the deep jungle, leaving the armed work force and the independent platoons at the jungle fringe to carry on the fight. While the MCP/MRLA were busily setting up their new infrastructure which closely involved the Orang Asli, the Security Forces were puzzled about the decline in MRLA initiated attacks on civilian, police, and military targets. The major directive on the change of tactics did not fall into the hands of the government forces until the end of 1952.[4] In February 1953, Templer wrote to Oliver Lyttelton, the Colonial Secretary,

> The Emergency is all pretty puzzling, though we know what their plan of campaign is. Their leaders and their brains are going deeper into the jungle, where they hope to be able to exist partly on jungle cultivation (which they are indulging in a big way with the newly formed Jungle Cultivation Corps) and partly on supplies . . . which they hope to be able to convoy in safely.[5]

The changes in tactics of the Colonial Government's armed forces also began to take effect. Following the decisions to discontinue resettling the Orang Asli, the Security Forces entered the jungle in the tribal areas to set up permanent posts with medical facilities and intelligence gathering capabilities. The Police Forts, as these strongpoints were called, were an idea based on two posts previously built by the PAAC at Lasah and Luckam in early 1951. The forts were to be built to dominate areas where Orang Asli were concentrated.

The indigenous inhabitants of the jungle were intended to be the pawns of both protagonists' tactical priorities. As Templer was to write later,

> And so the Department of Aborigines was born, and a pattern of jungle forts was built and supplied by air. It became possible to take some positive action—medical clinics, elementary schools, stores where they could exchange their jungle products for the simple luxuries. And the forts gave a certain sense of security against oppression.[6]

The presence of the forts and their garrisons was not just to service the Orang Asli; they were there primarily to offset any incentives offered to the Orang Asli by the MCP and as bases to strike at the MRLA cadres in the jungle.

Templer had bluntly declared in 1952, "The job of the British Army out here is to kill or capture Communist Terrorists in Malaya. . . ." He went on to include the Police Federal Jungle Companies, the Jungle Squads and the Area Security Squads of the Federal Police as participants in this stated objective.[7] The forts and the expansion of the Department of Aborigines were part of the plan to meet Templer's declaration about killing or capturing Communist Terrorists. The Orang Asli, in whose homelands the struggle was now to continue, would be involved in traumatic disruptions to their normal daily routines and life styles when the government's military forces attempted to carry out Templer's second exhortation.

The MCP, through a directive of September 1951, had also stated their intentions to win over the Orang Asli through incentives and promises of better treatment.

> We the Party and Liberation Army are the servants of the popular masses; at any moment we are ready to serve the masses and lead them to struggle for improvements in their livelihood. Without any exceptions we are similarly the servants of the masses of the nationality in the jungle areas; we must serve them well and lead them to struggle for improvements in their livelihood.

It continues with some noble expressions about educating the masses of the nationality in the jungle "so as to raise their enthusiasm in production in order to increase productivity."[8] In serving the Orang Asli the MRCP/MRLA were helping their own objectives. This in turn was to cause problems for the jungle dwellers who either assisted or evaded the MRLA when they attempted to establish cultivated areas and base camps in the tribal homelands.

Many Orang Asli did not side with the guerrillas solely because of threats or through fear as most official commentators imply. When interviewed by me, two Orang Asli, Bah Sepidi bin Belanda and Bah Dek, former members of the MCP Asal Clubs, gave some insight into how certain Orang Asli viewed the situation. The interview, held at the 19th Milestone on the Cameron Highlands Road in July 1990, generally dealt with their activities in the Asal organization, but a direct question on why they supported the MCP elicited an interesting reply. They claimed that the MCP promised they would eventually win the armed struggle with the help of the Orang Asli. In that event the MCP would ensure that the Orang Asli's rights to tribal land would be protected against encroachment by others. They would also assist the Orang Asli to obtain education where required as well as medical attention and ensure they had the necessary tools to till their land. It should be pointed out that both men were in the jungle with the MRLA from the early 1950's and Bah Dek was only thirteen years old when he first got involved with them.[9]

Casual conversations with other Orang Asli, who allegedly did not support the MCP, were sidetracked by the interviewees when questions of involvement with either side were raised. Some did say they were put off by atrocities by the MRLA against Orang Asli; others who were on the jungle fringe joined Home Guard or Special Constabulary units like their Malay counterparts. The MCP/MRLA were first to grasp the advantages of winning over the Orang Asli to their side and in late 1951 had begun a determined effort to win their loyalty through promises and material assistance. The Security Forces followed in 1953 with their planned wooing of the tribespeople they had previously maltreated through ignorance and lack of foresight. This struggle was to cause the Orang Asli more disruptions to their livelihood and pain and suffering to an isolated people who wished to be left to their own devices.

The Asal Organization

The development of the Asal Clubs or Asal Protection Corps by the MCP was a logical outcome of the September–October 1951 directives to win over the masses of the nationalities in the jungle areas.[10]

Any loose type of association with a group over which it did not have control would have been anathema to a tightly regimented body like the MCP. As previously stated, many of the MRLA had contacts with the Orang Asli during World War II when they were with the MPAJA, while others traded with the Orang Asli, or cohabited with, or married Orang Asli women.[11] Richard Noone claimed that his brother Pat "had given the Communists the key to the Senoi social behaviour pattern" which "lay in their doctrine of shared liability by all members of a group."[12]

The Asal Clubs mainly operated among the Senoi, the most populous of the Orang Asli groups, but there was some Asal Club activity among the Orang Melayu Asli in remoter parts of Negri Sembilan, Selangor, Pahang, and Johore. The Semalai around the Tasik Bera were subject to heavy pressure from the Chinese organizers of the Asal Clubs. Noone claimed that it took the organizers of the Asal movement two years to recruit thirty thousand Orang Asli out of a total population of fifty thousand. "By the end of 1953 they had dominated all the deep jungle groups from Negri Sembilan and South Pahang right up to the Thai border in the north."[13] Noone identified Low Mah as the chief Asal organizer[14] but Mr. Desmond Lawrence, a former senior member of the Perak Special Branch, told me that a State Committee member of the MCP in Perak, Ah Soo Choi, who was married to a Semai woman, was the overall controller. Ah Soo Choi had two assistants, Tet Meow in Perak and Low Sai in Kelantan, and he moved between both states organizing and advising on the setting up of the clubs.[15]

The structure of the clubs was loosely based on the principle of a Communist cell, without its strict discipline, and incorporating the Orang Asli social system of sharing and communal ownership. The objectives were:

(a) To act in a liaison role between the MRLA and the general Aboriginal population and disseminate MCP propaganda among the tribes.

(b) To collect information on Security Forces' activities in deep jungle areas and generally act as an intelligence screen.

(c) To provide guides, porters, couriers, and food cultivators for the MRLA and to build up a pool of reserves in those categories to be called on as needed. Some Aborigines were armed and operated with regular MRLA units.

(d) To purchase food and supplies in jungle fringe Kampongs for the MRLA and later from the police fort trade stores.[16]

The MRLA endeavoured to constitute each of the Asal units to the structure set out as follows: The Chairman of the Club was always an Aborigine. He was given the title "Datuk Pengerusi usually shortened to "Datuk Si." (These are Malay terms, Datuk is an honorific title and Pengerusi, a Malay word, means Chairman). The Secretary of the Club was invariably a member of the MRLA. He decided the agenda for all meetings and by coaxing or subtle threats, generally persuaded the Aboriginal members to decide matters the way he wanted. An Asal Club could consist of between six to twenty members, of whom two were CT and the remainder Aborigines. As far as possible, the MRLA would endeavour to persuade an Aborigine headman to become the "Datuk Si" of a club. The more influential he was, the better. However, in a number of cases when they were unable to persuade a headman, they would appoint a young, active, and well respected Aborigine with some influence to do the job. This was a situation the MRLA tried to avoid because it was divisive, causing some to side with the traditional headman and others, usually relatives and friends, to join with the young MRLA nominee. When they had to negotiate with tribesmen such as the Temiar and some Semai who had no conventional hierarchical structure, the MRLA organizers had to adapt the Protection Corps' structure to comply with variations in the local customs of the Orang Asli groups. The Communists were careful not to interfere openly with the Aboriginal social structure.

Many sources give descriptions of the workings of the Asal Clubs/Protection Corps.[17] All of these are by former members of the Security Forces or Colonial Administration. To try and get a view from the "other side" I asked both the Police Special Branch in Malaysia and Tony Williams-Hunt if they would put me in contact with Orang Asli or Chinese who had been in the Asal organization. Both introduced me to Bah Dek (currently a Special Government agent) and former member of the pro-MRLA group. Tony Williams-Hunt also introduced me to Bah Sepidi who had been Bah Dek's superior in the Emergency and now lived with his people in a village in the Cameron Highlands. Both described in detail the structure of their particular Asal group during the previously mentioned interview on 8 July 1990 in the Cameron Highlands. Bah Sepidi was the chosen Orang Asli leader of the group of thirty in the Sungei Jor-Sungei Sekai areas of the Cameron Highlands. This meant that their sector of operations straddled the main Tapah-Cameron Highlands Road on the way to Tanah Rata township. Bah Sepidi claimed he had been chosen to lead the group because the MRLA saw him as a courageous man who would endure hardship and had leadership qualities. His brother was the actual leader of their tribal clan, but was not active in the organization even though the MRLA had given him a shotgun. The Chinese gave Bah Sepidi the title of Chee Fei Poh (roughly translated as inspector).[18]

Bah Dek's and Bah Sepidi's platoon, which was larger and more heavily armed than normal, was controlled by two Chinese members of the MRLA, Choi Kau Ken, known as Awan and Wong Shu, alias Ayang. Both could speak the Semai dialect. They issued the weapons and ammunition; the unit had a bren light-machine gun, shotguns, rifles, sten sub-machine guns, and carbines with adequate ammunition. They met once a week at a pre-arranged rendezvous where they discussed security and how to get food. Attendance at this meeting was compulsory. There appeared to be little political indoctrination of the Semai at the gathering. They were given khaki uniforms but were not paid. Instead they received an allowance of one hundred dollars per person to buy food. They were not very clear about how often they received the allowance. All dealings with the MRLA were through the Chinese controllers. The Orang Asli were not allowed to see or enter any MRLA camp even though they were aware of its location. My informants claimed there were at first one hundred and fifty MRLA in the camp in their area but this number was gradually reduced to less than one hundred; they did not state why. The MRLA patrolled in groups of ten to fifteen men and frequently moved camp. They claimed there were Asal groups similar to theirs in all the river valleys in the main range area and at various times they did have contact with some of those other cells.

The major task of Bah Sepidi's party seems to have been obtaining food for the MRLA. On these foraging expeditions they went to the kampongs in the Tapah-Cameron Highlands area but not into Tapah itself. They went armed and in uniform at night. They paid the shop owners for the supplies and got provisions from Chinese, Indian, and Malay stores. In season they bought Durian fruit from Malay traders. Generally there was no difficulty in getting what they wanted. They were warned by the Chinese not to steal food and when dealing with other Orang Asli they were directed to ask, without threats, for any crops they needed and to pay for them. Orang Asli in their area, but not in the Asal, were requested to cultivate food for the guerrillas but away from their normal ladangs. Their band was never short of rations but they were aware that the Chinese MRLA in the area did go hungry despite their efforts to keep them supplied. The forays by the Orang Asli for food were quite brazen and they even claimed they walked through an SAS encampment at night on their way out for supplies.

Despite their concentration on providing supplies for the MRLA, the two interviewees did not regard their unit as a purely supply unit. They were heavily armed and although they claimed they were not an assault group, they were prepared to fight if necessary. They related two incidents, one an ambush at the fourteen mile post on the Cameron Highlands where they claimed to have killed two of three enemy ambushed: the third soldier fled.[19] The other contact was somewhere in the same area where they believed they killed the leader of an enemy patrol contacted in a surprise head-on clash. The Asal group withdrew when counter-attacked. In contrast to these militant actions they generally avoided contact with Security Force units. They had no wish to draw reprisals by indulging in aggressive action against troops or police. They considered the army more aggressive than the police and were particularly careful of the SAS even though they operated in small patrols. In answer to direct questions they said they ran when they knew the New Zealand SAS were in their areas. They were aware of the Maoris in that unit and their warlike reputation.[20]

The MRLA had an assault group in the camp in their locality which was used to carry out any killings of informers or uncooperative Chinese in their operational area. They too avoided combat unless forced to react to enemy pressure. Two Orang Asli, Bah Using and Bah Payong, were recruited into the assault group. Whether this was a sign of their military skills or just a token gesture was not stated. Even they were always accompanied by Chinese when they left the camp. They eventually surrendered to the Security Forces after killing their two Chinese "minders" sometime in 1958.[21] They shot the two one night at the seventh mile on the Cameron Highlands Road and gave themselves up to the nearest police post. They received rewards for the two dead Chinese and the weapons they handed over. Both became sergeants in the Senoi Pra'aq.

The Asal force to which the two informants belonged surrendered en masse in 1958. This included their two Chinese controllers who pragmatically accepted the fact that not only was the shooting war lost by the MCP/MRLA but that they were also outnumbered and in danger from their own followers if they did not recognize those facts. The whole group came out at the twenty-second milestone on the Cameron Highlands Road. The surrender had been arranged through intermediaries from the Police Special Branch in Ipoh. Trucks picked them up and took them to Ipoh where they were held in open custody, i.e., not put in jail but held in a compound. They were well treated and Protector of Aborigines in Perak, Mr. R. C. Corfield, looked after their welfare. He arranged for their transfer to Seremban for six months (they do not know why) and finally they were returned to a camp for Orang Asli at seven mile on the Cameron Highlands Road. There they received rewards for handing in their weapons and ammunition.[22] While Bah Dek was detailing how much each weapon was worth, Bah

Sepidi leaned over towards me and said with a wide grin, "They gave me three thousand Malayan dollars for surrendering, I was important."

Bah Dek joined the Senoi Pra'aq, which he eventually left in 1969 to become a Special Government agent among the Orang Asli, reporting to the Special Branch. Bah Sepidi returned to his village.

The interviewees' account of the structure of the Asal organization concurs with that from other sources with a few minor deviations. Allowing for the passage of thirty-five years and the possible egocentric inflation of the parts the two former MRLA supporters played in the accounts they related in their interview, their anecdotal reminiscences are as close as we can get to the facts other than from official sources.

However, in a recent letter received from Mr. Corfield, he stated:

> I feel that perhaps the aborigines exaggerated about their being so heavily armed. I never heard of any abos [sic] being armed with either Bren or Sten guns, and normally, if the CTs entrusted them with fire-arms, these were only shot-guns. This particular group were, however, thought to be more indoctrinated than usual, and after their surrender and the subsequent interrogation, it was thought wiser to send them to Seremban for a period. There were a number of reasons for this.
>
> Normally, abo groups, when contacted, were settled at one or other of the jungle forts, and individuals brought in for interrogation would live in the back of my house. There being insufficient space for this group at the house, the Police housed them in an enclosed compound during interrogation. As there was no intention of settling aborigines outside the jungle, we liked them to get back into their normal habitat as soon as possible. In this case, we were afraid that, if we sent them to one of the Perak jungle forts, they might be contacted again by the CTs, who might either tempt them back into their service, failing which, reprisals might have been taken against them. In Negri Sembilan, however, they would be settled into a jungle environment, but completely out of touch with their old friends. We also wanted to be quite sure of their change of heart, before allowing them to return to their normal stamping ground.

When I took over in Ipoh, there were seven CTs known to be dealing close with aborigines. Of these, six were eliminated, but the seventh, Ah Soo Choi always eluded my efforts, often by slipping across into Thailand, when we were getting information that might lead us to him. I was most interested to hear that he survived to the end. In a way, I feel glad he did survive.

As stated by Dawson, the MRLA had something like a two year lead on the Security Forces in trying to win over the Orang Asli. It was not until late 1953 that the Administration became aware of what was happening in the interior of the jungle.[23] The colonial and military intelligence services were conversant with the ties between the Orang Asli and the MCP/MRLA dating back to the Japanese occupation. What they were not aware of was the new sophistication of the organization the guerrillas were setting up among the tribesmen. The resources of the police and Special Branch were fully occupied in dealing with the Chinese squatters. Once Templer took a personal interest in the Aborigines he set the direction of the counter effort to block the MCP/MRLA, organizing and using the tribespeople for their own purposes.[24] The construction of the police forts was to play a crucial part in gaining the confidence of the Orang Asli.

The Forts

By building the police forts in tribal homelands, the Security Forces were not only intent on gaining a military advantage over their Communist opponents, but also on recovering the psychological advantage they had allowed the MCP/MRLA to gain through the Asal Clubs. The colonial power had recognized that just planting a paramilitary garrison in a certain location to subjugate a hostile or non-cooperative population was not enough. It was a futile gesture unless that presence was supplemented by positive benefits to the inhabitants. To win over the previously ignored or maltreated people required more than a display of force.

The Asal organizers took advantage of the administration's

Fort Brooke. Note Helicopter Landing Pad on left and gun-pit on right. Approx: 1954–55. *Unknown SAS*

Prestwick Pioneer Short Take Off Landing Aircraft (STOL) at jungle fort 1954 *Unknown SAS*.

Draconian efforts to resettle the tribespeople against their will. Other hostile acts such as the bombing of ladangs by the Security Forces helped the MCP to strengthen their contacts with the Orang Asli. Bah Dek and Bah Sepidi confirmed that their fellow tribespeople were aware of the atrocities committed by the MRLA against some of their kindred. They were also cognizant of the modified attitude of the guerrillas since late 1951. To the bulk of the deep jungle inhabitants, the MCP/MRLA were the only recognized authority in constant contact with them. This ubiquity, combined with a visibly superior weaponry, commanded obedience and cooperation from the various Orang Asli groups.

The Security Forces had to learn how to loosen this grip by a combination of a display of superior force and by provision of positive advantages for the jungle people before they could obtain their cooperation and eventually their full allegiance. The forts were the beginning of that process.

The establishment of forts in the tribal areas was first undertaken at the direction of the Perak State War Executive Committee (SWEC) in late 1952. These provisional forts were surveyed in that state in tribal lands where the Senoi populations were comparatively dense. The OC, 20 FJC, ASP John West was directed to choose the three sites and submit plans.[25] He chose the junction of the Legap and Plus rivers about twenty miles east of Kampong Lasah for the first one.[26] The second was at Kampong Temengor, to the east of Grik in Upper Perak and the third at Blue Valley Tea estate in the Cameron Highlands roadhead in Pahang.[27] Dawson claims that West's plans and locations were accepted by Perak SWEC and by the Emergency Planning Staff in Kuala Lumpur, with some reservations, which he does not specify. The forts were located in Temiar Senoi tribal lands which had previously been reconnoitered by H. D. Noone in 1934–35.[28] All three were in areas where there was a heavy concentration of Temiar. As Noone reported,

> In Legap, the Temiar from the furthest sources of the Plus are continually gathering; it is a recognised rendez-vous and of great importance therefore to the administration of the area, since one

night on the way, at Kuala Temor, will bring any officer who forewarns into touch with all the headmen of the Plus valley, for the head waters of the Plus open up like the fingers of an outstretched hand with the tips pressed against the Kelantan divide.[29]

The other two sites also straddled important transit and trade routes which would enable the garrisons to monitor the Temiar movements in those locations.

Despite the fact that the Perak SWEC had recognized that the policy of resettling Orang Asli outside their normal habitat was a failure, they continued in their efforts to experiment with "Influenced migration." Immediately following Operation League,[30] Fort Jor in the Cameron Highlands was patched together in May 1952 from a "collection of Public Works Department Labour Lines, long since abandoned because of the Emergency." The police garrison of forty men lived in tents and they were there to protect the evacuees from the Jelai Kecil brought out by the SAS. An Assistant Protector of Aborigines (APA) was stationed in the fort to advise the fort commander and assist with the administration of the Aborigines. Despite strenuous efforts by the authorities to make the resettled area a success it proved a failure due to unsuitability of the land for tapioca, the staple diet of the Semai evacuees. There were too many people settled too close together and they could not expand into the surrounding jungle which was the territory of the local Semai. Neither could they hunt in that territory and the small river would not provide fish.[31] General Templer visited the camp in September 1952 but "he was not impressed with the arrangements nor did he have a high opinion of the Aborigines who paid little attention to him and his entourage, as they were by now well accustomed to visitors of all descriptions."[32] They told him they were unhappy and wished to return home. It was a sign of the ignorance of the colonial government, at all levels, about the plight of the Orang Asli and their future usefulness in combating the MCP/MRLA, that they were not taken seriously. Instead more improvements were made to the fort, including the addition of a medical dispensary and trade store to the now newly constructed garrison quarters. By December 1952 the Semai evacuees at Jor had lost all interest in self help or cultivating the land and were content to live on the Government handouts. Some were allowed to return home in January 1953 and the remainder after May 1953 when a fort was established in their old tribal area. Fort Jor was abandoned in 1953.[33]

Even while the Fort Jor fiasco was being acted out, a police party under ASP West did march in, unopposed, to Legap in August 1952, taking three days to do so. The construction of Fort Legap commenced that month and was the model for the building of other forts. Local Orang Asli were used to build the huts and cut a dropping zone (DZ) for the air supply drops. They were paid for their labors with rations and tobacco in part, and the balance in cash was given to the headman for communal effort or to individuals for personal services. The headman shared the cash with his group or in some cases purchased supplies in Lasah or Ipoh which he distributed to his followers. The local populace were not very cooperative as the Asal organization, about which the police were unaware at that time, was active in the area. West received information from some "loyal groups living in the Temor, Perwor and Ternam river areas" about two Communist cultivators living in the Kuala Temor area. With a small patrol he located and killed the cultivators and recovered their weapons. The informants were paid five thousand Malayan dollars in reward money which resulted in more, not always accurate, information being supplied.[34] A game of cat and mouse ensued during the remainder of the time the fort was being built. The local Asal group's Chinese controllers threatened revenge for the killings and circulated rumors of large MRLA units in the area who would exact retribution for the deaths of their fellow Asal Club members. The police countered this by claiming they had a garrison of two hundred in and around the fort. The pragmatic West and Dawson recommended that those Temiar who supported them should be armed for their own protection, but this was rejected by the Perak SWEC.[35]

While the police and the MRLA were attempting to secure advantage for their side, during the time the fort was being constructed the Orang Asli were faced with conflicting loyalties to one side or the other. They had no ideological inclination toward either party. These uninvited strangers who had invaded their lands to obtain a military gain were attempting to persuade or force them to take part in a struggle which they had not initiated and which they found confusing. Each group of Orang Asli had to decide what was most beneficial for them and wherein lay the least danger to their welfare. Many had to live in temporary shelters away from their ladangs to avoid the attentions of either of the invaders. All through 1953 this situation would continue as more forts were constructed in jungle homelands. Most would be built in Senoi areas where the Asal organization was strongest and where the Orang Asli population was generally remote and at the same time at its densest.

It cost seven thousand Malayan dollars to complete Fort Legap, its DZ, and helicopter Landing Zone (LZ). Labor and most material had been provided by the local Temiar. Legap consisted of two large barrack type *atap* (plaited palm fronds) and bamboo buildings, an officers' quarters, canteen, medical and office block, kitchen, latrines, and a visitors' building for the transient Temiar. Surrounded by barbed wire it was reinforced by strong points (gun pits). There was an area for ball games on the LZ and the canteen, radio, and cardboard games e.g., jigsaw puzzles, provided amenities for the garrison. A weekly airdrop brought in supplies of fresh food and mail.[36] Most subsequent forts followed this pattern with some modifications such as smaller huts for sections (eight to ten men) instead of the large building. Some forts later included air strips for short take-off and landing aircraft (STOL) which took over the role of the helicopters in reinforcing or relieving the garrison, or to evacuate sick police, soldiers, or Orang Asli. By early 1954 there were seven of these forts, manned by the PJC, now redesignated Police Field Force (PFF) at strategic points in Orang Asli areas in the jungle.[37] Fourteen forts were completed by the end of the Emergency, most of which were in Perak, Kelantan, and North Pahang. The most southernly was Fort Iskandar near the Tasik Bera in Semalai territory near the Pahang-Negri Sembilan border.

The erection of forts in the tribal areas which were controlled by

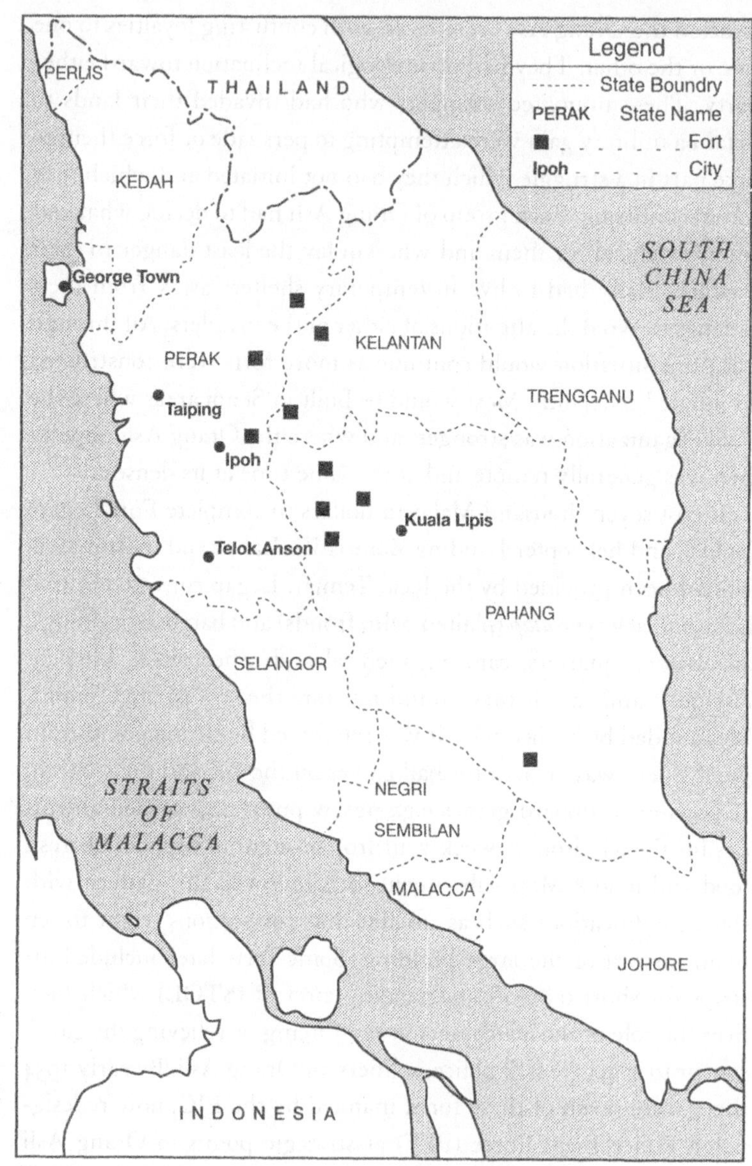

Map 3. Distribution of Jungle Forts, Malaya, 1953–1960

the MRLA through the Asal Clubs did not result in instant defections from the Communists to the Security Forces. The Orang Asli had to be convinced that the police and military were there to stay. They had seen patrols pass through their areas before which gave medical care and asked questions, while all the time the MRLA remained to emerge once the patrols had gone. Some information on MRLA movements was forthcoming from the Orang Asli because the forts were in their areas.

Despite the construction of forts in 1952–53, the major problem facing the Security Forces in positioning new forts and dealing with the Orang Asli was lack of knowledge about the location and numbers of tribespeople in the Main Range area of Malaya and the strength of the MRLA in that area. In October 1953 Malaya Command ordered a reconnaissance in force to get this information. This operation included the 22 SAS Regiment, a company of the Malay Regiment, and four Police Field Force platoons, supported by the fort garrisons in the area. The SAS were to gather information about the Orang Asli and on the MRLA formations in the deep jungle between Grik in Perak and Fraser's Hill in Pahang. Designated Operation Galway, it was also intended "to dominate Aborigines in fort areas." A further task of the SAS was to survey and recommend new fort sites.[38]

By the end of 1953 the Security Forces were establishing a permanent presence in Orang Asli homelands in the remote jungle. The MCP/ MRLA, through the Asal organization, had preceded them and enjoyed both a psychological and physical advantage through this prior dominant position among the tribespeople. It was the beginning of the struggle to win over the indigenous people of the remote jungle to support one side or the other. Despite their early advantages, the MCP/MRLA could not match the technology, manpower, and financial resources of the colonial government.

This superiority had been made possible in no small measure by the boom in rubber and tin prices due to the outbreak of the Korean war in 1950. The United States had begun to expand its strategic stockpile of those commodities, causing the price of rubber to jump from an average of $US 0.40 per pound in 1949 to a 1951 yearly average of $US 1.70 per pound after reaching a high of $US 2.20 per pound in February 1951. Tin reached £1,300 per ton in early 1951 as against £590 per ton in April 1950. The estimated total revenue from duties and taxes for 1951 was $273.7 million, the actual figure attained for the Malayan Government coffers was $443.4 million. In 1951 the estimate was $410.3 million, the actual sum received was $735.4 million.[39] Malaya, through its export earnings, was the principal earner of American dollars in the entire Commonwealth. Expenditure by the Government of Malaya on the Emergency increased as follows:

$US 4.620 million in 1948
$US 16.500 million in 1949
$US 19.980 million in 1950
$US 51.150 million in 1951
$US 69.300 million in 1952
$US 89.100 million in 1953.[40]

This boost to revenue and expenditure facilitated the purchase of equipment such as large troop-carrying helicopters (see Plate 5), the recruitment of more police to man jungle forts, and the rapid expansion of the Department of Aborigines. The government could now offer rations, medical care, and other advantages to the Orang Asli which could swamp any little assistance the MCP could promise them.

It was the employment of troop-carrying helicopters and extensive use of supply dropping aircraft, rather than the fire power of fighters and bombers, which was the prime reason the Security Forces were able to maintain a permanent presence in the jungle.

The Asal organizers had no answer to the superior airpower of the Government Forces, especially troop-carrying helicopters (gunships were not used in Malaya) and transport aircraft which moved personnel and material into the jungle swiftly and with immunity from ambush. Access by Orang Asli to medical attention in the forts and to the purchase of consumer goods from cash earned, either by working for the Security Forces or supplying information about the

MRLA, could not be countered by the Asal Clubs. The jungle was still relatively safe for the MRLA in 1953 but by the end of that year the Security Forces had finally recognized that the key to domination of the deep jungle was by the control and cooperation of the Orang Asli. That situation would not come about without hardship to many of the tribespeople and fatal consequences to others.

The Department of Aborigines

Following the death of Peter Williams-Hunt in June 1953, an editorial in the *Straits Times* declared:

> There should be some searching of consciences in Jalan Rajah.[41] Much of Williams-Hunt's energy, until General Templer took personal interest in his work, was spent in convincing Civil Servants that money for Aborigines and for Museums and Archaeological investigations was not money wasted.[42]

Williams-Hunt's frenetic efforts to help his charges were beginning to show some progress at the time of his death. It must be accepted that he was a man of his times when we view his association with the Orang Asli. Despite the fact that he married a Semai, his attitude to the tribespeople was that of a benevolent father rather than an equal. They were his charges for whom he was responsible and he saw it as his duty to guide them in the manner he considered to be good for them and for the government on whose behalf he had taken on the task. Even after World War II there were still well-educated young British men, like Williams-Hunt, who considered it their duty to take up the "white man's burden" and bring what they considered the benefits of British administration to lesser races. After his appointment as adviser on Aborigines he worked tirelessly for them. His paternalistic attitude to the Orang Asli and his plans for their future welfare, as he saw it, were summed up in a speech to the Rotary Club of Kuala Lumpur in February 1950.

> The lines I expect to follow are to settle the wanderers and tie down the shifting agriculturists to one place by encouraging the planting of fruit orchards. We can help them start their own Kampongs and help them on the best way to grow food economically. They could have their own schools in their own language and they could be encouraged in their arts and crafts, for we want to keep them as aborigines and not as fifth-rate Malays. Later settled groups could become Malayan if they wished but there would be no pressure.[43]

In the same speech he predicted the extinction of the Negrito (Semang) tribes within one hundred years.[44] He also stated in 1952 that he was not in favor of putting the Orang Asli in reserves except in the initial stages of "an advancement scheme." "Given a fair chance the Aborigines have the ability to advance and it is possible that artificial boundaries will not always be respected."[45] Because of the demands of the Emergency he did not have an opportunity to put his ideas into practice before his accidental death in June 1953. Whatever we may think of Williams-Hunt's ideas (with the benefit of hindsight) there is no doubting his dedication to improving the lot of the Orang Asli despite lack of funds and lack of staff. Williams-Hunt was in essence the Department.

In addition to his duties as Adviser on Aborigines he was also appointed Director of Museums in 1951.[46] Added to his anthropological researches he now had the responsibility for the investigation of archaeological sites and collection of antiquities including Orang Asli craft work. Photographic evidence of his archaeological endeavors is currently held in the library of the School of Oriental and African Studies of the London University.

He lobbied hard for the implementation of an Aboriginal Peoples Ordinance based on the Perak model Pat Noone had successfully managed to have promulgated in that state in 1939.[47] He was prepared to use anybody whom he considered could help his cause. In 1950 he was censured for privately contacting Captain Hussain bin Onn, of UMNO to enlist his good offices in getting support for the proposed ordinance.[48] He wrote articles and letters tirelessly and travelled extensively in an effort to convey his message regarding the need to treat the Orang Asli with friendly under-

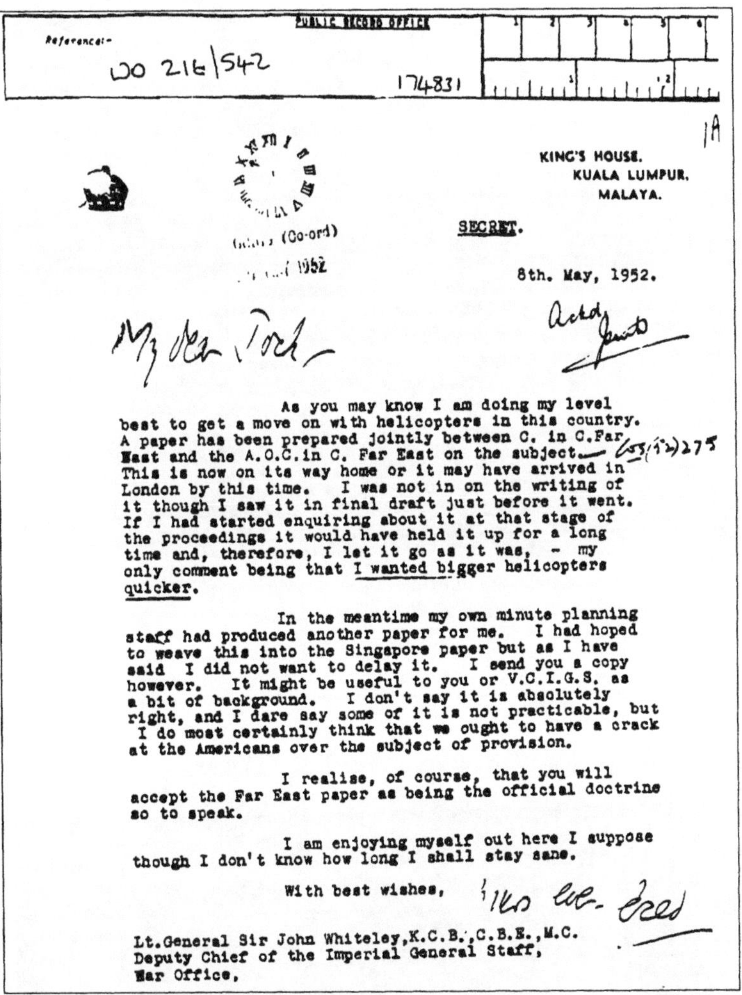

PUBLIC RECORD OFFICE

Reference:- WO 216/542

174831

1A

KING'S HOUSE.
KUALA LUMPUR.
MALAYA.

SECRET.

8th. May, 1952.

My dear Tock

As you may know I am doing my level best to get a move on with helicopters in this country. A paper has been prepared jointly between C. in C.Far East and the A.O.C.in C. Far East on the subject. This is now on its way home or it may have arrived in London by this time. I was not in on the writing of it though I saw it in final draft just before it went. If I had started enquiring about it at that stage of the proceedings it would have held it up for a long time and, therefore, I let it go as it was, - my only comment being that I wanted bigger helicopters quicker.

In the meantime my own minute planning staff had produced another paper for me. I had hoped to weave this into the Singapore paper but as I have said I did not want to delay it. I send you a copy however. It might be useful to you or V.C.I.G.S. as a bit of background. I don't say it is absolutely right, and I dare say some of it is not practicable, but I do most certainly think that we ought to have a crack at the Americans over the subject of provision.

I realise, of course, that you will accept the Far East paper as being the official doctrine so to speak.

I am enjoying myself out here I suppose though I don't know how long I shall stay sane.

With best wishes,

Lt.General Sir John Whiteley,K.C.B.,C.B.E.,M.C.
Deputy Chief of the Imperial General Staff,
War Office.

Plate 5. Letter from Templer to Deputy/CIGS re Helicopters

standing to keep them from being suborned by the MCP/MRLA. His book, *An Introduction to the Malayan Aborigines,* was written, he said, as "a somewhat horrid child of necessity hurriedly put together for the information of the Security Forces."[49] In spite of its faults, for those of the Security Forces who bothered to read it, it was a useful tool when dealing with the Orang Asli. It continues to be a very useful reference book for students researching the involvement of the Orang Asli in the Emergency.

Supply Dropping Zone (DZ) in primary jungle 1950–51. Note fluorescent identification panel in right center. *E. C. V. Peacock*

Testing loads on Orang Asli porters 1950–51. *E. C. V. Peacock*

Williams-Hunt was invariably welcomed by most administrators and Security Force officers who were in contact with the Orang Asli and who appreciated his knowledge and advice. As an example, in reply to his request to the State Secretary Selangor to review the possibility of the appointment of a Protector of Aborigines in that state, the six District Officers contacted all supported Williams-Hunt's proposal when he asked for comments.[50] These officers were Malay and British. I met Williams-Hunt in 1951 when he was visiting the PAAC at Lasah where his reception was wholehearted, and his enthusiasm, when speaking about the Orang Asli, contagious.

In 1950 he put forward a proposal for the appointment of Aboriginal Affairs Staff in the states as follows:

Pahang	23
Johore	6
Perak	11
Kelantan	23
Selangor	3
Negri Sembilan	8
Trengannu	8
Malacca	2
Kedah	8

This included clerks, field teams of Aborigines, and medical dressers.[51] It was a vain hope at that time and apart from Perak, Pahang, and Kelantan who did appoint whole or part time State Protectors, little action was taken despite support from DOs and others in contact with the Orang Asli.

Pamela Gouldsbury, who was to become Assistant Adviser in 1953, related an example of the dark side of Williams-Hunt's paternalistic attitude to "his" Orang Asli. She does not give a date for this incident but it must have been in late 1951 or 1952. He had decided to pay a surprise visit to a group of Semai some distance from his wife's ladang. Just before he got to their ladang, he saw them fleeing when they sighted him dressed in jungle green uniform instead of his usual loin cloth. Next he was fired on by two Chinese guerrillas.

Furious at his narrow escape he led a military operational unit to the settlement. The inhabitants again fled and one of the two guerrillas was wounded. His pride was hurt because "his people" behaved in such a manner, fleeing from him and sheltering two MRLA.

> Peter then decided the group concerned must be taught a lesson and thus he supervised the breaking of all their blow-pipes, burnt various seed, both rice and corn, and generally wrecked the ladang. This was on the grounds that it would make it uninhabitable as a staging post for the guerrillas in future and also show the aborigines they could not behave in this fashion and get away with it. All most salutary.[52]

Gouldsbury who at this time had set up a private clinic for Orang Asli in Tapah went on to claim she had later assuaged the group involved and persuaded their headman to pass information on guerrilla movements to the police while still allowing the MRLA to transit the ladang. The Communists discovered his duplicity about a year later and killed him after five days of torture.[53]

Late in 1952, when the Malayan government finally realized it had to pursue the MRLA into the deep jungle, the Department of Aborigines finally began to receive due recognition at the highest level.

> Gerald [Templer] had decided that, if the aborigines could not be successfully resettled, the only answer was to bring the administration to them. A programme for the construction of jungle forts was launched, carefully sited in key deep jungle areas, from which an attempt to control the aborigines could be made.[54]

As well as the hardware such as helicopters, light aircraft, and transports to supply the forts, a key element was the presence of Department of Aborigines' officers who could speak Orang Asli dialects and communicate with them. Templer wrote to Secretary of State for the Colonies Oliver Lyttelton on 3 November 1952, "A contest is going on between us and the Communists over gaining the confidence of the Sakai. We're both very hot on Sakai welfare."[55] Crucial to the success of that contest was the involvement of the Department of Aborigines. By July 1952 the staff of the Department had grown to ten, including as Assistant Adviser Jill Redwood, a qualified anthropologist.[56] This took some of the strain from Williams-Hunt and he was able to proceed on leave to England, with his wife, in October 1952.[57]

Despite his apparently close contacts with the Orang Asli, through marriage and in his official capacity, Williams-Hunt failed to detect the activities of the Asal organizers which were taking place at the same time as he was recruiting the tribespeople to act as porters and guides for the Security Forces. At no time does he make a reference to that movement in his official reports or talk to interested bodies. There is no comment in his book about the MRLA Asal cells and I suspect that the Adviser did not think that "his people," in what he refers to as unprotected areas, were capable of being organized into any kind of disciplined body. His advice to the Security Forces was, "The initial approach to an Aboriginal Group must be unhurried rather as if one is dealing with semi-tamed animals."[58]

Neither does Gouldsbury refer to the Asal organization. She prided herself on her close contacts with the Semai through a very successful voluntary welfare organization she set up in South Perak (Tapah) in May 1952. In her curriculum vitae she claimed "3000 aborigines were seen or visited the clinic every month." She contended that Orang Asli from as far away as the Jelai area in Pahang visited her.[59] Both she and Williams-Hunt were aware of close ties between some Orang Asli and the MRLA and following her appointment as Assistant Adviser on Aborigines in September 1953, Gouldsbury was aware of some organized efforts by the MRLA to keep Orang Asli in deep jungle areas on their side, but still did not seem to grasp the systematic way they were being recruited. Much useful military intelligence was gleaned from the tribespeople by the Department under Williams-Hunt, but he and his Departmental Officers, federal and state, failed to detect the methodical planning behind the Asal movement. "His people" obviously did not tell him, and it was not until after his death that the ramifications of the Asal Clubs came to light through intelligence gathered by police and Aborigines Department staff in the forts from Orang Asli, through captured documents, and through surrendered guerrillas.

Just when his personal and operational life was about to blossom, Williams-Hunt died. His son had been born only three weeks before, he was finally being recognized professionally outside Malaya by his peers,[60] the policy of resettlement of Aborigines which he had opposed so strongly had been dropped, and the Government of Malaya, particularly General Templer, appreciated the importance of his Department's part in the future defeat of the MCP/MRLA in the jungle. Others were to gain the benefit of his years of hard work, in adverse circumstances, for the people he regarded as his own.

Both Williams-Hunt and Gouldsbury offer the same explanation for the Orang Asli's alliance with the MRLA. They were misguided "and had been convinced by the Communists that the Emergency was a continuation of the Japanese war."[61] Gouldsbury claimed that the guerrillas had persuaded the tribespeople that the aircraft they saw were Communist, searching for the remains of the British Army hiding in the jungle after being defeated by them.[62] Both Bah Dek and Bah Sepidi denied that they ever believed that propaganda and the question arises as to which group was fooling which.[63]

The machinations involved in the eventual appointment of a successor to Williams-Hunt are quite illuminating about the autocratic control of Templer and the dubious personal style of some of the staff and government servants surrounding him. John Blacking, a young, well qualified anthropologist from King's College, Cambridge, was appointed as the new Adviser.[64] He was Templer's own choice.[65] Blacking, a flamboyant former Coldstream Guards officer had served his national service in Malaya in 1948–49, and had become friendly with Williams-Hunt whom he had accompanied on some of his journeys into the jungle to contact Orang Asli. Blacking arrived at Singapore Airport in a blaze of newspaper publicity "dressed in chocolate brown suit and trilby, with a pink carnation in his buttonhole and rolled umbrella in the crook of his arm."[66] The same papers reported his dismissal on 2 November 1953, "because the Government considered him unsuitable for the job."[67] Cloake states that Blacking threw out most of the material gathered by Pat Noone and Williams-Hunt on the Orang Asli, gave Templer a lecture on military strategy, and "told Gerald's and McGillvray's [the A-High Commissioner] Private Secretaries how the political situation should be handled [starting by pensioning off the Rulers]."[68] Gouldsbury, who had been appointed Assistant Adviser replacing Jill Sargent nee Redwood, and was in fact Acting Adviser, does not mention him in her book. She does intimate that she was responsible for the appointment of R. O. D. Noone through a personal approach to Templer.[69] Cloake claims it was Templer's own idea.[70]

In articles in the local papers, Blacking explained his views on how he thought the Orang Asli should be won over.[71] The Security Forces would have to study and adopt Orang Asli cultural values when dealing with them. There was a need to find out who the real leaders were; "Real leaders are not always those who talk the most." Without the cooperation of the real leaders, outsiders generated only friction and offended the key men. The social structure of the Aborigines needed to be followed, and they appealed to in their own language. The Orang Asli did not want to leave their homelands and would be dealt with there. "In order to win them over decisively and finally, we must make an appeal which strikes at the very roots of their spiritual life." Real knowledge about the tribespeople could only be gained by considerable amount of scientific research rather than an obsession with the immediate problems of the Emergency and looking for instant solutions.[72] Obviously this approach was too esoteric for the pragmatic military and police commanders who were looking for quick, decisive solutions to the problem.

In an exchange of correspondence with me, Blacking outlined the circumstances that he claimed had led to his unjust dismissal. He denies that there were any notes by Pat Noone for him to destroy, and claimed that if there had been he would have had them published as he "longed to find them." Richard Noone confirms that his brother's notes were lost to the Japanese during their occupation of Malaya. One collection had been burned by them, the others were lost in a Japanese attack and disappeared.[73] Blacking went on to say he had been sacked by Templer because he wanted to do research among the Orang Asli. He claims "Templer wanted me to woo Aboriginal women out of the jungle with anything I suggested, 'Elizabeth Arden' face creams, lipstick, perfume, anything you like Blacking. But get the women out, and the men will follow, what?" Blacking went on to say that Templer was speaking to him as one military man to another. He, on the other hand, had been to Cambridge since his military service. He had also met Peter Williams-Hunt and his wife, which apparently had changed his view towards the Orang Asli, with the result that he regarded Templer's remarks as displaying an ignorant and unfeeling attitude towards the tribespeople. He argued with Templer hoping to get over at least part of his viewpoint before he had to act eventually. He did not expect to be summarily sacked. Blacking further claims he went to Malaya a "high Tory" and admirer of Templer but then he ran foul of Gouldsbury whom he considered overly concerned with security. "She even locked the lavatory paper away." He was caught in the toilet one day, minus paper, so he searched all the cupboards for some, including one she kept locked. He alleges because of that incident, Gouldsbury thought he "must be a Commy." As a consequence he was interrogated "by the despicable Hugh Storey (Templer's Secretary) who had been rather more than an acquaintance at Cambridge." Storey, whom he accuses of being two-faced and typical of a certain type of Wykehaimist, had also been a member of the Labour Party at Cambridge but had "changed his spots" to curry favour with Templer and his daughter. Blacking frankly admitted his friendship at Cambridge with Chinese, "all Communists of course!!" This information he claims to have been passed back to Templer "completely reinterpreted." Blacking concluded the letter by writing:

> It makes me very sad to recall those days. I looked forward to a lifetime in Malaya. I fell in love with the place and its people in 1948/9, and I don't think I ever got over it completely.[74]

Blacking in a later letter expressed the opinion that by his dismissal he had joined a distinguished company of people who had been dismissed by Templer, such as Hardy Amies and Konrad Adenauer.[75] In the same letter he expressed the belief that Templer realized he was right because Robert Bonley (sic), Head Master of Eton, mentioned his name to Templer who spoke very warmly of him. Templer also expressed interest in what Blacking was doing in South Africa.[76]

Whatever Templer's later opinion of Blacking may have been, he quickly replaced him with another candidate whom he considered more suitable, R. O. D. Noone, younger brother of H. D. Pat Noone. A member of the Federation Intelligence Committee in 1953, Noone had applied for the vacancy after Williams-Hunt's death. The Director of Intelligence would not release him but the Chief Secretary telephoned in October 1953 to tell him he had the job. As Noone describes it, following the telephone message he was summoned to King's house to see Templer. Following his affirmative reply to the High Commissioner's query on whether he wanted the post, Templer said,

> Noone, what I don't want is a desk man. Nor do I want a purely scientific type—though of course your knowledge of anthropology and experience of these jungle tribes in particular would be of great value.[77]

Gouldsbury approved of the appointment and in her book takes the credit for persuading Templer to employ Noone.[78] From the Federal Administration's point of view there was no doubt that "Dick" Noone was the correct choice. By 30 November 1953 he submitted a paper to the Director of Operations Committee advocating:

> An expansion of the Department to enable it to meet additional commitments resulting from the Emergency. This was to include an Intelligence Section, and a Supply Section (Q Section) in addition to a massive recruitment of field staff for work in the forts.
>
> Civic courses for the Orang Asli to counter MCP propaganda.

Schools in the forts and at the Research Centre at Selayang. Medical dispensaries manned by trained Field Assistants in the forts and at the centre.

Shops for the sale of goods to the Orang Asli at the forts and to buy and sell Orang Asli artifacts.[79]

Following acceptance of his recommendations by the Committee, funds were allocated for an immediate recruitment of ninety extra staff for the Department.[80]

Templer appointed his Chief of Staff (Operations) to chair a committee which reviewed the department's progress. It laid down the various responsibilities in which policy was a Federal matter, and the day to day execution of policy a SWEC function. "It developed programmes both for the collection of intelligence from the aborigines and for effective efforts to counter the Communist indoctrination they had received in the jungle."[81]

The new departmental head was soon able to claim some spectacular successes in his dealing with the Orang Asli. He and Pamela Gouldsbury came to the conclusion that they would make no headway in winning over the Semai in the Batang Padang region of South Perak until Bah Pelankin was killed. Bah Pelankin was the most notorious of the Senoi-Semai supporters of the MRLA and the most feared by his own people. His part in the massacre of thirty-four of his fellow Semai in the Cameron Highlands was such an abhorrent act that it is difficult to understand his motivation. All the Semai I met during my research trips to Malaysia in 1988 and 1990, who were old enough to have experienced the Emergency, knew of him and his commanding influence during the early days of that conflict. Some of the older ones claimed he had assisted the MPAJA. Spencer Chapman wrote of "Pa Blanken, the intelligent and influential leader of the Bot Sakai at the foot of the Cameron Highlands Road" who assisted him in his wartime ordeal behind the Japanese lines. He described Blanken as shrewd and a wily hunter who had been lent a shotgun by the Cameron Highlands guerrillas.[82] All the Orang Asli I met who knew him or of him were adamant that Pelankin personally had never killed anyone but was responsible for many deaths among his own tribal group. He simply directed the MRLA to kill those he pointed out. Why he killed his own people is not known. Ruslan bin Abdullah suggested, (in a conversation with me in July 1990), that he was mentally unbalanced, but that only expresses a personal viewpoint.

Noone wrote that there was a big (unspecified) reward for eliminating him.[83] Gouldsbury claimed that she had had discussions with some Semai about the capture of Pelankin, but they had replied:

> "The One" [only one Semai would call Pelankin by his name] is filled with evil and his spirit is in league with the spirits of evil.[84]

She then agreed with them that he should be lured into a trap and killed. Gouldsbury intimated that she had organized the Semai to kill him. Noone wrote that he and Gouldsbury had persuaded a particular headsman who was a Home Guard to do the killing.[85]

Bah Dek and Bah Sepidi had a different story. Their account was also supported by Udah, Sabek, and Bah Hoi. They claimed that two Semai Orang Asli Home Guard were on leave and had gone hunting in the jungle. The two, Bah Wan and Bah Chong, spotted Pelankin alone in the jungle in the Raub area of Pahang. He was about to cross a log spanning a stream. They were surprised to see him without the armed Chinese escort who had invariably accompanied him in the past few years. They debated whether to call on him to surrender but decided that if he did he might be allowed to live in return for the valuable information he could give. Also he was known to have escaped before when captured.[86] They surmised that he may have shed his escort and was coming in to surrender. Taking no chances they waited until he was at point blank range and killed him with shotgun blasts. He was killed on 1 December 1953.[87] Whether the Noone-Gouldsbury version or the Bah Dek-Bah Sepidi version of the killing of Pelankin is correct is not the issue. What emerged from that killing was that the Orang Asli were now turning on their own kind who supported the MRLA. One murderous Semai was killed in cold blood by fellow Semai either for reward or revenge or both. Pelankin's reported homicidal tendencies and the action of his killers were hardly that which could be expected of a gentle, timid people.

There were other incidents of direct violence by Orang Asli against their fellows. Chawog, a Semai from the Betau River area in Pahang, had a reputation, like Pelankin, for killing his own people.[88] Short claimed that Orang Asli Asal members had a mutual protection pact with their fellow, non-Asal or pro-government tribesmen. This pact bound both parties to look after each others' interests, irrespective of which of the opposing forces, the MRLA or the Security Forces, eventually won the struggle they were waging in the Orang Asli homelands. Chawog broke the pact by killing two pro-government Aborigines whom he suspected of informing against him. "This so incensed the friendly [i.e., pro-government] groups that within a week they shot him in the act of stealing a pro-government headsman's wife."[89] Noone claims that he asked for volunteers from the Semai to kill Chawog for crimes against his own people; eight Semai volunteered. "A week later, in late September 1954, I received the news that Chawog had been shot by them as he came out of a house in which he had spent the night with a woman."[90] *The Straits Times* reported that he was visiting a woman thought to be his wife. "A second terrorist was wounded as he dashed from the hut but managed to escape." Chawog managed to fire his shotgun before he was shot dead. The newspaper claimed the patrol fled superstitiously from the scene "aghast at the deed it had committed." It was more likely the killers used their discretion and got out fast before some well-armed MRLA arrived. Director of Operations General Bourne sent a message of congratulation to the patrol of Aborigine auxiliary policemen who killed Chawog.[91] It is not recorded whether they received a reward for the killing.

While official dispatches, newspapers and Security Force participants' accounts of the Emergency are replete with reports of Orang Asli attacking police or army patrols and in other instances MRLA personnel, they are less informative about the internecine clashes among the tribespeople. As Tony Williams-Hunt said in his letter on the Bidor massacre, many killings of Orang Asli went unreported. That comment would have applied even more to the slaying of tribespeople by their fellows. Not only would the authorities be unaware of intertribal clashes but also one group of the Orang Asli would not necessarily be aware of what had occurred in another area. Some of the Semai I interviewed had never heard of Chawog even though he too was a Semai.

There may have been more to the deaths of Bah Pelankin and Chawog than just revenge by irate Orang Asli. It does seem strange that two of the MRLA's staunchest allies were ambushed when they were either alone or with a minimal escort. It is quite possible they had outlived their usefulness to the guerrillas and were expendable. After October 1951 there was a new attitude of cooperation not confrontation by the MRLA toward the Orang Asli. They now needed the assistance of the tribespeople in helping with their plans for expanded cultivation in the deep jungle. Pelankin and Chawog were feared and hated by their fellows for their cruel and arbitrary treatment of the jungle dwellers. Did the MRLA expose these two erstwhile allies to vengeance by those who hated them by withdrawing their escorts? Their movements would have been known as they travelled from settlement to settlement away from MRLA base camps. Once they were out of the way, relations between the guerrillas and the Orang Asli would be less strained and blame for previous atrocities could be attributed to the dead men.

The deaths of the two pro-MRLA Orang Asli leaders and the October 1951 directive did not prevent other atrocities against the tribespeople by the Communist insurgents. In the Kampar district of Perak, a party of three Aborigines stumbled upon a camp occupied by about forty MRLA in late December 1953. Two of the tribesmen were killed by gunfire, the third escaped.[92] A further incident, in March 1955, involved the abduction of seven Orang Asli women in the Tapah district of Perak. The survivors reported three of their number were killed because they were suspected of being Home Guards.[93]

These deaths often resulted from aggressive actions by the Orang Asli against the MRLA. An unusual occurrence was the killing of a guerrilla by blowpipe darts in January 1954. It was the first such killing since the beginning of the Emergency. The Orang Asli had

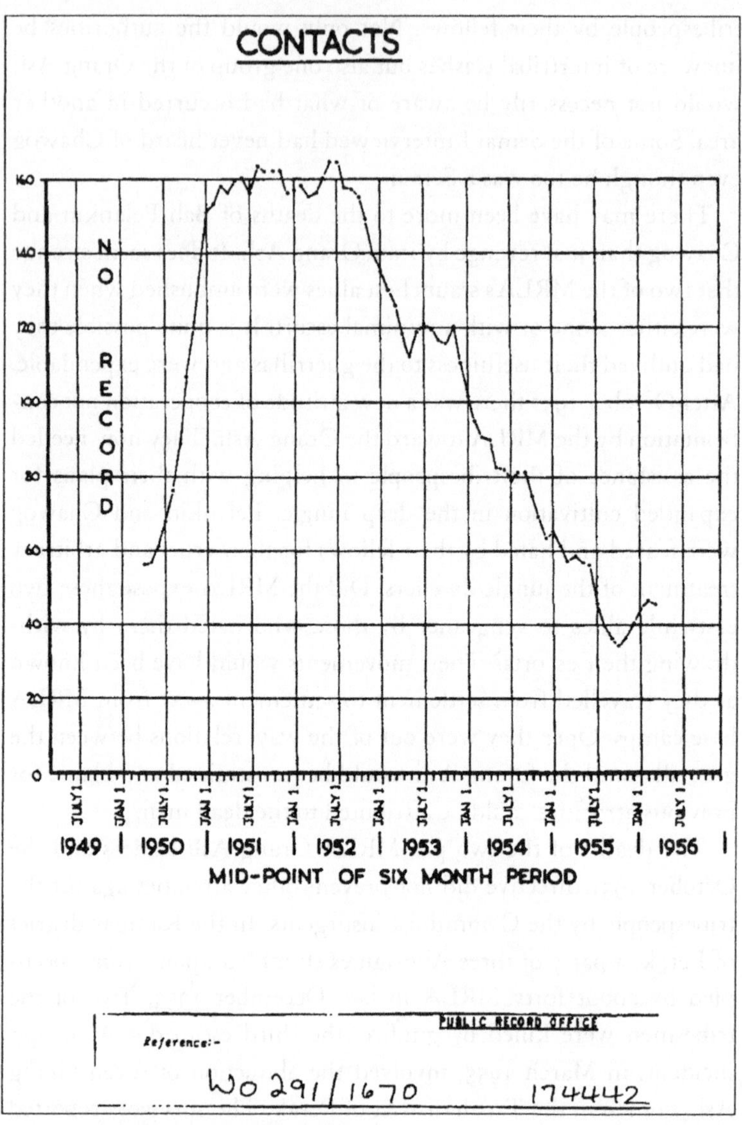

Plate 6. Fall Off in Hostile Contacts

guided a Security Force patrol to a MRLA camp. The occupants fled when an aircraft flew overhead. The Orang Asli stalked them and killed one with three poisoned darts from their blowpipes. They claimed the victim died instantly.[94]

Despite the Security Forces concentration on obtaining the support of the Orang Asli by peaceful means from 1953 onwards, they too had clashes with hostile tribesmen. In August 1954 a reported fifty Aborigines made unsuccessful attacks with blowpipes against an SAS patrol east of Ipoh. The SAS did not have any casualties but two tribesmen were killed and three wounded. The patrol alleged that the attackers were directed by a "uniformed terrorist."[95] In the Tanah Rata area of the Cameron Highlands in June 1956 an Aborigine guiding a Chinese guerrilla took a shot with his blowpipe at a Security patrol. He missed and was shot dead. His companion was wounded and escaped.[96]

As 1953 drew to a close the battle lines had been drawn. The withdrawal by the MCP/MRLA-fighting units into the jungle in 1952 gave the government forces time to regroup and reorganize. Because of the dramatic decline in MCP/MRLA initiated aggressive incidents (see Plate 6) the Security Forces were able to rethink their tactics and plan countermoves. They were winning by default, but they still had a long way to go to finish off a determined enemy. In April 1953 Templer made his famous remark to Homer Bigart of *The New York Herald Tribune,* "I'll shoot the bastard who says this Emergency is over."[97]

If ever the MCP had a hope of a military victory, the October 1951 directive had scuttled whatever chance they may have had. They were now fully on the defensive and many MRLA units depended on their ties with the Orang Asli, particularly in the Main Range area, to survive. On the government side, the battle had developed, in the main, into a clash of small patrols out of contact with their headquarters, much to the chagrin of senior officers.[98] Caught between the opposing combatants were the Orang Asli who were wooed by both sides. The possibility of the jungle dwellers avoiding active involvement in the conflict was shattered in 1953, the fateful year; the year which heralded a heavy commitment by the protagonists to gain the upper hand in controlling the Orang Asli homelands.

Notes

1. *Arkib Negara,* MUS 11/51.

2. *Federal Legislative Council Proceedings,* March 1953–January 1954.

3. PRO. Kew, CO 1022/187.

4. In an interview in June 1990 with former ASP Lim Cheng Leng, Malayan Police Special Branch, he suggested that these Politbureau directives may have fallen into the hands of the Security Forces before the end of 1952. There was a tendency in the early 1950's for the Intelligence Services to give low priority to interpreting roneod or printed documents captured from the MCP. This was due to shortage of staff and the fact that most of the typed material was propaganda. The efforts of the translating and evaluation staff was concentrated on captured hand-written notes, usually on rice paper, which contained day to day instruction for MRLA operations. Some MRLA units did not get the directives until late 1952 and some first learned of it when it was published in the *Straits Times* (to the SF's chagrin) on 28 October 1952.

5. Cloake, 255.

6. Gouldsbury, Foreword by Templer.

7. Director of Operations, *The Conduct of Anti-Terrorist Operations in Malaya,* 1st Edition (Kuala Lumpur, 1952), Foreword.

8. PRO. Kew, CO 1022/187.

9. This interview was held in the presence of Bah Toneh (A. Williams-Hunt) and his step-father, Bah Akeh, on 8 July 1990. It will be referred to quite substantially in another context in this chapter. This and one other interview with the survivor of a massacre of his people, were the most candid I had. When government officials were involved, replies were evasive and interviewees were reluctant to discuss anything to do with the Emergency.

10. R. O. D. Noone, 151: *Asal,* meaning "original" in Malay, was the term the Communists adopted for the Aborigines in preference to the derogatory term Sakai, which was still in official use.

11. Sel. Sec., 1411/1950.

12. R. O. D. Noone, 152.

13. Ibid., 152. Here again we strike the problem of how many Orang Asli there were in Malaya in the 1950's. Noone seems to favor a figure between that of the 1947 census (34,737) and Williams-Hunt's estimate of 100,000. The 1960 census gave a population of 45,900. Carey, 9.

14. Ibid., 154.

15. Interview in Ipoh, in October 1988, with Mr. Lawrence. There are a number of explanations for the apparent discrepancy. Low Mah may have been an alias for Ah Soo Choi or the latter may have been appointed

later. Ah Soo Choi was alleged to be still active in the jungle up until December 1989 when Chin Peng signed an undertaking with the Thai and Malaysian governments to cease armed conflict against both countries. I met Ah Soo Choi, at Betong and Yala, in South Thailand, on 14 September and 28 October 1994 respectively. On both occasions he denied that he or anybody else was the overall organizer of the Asal Protection Corp.

16. The information on the objectives of the Asal Protection Corps and their structure was supplied to me in 1988 in correspondence and discussions with Ruslin bin Abdullah of Kuala Lumpur. He was formerly a Police Lieutenant in the early 1950s, then an Assistant Adviser on Aborigines, a Squadron Commander and later Commanding Officer of the Senoi Pra'aq.

17. See also R. O. D. Noone, 152–65, Short, 447–49, 453–55, Holman, 152–53, Carey, 310–12, Dawson, 118–22, for further descriptions of the Asal organization.

18. I wrote this down phonetically as Gee Wei Poo during the interview. Superintendent Chung Choon Soon of the Special Branch in Ipoh gave me what he believes is the correct title (shown above) and the translation.

19. In November 1953 a three-man patrol of the 22 SAS was ambushed in the Cameron Highlands area. Two of the patrol were cooks, normally non-combatants, who were on their first patrol with an experienced NCO. The NCO and one cook were killed in the first burst of fire, the third man followed laid down procedure for contact with a much stronger force and disengaged (euphemism for cleared out). This is possibly the same incident. See *S. T.*, 3 November 1953. I spoke to the survivor soon afterwards.

20. It must be taken into consideration that the New Zealanders arrived in Malaya in late 1955 when the MRLA were very much on the defensive which of course would be known to the Asal groups. They also considered it was counter-productive to attack the SAS or the Police Forts because it only drew attention to their presence, something they wished to avoid following the 1951 directives.

21. The narrators were vague about dates but not locations. This is no reflection on the intelligence or memories of these two men, but it was their normal cultural practice to relate times to natural or unusual phenomena rather than the more advanced societies' use of calendar dates.

22. The rates were M$300 for a firearm, 50 cents for a bullet, $50 for a hand grenade.

23. Dawson, 201.

24. Cloake,256–58.

25. Dawson, 171. 20 Field Jungle Company (FJC) was formerly the

PAAC which had a depth of experience in dealing with Orang Asli in remote jungle. The PAAC also previously had forts at Lasah, a Kampong on the jungle fringe, and Fort Luckam, located in the jungle on the Sungei Plus, which was closed in late 1951.

26. This was formerly an SAS training camp in which I spent some weeks in early 1951. At that time our attitude to the Orang Asli was ambivalent, we used and paid for their services as porters and to help with clearing the jungle, but we did not trust them.

27. Strictly speaking, West was out of bounds locating his fort in another state. However it was a pragmatic decision based on the fact that the Senoi and other Orang Asli moved freely over state boundaries which they did not recognize.

28. H. D. Noone, 14–20.

29. Ibid., 15.

30. See Chapter 2.

31. Dawson, 187–88.

32. Ibid., 191–92.

33. Ibid., 191–96.

34. Ibid., 200–06

35. Ibid., 204–06.

36. Ibid., 206

37. PRO. Kew, CO 1022/475. Telegram from Fed. of Malaya 14/12/53 to Secretary of State.

38. PRO. Kew, GO2608, Sitrep. 287, 27 October 1953, FARELF to War Office. Annual Report 1954, 412–3. *S. T.,* 25 November 1953.

39. Stubbs, 108–09.

40. *Weekly Press Summary,* Government of Malaya, 15 August 1953, and *Annual Report* 1953. Figures do not include the UK Treasury contribution to the Emergency.

41. Site of Head Quarters of Malayan Civil Service in Kuala Lumpur.

42. *S. T.,* 16 June 1953.

43. *M. M.,* 15 February 1950.

44. See A. G. Gomes. *Ecological Adaption and Population Change: Semang Foragers and Temuan Horticulturists in West Malaysia* (Hawaii, 1982). This shows that Williams-Hunt's hypothesis on the Semang was not correct because of changes in their lifestyle since the 1950s.

45. Williams-Hunt, 79.

46. *Arkib Negara,* MUS. 11/51.

47. Refer to H. D. Noone, 61–73 for outline of this Ordinance. A copy of the Federal Ordinance is in the Appendix.

48. *Arkib Negara,* 12354/50. I was unable to obtain a copy of Williams-Hunt's letter.

49. Williams-Hunt, 4.

50. Sel. Sec., 1988/50 (3).

51. *Arkib Negara,* 12663/50.

52. P. Gouldsbury, 50, 51. Although much of Gouldsbury's book is anecdotal it is useful as a record of how she viewed the Orang Asli and the MCP/MRLA.

53. Ibid., 55.

54. Cloake, 257.

55. Ibid., 257.

56. *Arkib Negara,* MUS 118/53.

57. *M. M.,* 6 November 1952.

58. Williams-Hunt, 93.

59. *Arkib Negara,* F S 8916/1952.

60. *The Times,* London, 16 June 1953. In an obituary, Mr William Fagg, Honorary Secretary of the Royal Anthropological Institute, wrote that Williams-Hunt, like H. D. Noone before him, had a sure gift of obtaining the confidence of the Aborigines. He (Hunt) "developed methods and techniques more rigorous in many ways than those in common use by anthropologists today. It will be hard indeed to find a successor to him, but it is urgently needed, on scientific as much as on strategic grounds."

61. William-Hunt, 91

62. Gouldsbury, 128.

63. This story was a generally accepted belief in Malaya at the time. During my sojourn there I accepted it as valid although I never heard it from any Orang Asli source. On reflection it does seem somewhat unbelievable that even the most naive indigene in the remotest part of the jungle could have been fooled for very long. The constant airdrops to the Security Forces operating in their areas where they would see the soldiers or police collecting supplies in the dropping zones, which those same Orang Asli may have assisted in cutting, would have made them question the story. Again all the Security Forces had Orang Asli porters and guides in deep jungle operations who knew their supplies came by air. Even if they were not of the same ethnic group as the people in the operation area there was contact and the locals could see where they got their supplies. Local Orang Asli were frequently used to carry out parachutes to road heads and were paid for this work. Dawson, 209.

64. *S. T.,* 13 October 1953.

65. Cloake, 257.

66. *S. T.,* 16 October 1953.

67. Ibid., 2 November 1953.

68. Cloake, 257, also CO 1022/475, 14 February 1953. Telegram from Federation of Malaya (name of sender indecipherable) to Colonial Office.

69. Gouldsbury, 113–15.

70. Cloake, 257.

71. *M. M.*, 2 November 1953 and 6 November 1953, *Straits Budget*, 3 December 1953.

72. *S. B.*, 3 December, 1953.

73. R. O. D. Noone, 142–43.

74. Letter: Blacking to Leary, 7 July 1988.

75. I am not aware of the Hardy Amies incident but Adenauer's dismissal from his post as Ober-Burgermeister of Koln in 1945 is described in detail by Cloake, 159–62.

76. Letter: Blacking to Leary, 1 September 1988. Blacking became Professor of Social Anthropology at The Queens University in Belfast following a controversial career in South Africa. He died in 1990.

77. R. O. D. Noone, 147.

78. Gouldsbury, 114–15.

79. *Arkib Negara*, F S F35400/54. This is actually an extract from a draft of the Department's submission to the Member for Home Affairs for the 1953 Annual Report which incorporates the recommendations.

80. Cloake, 257–58.

81. Ibid., 258.

82. Spencer Chapman, 240–41. The similarity in the pronunciation of the two names and the description lead me to believe this was Bah Pelankin.

83. R. O. D. Noone, 164.

84. Gouldsbury, 138.

85. R. O. D. Noone, 164.

86. *S. T.*, 4 December 1953. No information located on Bah Pelankin's previous place or date of capture.

87. Ibid., 4 December 1953.

88. R. O. D. Noone, 172.

89. Short, 453–54.

90. R. O. D. Noone, 172–73.

91. *S. T.*, 26 September 1954 and PRO. Kew, CO1033, 7 September 1954.

92. PRO. Kew, DEFE 11, Security forces Weekly Intelligence Summary No.191, for week ending 31 December 1953.

93. Ibid., DEFE 11–105, Telegram from High Commission to Secretary of State for the Colonies, 12 March 1955.

94. *S. T.*, 27 January 1954.

95. *S. T.*, 1 August 1954. These attacks took place during Operation Termite when seventy tons of one thousand pound bombs, followed by rocket, cannon and machine gunfire were used to "blast" the jungle in the

area. Some fifty aircraft, one hundred and eighty parachutists (SAS), elements of five infantry battalions, an artillery battery, two platoons of police, the Special Operations Volunteer Force (surrendered MRLA), and eighty armed aborigines were used in the operation.

96. Ibid., 29 June 1956.

97. Cloake, 261.

98. Ibid., 243.

CHAPTER 5

The Senoi Pra'aq and the Arming of the Orang Asli

THE SENOI PRA'AQ was not the first armed Orang Asli pro-Government paramilitary unit established during the Emergency. Udah Mat bin Long Sohr from Kampar in Perak stated that the Orang Asli in his settlement were engaged as an armed uniformed unit to protect a local mine as early as 1949. Senior serving officers and a former officer of the Special Branch in Ipoh, as well as Orang Asli who heard his comment, have accepted it as being correct. Special constables were recruited for guard duties from the beginning of the Emergency in June 1948[1] so his assertion appears to be a reasonable one. Normally the specials were Malays but clearly some were Orang Asli for a Sakai special constable in Kampar, Itam bin Alang, received three months detention for desertion in August 1949.[2]

There were various reports in the early days of the Emergency of armed Sakai being with MRLA units. On 10 May 1949, an armed Sakai was reported to have been with a party of MRLA who confiscated an identity card from a Malay rubber tapper.[3] In June, a Sakai guide for the guerrillas surrendered, bringing in his Japanese rifle and ammunition.[4] Some of the reports on armed Orang Asli alleged to be MRLA supporters were dubious. In January 1950, "A Sakai bandit gang with a small liaison party of Chinese bandits was attacked in a camp in the Kuala Lipis area of Pahang yesterday." The only weapons recovered were blowpipes, and a quantity of food was found. The conclusion drawn was that the MRLA were using the area for growing crops.[5] This was hardly conclusive proof that the tribespeople were a "bandit gang."

The PAAC

The Perak Aborigines Area Constabulary (PAAC), established in March 1950, had Orang Asli making up ten percent of its numbers. These tribal recruits had access to more powerful weapons than the single barrel shotguns that were the principal weapon of their fellows in Special Constabulary units. The unit was issued with standard .303 rifles, carbines, sten-guns, and bren-guns. Although some of these weapons were old and in poor condition they were still an advance on shotguns. Many of the Malays, who formed the bulk of the unit, were related to Orang Asli or in some cases were actual Orang Asli who had embraced Islam and regarded themselves as Malay.[6] The presence of Semai and Temiar tribesmen in the PAAC was one of its strengths. This enabled patrols to re-establish contact with many groups in the interior who had fled there to escape resettlement.[7] As previously stated, this unit including its Orang Asli members was incorporated into 20 Police Field Jungle Company in 1952 where its personnel were re-trained and re-equipped with better weapons and accoutrements.[8] This police company incorporated the first group of Orang Asli who were to be armed and equipped on a par with the best of the paramilitary police in the Emergency. Despite the obvious capabilities of the Orang Asli in a well trained force, it was to be some time before the Security Forces took maximum advantage of this competence and formed a wholly Orang Asli unit armed with up-to-date weapons.

Orang Asli Armed Guards and Police Units

Even though the tribesmen, recruited as Kampong settlement guards, special constables or home guards, were poorly armed and trained they still gave a good account of themselves when they were involved in armed clashes with MCP armed units. Some examples have been given in previous chapters but there were others which again showed that all groups of Orang Asli could be aggressive. Most of those skirmishes were fought by Orang Asli acting on their own without European or Malay leadership. While most of the Malay special constables had been conscripted under the 15 December 1950 manpower regulations, the Orang Asli were volunteers, being held to be exempt from conscription. This contrasted with many Chinese who were not Malay citizens at the time and who objected to being inducted into the police or military. Six thousand decamped to Singapore and several thousands to China to avoid being called up.[9]

Orang Asli police units were capable of determined resistance and had shown ability to fight off better armed attackers who also had a superiority in numbers. "Ten CT yesterday ambushed five Sakai Auxiliary Policemen in the Tapah area of Perak, but the Sakai put up a tough resistance." In the action, two Orang Asli were wounded but they put their attackers to flight, wounding one of them. The following day, one of the ambushed tribesmen led a patrol of the 1st Manchester Regiment to the ambush area where they followed a blood trail and killed the wounded guerrilla. It was later discovered that the ambushed police had also killed another whose body was found a few days later.[10] The Orang Asli continued to display their ability to act independently and often with flair and consummate bravery against the MRLA and their allies. As demonstrated in previous chapters the motives of the jungle people were sometimes mixed and varied from revenge or reward to self-defense. The violent acts were not confined to any one group of Orang Asli or any one area. Two armed MRLA were killed by Orang Melayu Asli in the Mersing area of Johore in October 1953. The guerrillas, who were armed with rifles, demanded food and threatened to shoot if they did not get it. The villagers killed them with their machetes in a surprise attack.[11]

Individual Security Force officers, such as ASP John West, who had experience of the Orang Asli in the jungle, were quite prepared to arm those who had shown themselves to be cooperative. He realized that this cooperation was dangerous for those who had displayed it and that they should be given weapons to protect themselves against the MRLA.[12] While small groups were supplied with shotguns, there was no real effort to form an Orang Asli unit armed with modern weapons to operate in the interior jungle areas. Even after the MCP October directive was finally found and the strength of the Asal Organization among many Orang Asli was realized, there was no concentrated attempt to use the skill of the tribespeople in the jungle to counter the MRLA. There is no doubt that many of the resettled Orang Asli would have welcomed the opportunity to return to the jungle as paid, armed para-military rather than spend their days idling in the resettlement camps.

The Iban trackers who had been recruited from Sarawak to act as scouts for the Security Forces were formed into their own regiment, the Sarawak Rangers, in March 1953.[13] Surrendered MCP/MRLA were recruited into their own unit, the Special Operations Volunteer Force (SOVF), in May 1953. Officered mainly by European volunteers from the police, they were used to hunt their erstwhile comrades. That unit grew out of two squads of Surrendered Enemy Personnel (SEP) formed in Pahang in 1952 with Police Lieutenants in charge.[14] Why the jungle-wise Orang Asli were not formed into a paramilitary unit, to be used in their natural environment before late 1956, is difficult to understand. They did not commence operations as an official unit until 1958.[15]

Conflicting Attitudes

Even though Williams-Hunt relied on his Orang Asli guides to protect him against attack during his jungle forays, he did not arm them. It is doubtful whether he would have supported arming an

Orang Asli unit during his term as adviser on Aborigines. His paternal and protective attitude towards "his people" precluded him from doing so and in his book, *An Introduction to the Malayan Aborigines,* he did not give any such indication. His emphasis was on protecting Aboriginal guides and porters and in ensuring they were kept out of the line of fire. His statement that "Aborigines are not very happy when being fired at. . . ," makes it appear that there was something wrong with them because they were afraid of being wounded or killed.[16] His attitude towards the Orang Asli fighting prowess was reflected in that of most Government and Security Forces administrators who had dealings with them. The jungle people were fine to use as guides and porters but not as armed auxiliaries.[17]

There were rumors of tribespeople using blowpipes against Security Force patrols, but they were questionable. That excuse could be used to justify burning down huts and even killing some of the fleeing inhabitants by panicky and inexperienced patrol commanders. In March 1949 twelve Sakai shelters were burned by Security Forces in the Gua Musang area of Kelantan because they were believed to have been used by bandits.[18] It was true that some armed Orang Asli had fired either on MRLA units, or the police or army, but these incidents were regarded as aberrations. The myth of the timid, peaceful people in the jungle who were sometimes manipulated by the MRLA persisted all through the Emergency. Mass resettlement of the tribal groups which had not resisted tended to confirm the belief in their peaceful timidity. Even if they fled to escape the mass movement, that was regarded as the act of a wild, frightened people who did not know what was good for them.

As the ramifications of the Asal movement, among the Senoi in particular, began to become clear to the Security Forces, preconceived views of the Orang Asli as non-belligerent people began to change. Dawson claimed that police patrols under the command of ASP J. West and Lieutenant Wilson, captured documents in December 1952 detailing the activities of the Asal Organization in the whole of the Temiar-Senoi territory. The patrols were guided to an MRLA camp on the River Sulieh by a former pro-MRLA head-

SAS Patrol on stand-by for an operational parachute jump into primary jungle, Sungei Besi 1953. Note white canvas bags strapped to parachute harness on their right sides. This held some 50 meters of webbing used to abseil out of tree tops to ground. *Unknown SAS*

Police Aborigine Guards (PAG) at jungle fort 1953. *Unknown SAS*

man, Allang Sulieh. Although the attack on the MRLA position did not result in any MRLA casualties, the fleeing guerrillas left all their papers and supplies behind. Shortly after the attack two armed pro-MRLA Temiar couriers surrendered with their weapons, after which some other weapons they had been given were recovered. The Orang Asli received unspecified rewards for their cooperation.[19]

The problem facing the police was how to protect the cooperative Orang Asli on the Sulieh who were fearful of the reprisals from the female Asal leader in the area, Ah Chu, and her group. In this instance, the Temiar were resettled outside the jungle which was an unsatisfactory solution for the Orang Asli and the police. If the MRLA were prepared to arm their tribal supporters, why should the Security Forces not do so?

Change of Policy

A new policy, *The Director of Operations Instruction No. 17,* entitled "The Control of Aborigines in Malaya" was promulgated on 20 January 1953. Major changes to existing methods were proposed. Orang Asli home guards would be recruited and armed to protect their own areas. Aborigines would no longer be forced to leave their homelands but would be encouraged to move closer to the police forts established for their protection in their homelands. Even if they did not do so they would still be allowed to continue their normal way of life. Almost immediately the Temiar in the vicinity of Fort Legap were issued with twenty single-barrel twelve bore shotguns with twenty-five rounds of ammunition each, and a further twenty guns were issued shortly afterwards.[20] The accelerated recruitment of staff for the Department of Aboriginal Affairs has already been mentioned and their presence in the forts helped to assist with training the Orang Asli. An SAS engineering officer, Major E. C. V. Peacock, was now employed in choosing fort sites and constructing the new forts while the police organized the Orang Asli labor in the actual erection of the buildings.[21] SAS fighting patrols actively patrolled the area to prevent MRLA attacks on the builders. The troop-carrying helicopters, flown by navy pilots, which had been requested by Templer were used to move the troops into the jungle and evacuate the sick. Training of the gun-carrying tribesmen concentrated on weapon maintenance and target practice. It was considered that they did not need to be taught jungle tactics because their familiarity with their surroundings gave them a tactical advantage over hostile intruders.[22]

It should be understood that some Orang Asli had their own shotguns which they used for hunting. These gun owners caused problems for both sides in the Emergency because they could be shot if they ran into patrols of MRLA or Security Forces. A captured MRLA instruction explained the dilemma some of the guerrillas faced and their suggested solution. It was recommended that the shotguns be confiscated "because the enemy may make use of them at any time." Before collecting the weapons, the unit doing so should check if "these arms were bought by them [Orang Asli] or issued by the British Imperialists." The full market price should be paid, not ten dollars, because that amount would be insufficient and cause the Orang Asli to turn against the MRLA. They should also be asked to persuade their friends to sell their guns to the MRLA. "At the same time we have to dissuade them from coming into the jungle for hunting as we may mistake them for our enemy. We must try to find out their difficulties and direct them in their cultivation which is the most important thing at present."[23]

Six jungle forts were established in 1953[24] with a consequent increase in the number of Orang Asli being brought under government control. To hand out arms to the increasing members of cooperative tribespeople so that they could protect themselves from the MRLA required that they be organized into a disciplined, uniformed force. The police platoons in the forts and the SAS patrols operating in the area could not give full-time protection. The Orang Asli in their own areas could use their knowledge of the terrain and their ability to move quickly and silently to good effect in guarding their settlement.

Although still not established in a formal, armed, body, the

Orang Asli in the remoter areas (armed by West and Dawson) gave some return for the trust placed in them. The Temiar from the Sulieh, under Allang, returned for a visit to their old ladang and saw an Asal Organization member there. With permission from the police commander at Fort Legap, Allang Sulieh led an armed Temiar patrol to the site and killed the unarmed man. This fact was verified by a police patrol from the fort, who followed the Orang Asli.[25]

The PAG

Although more Orang Asli were being armed, there was still no cohesive body formed in the fort areas. Both the police and the SAS were making use of surrendered tribespeople, in particular Temiar and Semai who had been in the Asal Protection Corps, to track down their former comrades. Many of these former MRLA supporters were armed at the initiative of individual local commanders and efforts were made to give them some military training. They were also issued with the Security Forces' jungle green uniform. In late 1954 the Finance Committee of the Federal Legislative Council voted to spend nineteen thousand dollars for the remainder of the year to raise and equip part-time police Aboriginal guards (PAG) for the purpose of protecting Orang Asli settlements. Although the PAG were designated as Home Guards for administrative purposes, the fort commanders retained tactical control.[26]

There were tensions between the various Security Forces groups dealing with the Orang Asli and differing views on the methods to be used to win them over in order to use them against the MRLA. The expansion of the Department of Aborigines and the support it received from Templer made it the prime mover in controlling and deciding how they should be handled. The army used the SAS Regiment to keep the pressure on both the Orang Asli and the MRLA in deep jungle areas by remaining in an area for up to fourteen weeks with numerous small patrols constantly traversing the immediate location. These locations were usually where a fort was to be built, following recommendation from the SAS squadron commander, and Major Peacock's expert advice. After the fort had been built, the SAS patrols covered the ground outside the orbit of the police garrison's protective patrols to adjacent ladangs.

Individual police officers such as Dawson were critical of the operational technique employed by the SAS. He considered that they plunged into the jungle without first gleaning the necessary information from the local inhabitants. All they did, he claimed, was stir up the local MRLA, with little success; tactical surprise was lost by using a five day air supply cycle and the use of helicopters to evacuate the sick and wounded.[27] The Department of Aborigines considered that their staff were the only ones who could interrogate friendly or formerly hostile Aborigines. They were successful in keeping out the Special Branch, whose job it was to deal with interrogation, until after the Emergency was over.[28] All three bodies were involved in arming Orang Asli for their own purposes and for different reasons. Gradually the tensions between the groups dissipated as each accepted the other's specialist role. Much of the success of the cooperation between the parties was due to the respect and friendship that grew up between individual commanders in the field. Noone was glad to have the cooperation of the SAS in training his armed Orang Asli. The police were generally pleased to have the assistance of the Department of Aborigine's field officers to liase with the Orang Asli.

By January 1955 there were seven operational sections of armed PAG among the Orang Asli tribes.[29] Their role was still part time and confined to protecting their own settlements. As detailed in Chapters 3 and 4, they had justified the trust placed in them by eliminating the two most wanted pro-MRLA Orang Asli leaders, Bah Pelankin and Chawog, in addition to various MRLA members.

Noone decided to conduct trials with ten Temiar who were former members of the Asal Protection Corps, to establish whether they could be trained as a fighting unit in the style of the SAS. They were attached to D Squadron 22 SAS and their training was undertaken by experienced NCOs under the overall supervision of Major John D. Slim. Armed and equipped with modern weapons, uniforms, and the other accoutrements of a soldier of the time, they proved apt pupils. In early 1956 more Orang Asli, including Semai, were recruited for training. Among one of the first trainees was Batanga, a Semai reputed to have been with the MRLA ambush party which killed High Commissioner Sir Henry Gurney in 1951.[30] In September 1956 reports about a "Temiar Squadron of veteran sharp-shooting aborigines" appeared in the press. The Chief Minister, Tunku Abdul Rahman, was reported to favor the project which was designed to form a fully fledged battalion on the lines of the Sarawak Rangers.[31] The Adviser on Aborigines lobbied for the formation of an independent unit for these trained groups of Orang Asli. He claimed they were restricted in their ability to prove their worth by being forced to operate with Security Force units.[32]

Meanwhile pressure continued on the MRLA and those Orang Asli who continued to support them. Even though an amnesty was announced in September 1955 for any MCP/MRLA who wished to surrender, and abortive peace talks were held at Baling between Chin Peng and the Chief Minister Tunku Abdul Rahman in December 1955, the jungle war continued unabated.[33]

In a review of the Emergency situation at the end of 1954 the Director of Operations estimated there were thirty-five hundred Aborigines "not yet under control." The report continued, "There is a continuing need for more parachute units of the regular volunteer SAS type for operations in deep jungle. It has been clearly shown that British troops are the most successful in deep jungle where contact with and winning over of the aboriginal population is an important component of success." It also stated in the review "that the Malay/Aboriginal element of the Home Guard is a reliable force. Steadfast and patient and that its initiative is increasing as added scope is given to its offensive potential."[34]

In an Appendix to the same report, a breakdown of "Communist Terrorists" remaining in Malay was given, state by state. This showed that the majority were in the states with the largest Orang Asli populations.

Kedah	425
Penang	50
Perak	1110
Kelantan	130
Trengganu	30
Pahang	750
Selangor	350
Negri Sembilan	490
Malacca and Johore	965
Total	3950[35]

The dichotomy between the supporters of the "big battalion" concept and the supporters of the small patrol tactics in the jungle was causing problems in winning over the Orang Asli. In July 1956 a New Zealand SAS patrol killed four and wounded one of five MRLA they contacted near Fort Brooke in Perak. They were led to the vicinity of the camp by an Orang Asli guide supplied by one of the local headmen, Busu. This was a simple infantry style operation with a relatively small group of men.[36] In another incident two Orang Asli home guards, Bah Kampa bin Busu and Long bin Bunga, out hunting boar near Kampar, killed one of two terrorists who fired at them. Armed with shotguns Busu and Bunga hid behind trees until their assailants were close; they fatally wounded the leader, Ah Kwan, who was armed with a rifle, and wounded his companion. They shared a reward of $2100 for their deed and received a badge of valor.[37] In contrast, after a bombardment by the Royal Artillery and an air attack by four Venom jet fighter bombers, which dropped eight thousand pounds of bombs and rockets on the target, one Asal controller—a Chinese named Mang Kali and his armed aboriginal bodyguard—was killed by a Gurkha patrol in the Cameron Highlands.[38] The cost-effectiveness of the contrasting operations, including the effectiveness of the Orang Asli Home Guard in a classic jungle contact, must have had some impression on senior Security Forces officers and would have assisted Noone in his lobbying for an Orang Asli fighting unit. The results obtained from the high cost of firing artillery combined with the use of expensive combat aircraft to drop explosives into the jungle, would have been compared by senior officers with the success of the New Zealand patrol and the Home Guards with limited numbers and small arms only.

The Senoi Pra'aq

The Senoi Pra'aq was finally established in September 1956. The platoon-size unit of thirty men in three sections of ten men each was commanded by R. O. D. Noone. There were two sections of Semai and one Temiar; each section was commanded by an Orang Asli Sergeant elected by the men in the section. Discipline was based on consensus but any breach resulted in the offender being asked to leave the unit. They were uniformed in standard jungle green with a red beret. Their badge was crossed blowpipes with a *Seladang* (wild buffalo) head in the middle on a green background with crossed dart quivers underneath. In contrast to the symbolic blowpipes on the badge they were armed with modern weapons. Pay rates were the same as the police and they were paid, administered, and rationed by the Department of Aborigines. Operational control was vested in the local military commander in the areas where they operated.[39] Within twelve months the unit had grown to three squadrons of sixty men each, commanded by Europeans from the Department of Aborigines who had previous paramilitary experience.

There was still a reluctance to utilize them in other than a reconnaissance or tracker role. The old beliefs about the timid, nonaggressive Orang Asli were hard to shake off. This was despite the fact that there was ample evidence of the willingness of the tribesmen to take aggressive action against those whom they saw as enemies, whether they were MRLA or Security Forces. The myth of Orang Asli timidity was fed by trivializing reports in the media of their behavior following armed clashes between poorly armed tribesmen and the better armed MRLA or Security Forces. The Orang Asli were generally reported as "fleeing in superstitious terror"[40] from the deed they had committed, or other such terminology, whereas Security Forces "bravely fell back" or "took up stronger positions" (See Chapter 4, fn 19). In one action involving the SAS in late February 1951, a major of the Malayan Scouts (SAS Regiment) and his bodyguard stalked and killed a Chinese MRLA sentry. They grabbed his rifle, quickly searched his body for documents, and then took to their heels and ran from the scene as quickly as they could to join their comrades some four or five kilometers away. They, like the Orang Asli, had no intention of foolishly hanging around waiting for a counter-attack from a superior force. Nobody accused them of fleeing in superstitious terror.[41]

There are comments also from Security Force sources of the reluctance of Orang Asli informers or guides to take part in assaults on MRLA camps they had located for the attackers.[42] There were very good reasons for that disinclination to expose themselves to danger. In many instances they had placed themselves and their families in jeopardy by pointing out the MRLA position. The Security Force did not always succeed in eliminating the inhabitants of those camps and the tribesmen were very much aware of that fact. If they were seen by an escaping guerrilla, their lives and those of their families could be forfeit. Furthermore, the guides were sometimes unarmed, and even if they were armed it was only with an inferior single barreled shotgun against trained, ruthless enemies, often with light machine guns, submachine guns and better personal weapons than theirs. The people whom the Orang Asli had guided to the target area were well-armed, trained and able to handle the situation without assistance.

Why should the jungle dwellers expose themselves to unnecessary danger? In the case of the Senoi Pra'aq, however, its members considered they were as well trained and armed as their opposition. They had the added advantage of being able to move quickly and silently in the jungle and could carry rations for sixteen days without resupply.[43] They were in fact ideal counter-guerrilla jungle fighters. As Noone wrote:

> I had been badgering the Director of Operations to allow the Senoi Pra'ak to operate independently. . . . I argued that although pacific

by inclination they could become implacably aggressive once they believed in the necessity for such a course and the justice of it . . . I succeeded in getting the Director of Operations to allow us to have a go on our own.[44]

By the time the unit was allowed to operate independently in 1958, the Emergency was nearly over. The MCP/MRLA military operation had been reduced to a mere nuisance and the handful of MRLA left in peninsular Malaya were no longer a threat to the new Malayan State which had achieved its independence in 1957. It was ironic that the formation which was the most successful in clearing out some of the remaining guerrillas in 1959–60 came from those people whom the MCP/MRLA believed would be their allies and help them retain control of the jungle when they decided to withdraw their main strike force into the forests in October 1951.

The first recorded "kill" by the Senoi Pra'aq was during a combined SAS-Senoi Pra'aq ambush in Perak in March 1958, when two MRLA members walked into the ambush position and one was killed. The Orang Asli who took part in the successful action were rewarded by a visit to naval, army, and military establishments in Singapore and as much of the city as they could fit in in a short visit.[45] Noone claimed they had eliminated eight terrorists and they had won over two hundred Semoq Beri tribespeople in 1958.[46] They took over the role of the SAS regiment which had detached one of its squadrons for another colonial war in Oman, to where most of that regiment followed later. Noone claimed that the Senoi Pra'aq's "record of terrorist eliminations was higher than any Security Force unit, Commonwealth or Federal in 1959–1960."[47]

The Senoi Pra'aq illustrated the failure of the MCP/MRLA to control the Orang Asli in the jungle. The guerrillas were capable of cultivating their own crops within the jungle but without the full cooperation of the Orang Asli they could not hope to do so without Security Forces locating and destroying them. The Asal Protection Corps concept had been cleverly conceived and had a good start on the counter measures of the government forces. Its lack of success lay in the Politbureau's failure to allow for the technological changes in weaponry and equipment that had taken place during and since World War II. Chin Peng and the other members of the Politbureau believed that the same situation would apply in the jungle as had during the Japanese occupation. The MRLA cadres would stay in the jungle indefinitely, emerging when the time was opportune for another armed onslaught. They had outlasted the Japanese during the occupation, and expected that the Security Forces would follow the Japanese example by blundering around the jungle for a week or two, attain some limited success, and then return to base.

There was a mistaken belief that the Royal Air Force would continue to bomb Orang Asli ladangs, and this would strengthen the ties between MRLA and Orang Asli groups. The "nationalities of the masses in the jungle" could be won over and trained to cultivate, carry and guard. The more aggressive ones could be taught to fight for the benefit of their powerful ally, the MCP/MRLA. What the guerrillas did not expect was the ability of the Security Forces to remain in the jungle. The Security Forces' air superiority, which allowed for the supply of everything the Government Forces' patrols needed by regular air drops was unexpected. Once the large troop-carrying helicopters arrived in 1953, the police and military mobility into, within, and out of the jungle was far quicker than any Orang Asli or MRLA group. SAS paratroop drops into the jungle bore the element of surprise. The tribespeople soon realized where the real power lay and from what source they could obtain the greatest advantage. They were paid, rationed, and rewarded for their work for the Security Forces or for informing on the MRLA. The government representatives in the forts supplied medicine and even evacuated the very sick to hospital. The Orang Asli women were not molested and the men were not maltreated as the Asal Group organizers warned they would be. Former members of the Asal clubs were rewarded for bringing in their weapons and informing on their controllers. They saw or knew of their erstwhile Chinese-Asal overseers being killed or surrendering. Cooperative Orang Asli were gradually being armed and finally the Senoi Pra'aq was established on a par with the other paramilitary units in the Security Forces. There was no shortage of recruits from all

Orang Asli groups to join this fighting unit. It is difficult to understand how the myth of Orang Asli pacifity could still be sustained.

Notes

1. Short, 124–28
2. *S. T.,* 19 August 1949.
3. Ibid., 10 May 1949.
4. Ibid., 10 June 1949.
5. Ibid., 18 January 1950.
6. Williams-Hunt, 78, Dawson, 146 passim, Short, 442 and conversations with PAAC officers in 1951.
7. Dawson, 154–55.
8. Ibid., 168–69.
9. Short, 252 and 300–303. In February 1952 Moto bin Jaal, an Orang Asli, was charged in Seremban court for failing to appear for a medical examination as required by the Manpower Regulations. He pleaded that he was illiterate and understood only a small amount of Malay. The magistrate referred the matter to the OCPD "as he thought Sakais were exempt from the call up," (*S. T.,* 15 February 1952).
10. *S. T.,* 8 and 14 November. 1952, also PRO. Kew, CO 1022/16, Weekly Intelligence Summary, 20 November 1952.
11. *S. T.,* 29 October 1953.
12. Dawson, 205. In contrast to Dawson and West, some police officers were contemptuous of the Orang Asli's capability as armed auxiliaries. Follows, 101, tells of the Police Aboriginal Guard (PAG) at Fort Brooke setting off with five days' rations "breathing fire and slaughter but as soon as they were out of sight they would settle down in the nearest ladang." There they would eat the rations and then return to the fort "and spin a yarn about how far they had patrolled." He continued: " I soon got wise to their little game and put an end to it."
13. *S. T.,* 12 March 1953.
14. Cloake, 248 and *S. T.,* 19 May 1953. One shortcoming of some of the original SEPs was their inability to speak Malay or English. A former SAS trooper told me of an operation in 1951, where his squadron was accompanied by two armed SEP who were supposed to show where their former camp was. Neither could speak the other's Chinese dialect or Malay. Nobody in the SAS unit could speak any Chinese dialect. Not even sign language could overcome the problem of two guides who could not communicate fully with each other and could not communicate at all with any of the soldiers. The camp was not located.

15. R. O. D. Noone, 200, also *S. S.*, 15 September 1956, and 15 February 1957.

16. Williams-Hunt, 98.

17. Follows, 101. He claimed that PAG were far more useful as guides than as armed auxiliaries.

18. *S. T.*, 14 March 1949. See also Dawson's account of an attack on a Sakai hut in Chapter 3.

19. Dawson, 218–19 and PRO. Kew, CO1022/16, Weekly Intelligence Summary 136, week ending 11 December 1952. Allang was referred to as Sulieh to distinguish him from another Allang at Legap known as Allang Legap.

20. Dawson, 222, passim.

21. Letter, Peacock to Leary.

22. Dawson, 231–32.

23. PRO. Kew, CO 1022/16, Weekly Intelligence Summary for week ending 23 October 1952.

24. PRO. Kew, WO 874, 1954–55. Situation in Malaya, 52/7416, letter from Director of Operations to Chief of Imperial General Staff (CIGS).

25. Dawson, 234.

26. Ibid., 252. Village Home Guards were originally formed in 1951 to protect the new villages. Often unarmed they patrolled the perimeter wire and advised of any gaps in the wire or suspicious tracks in the vicinity. Later they were armed to accompany police on patrols and handed back their weapons after each patrol. Finally those who were seen as reliable were allowed to take their weapons home. By 1953 there were over two hundred thousand Home Guards, some forty percent of these were Chinese. See Short, 293, 411–15.

27. Dawson, 226–27. The SAS literally plunged into the jungle in some of their operations. They had evolved a parachute jungle technique for parachuting into primary jungle, similar to that used by forest fire fighters in Canada and the United States.

28. Desmond Lawrence, former 2i/c Special Branch, Perak, claimed that the Special Branch was not allowed into the forts to interrogate Orang Asli until 1963. Orang Asli in the more settled areas were in contact with the Special Branch. Former ASP Lim Cheng Leng during a personal interview with me and later by letter, claimed that he "ran" two Orang Asli couriers, employed by the MRLA, whom he had turned. They operated in the Kuala Pilah area of Negri Sembilan in 1953. They were Orang Melayu Asli, and the two, Batin Baa and Batin Noh are now deceased. They allowed the Special Branch to copy the documents they were carrying for the MRLA. The operation resulted in the elimination of eleven MCP/MRLA members including a District Committee member and a

Branch Committee member. The Orang Asli used public transport between their MRLA rendezvous points.

29. *S. T.,* 19 January 1955.

30. Information obtained from Tuan Syed Zainal Abadin Alsagoff KMN, CO., Battalion 20 Police Field Force Senoi Pra'aq at Bidor, Malaysia, 29 September 1988. Tuan Syed joined the Senoi Pra'aq in 1957 after joining the Department of Aboriginal Affairs in July 1955. Also see R. O. D. Noone, 200. Lee Ang Sin was the bodyguard to Siu Mah, the commander of the fifty member ambush party that killed Gurney. He is believed to be the sole survivor of that group. At a meeting with him in Yala, South Thailand, on 28 October 1994 he stated that he did not know Batanga and that there was no Orang Asli in the ambushcade.

31. *Singapore Standard,* 15 September 1956.

32. R. O. D. Noone, 200.

33. Short, 459–71.

34. PRO. Kew, DEFE 11–105(a), Director of Operations 40/19, to War Office, Review of Emergency situation in Malaya at the end of 1954, 10 January 1955.

35. Ibid., Appendix B.

36. F. Rennie, *Regular Soldier. A Life in the New Zealand Army* (Auckland, 1986), 191–92.

37. *S. T.,* 11 September 1956 and 15 September 1956. The two Busus mentioned above were different people.

38. *M. M.,* 26 September 1956, and *S. T.,* 26 September 1956. The report claimed that the Gurkhas were amused to find several pairs of new brassieres and panties in Mang Kali's pack.

39. Paper, *The Senoi Pra'aq: A Brief History and Description* (Kuala Lumpur, 1966). Short, 493–94 and fn. *S. T.,* 15 February 1957.

40. *S. T.,* 26 September 1954. Describing the killing of Pah Chawog by an Orang Asli patrol it said, "Seconds later the superstitious patrol of auxiliary police which had shot him was fleeing from the scene aghast at the deed it had committed."

41. Eyewitness account by Malayan Scouts personnel and personal involvement following that action.

42. In a letter to me a former New Zealand SAS Troop Commander, I. Burrows, described how Orang Asli under Uda bin Pangoi also known as Alang, a former Asal member, were willing to guide his troop to MRLA camps but never took part in the assaults on those camps.

43. This was based on the new SAS air supply system devised in 1955–1956. Before late 1955 the SAS, like other units depended on a five day re-supply cycle for rations, replacement clothing, and other supplies. Gradually by experimenting with lighter ration packs, more concentrated

foods and discarding luxuries such as boiled sweets, lemonade powder, and other such items, they reduced the weight of the daily ration. They also relied on two meals per day. By increasing the weight of the personal packs they carried and re-distributing the rations about the body in pockets and on the waist belt, they were able to carry fourteen days rations. This allowed them nine or more days extra in an area before an air drop gave their presence away to Orang Asli or MRLA.

44. R. O. D. Noone, 200. Pra'aq was spelt Pra'ak in the early days of the unit but the "k" was changed in the new spelling to "q."

45. *S. T.*, 18 March 1958, *S. S.*, 3 and 4 July 1958.

46. R. O. D. Noone, 201.

47. Ibid. There were 115 MRLA eliminations in 1959 of whom 21 were killed, 8 captured, 86 surrendered. In 1960 13 were captured, 6 surrendered. The total eliminations were shown as 29 but the figures do not add up. Short, Appendix. 508.

CHAPTER 6

Merdeka and the Bureaucracy

THE DECLARATION OF Malayan Independence, *Merdeka,*[1] in 1957 did not mean an abrupt end to British involvement in that country. Some senior positions in both federal and state civil services were retained by their British occupants until their Malay successors were trained to take over.[2] The policies of the British incumbents were thus carried over into the early period of *Merdeka,* and even when Malayans replaced the colonial bureaucrats, it took some time for them to get their new ideas implemented. The ongoing effects of some of these policies on the Orang Asli, leading up to *Merdeka* and on to the end of the Emergency in 1960, will be discussed in this chapter.

Merdeka and the Orang Asli

The advent of *Merdeka* did not evoke the same euphoric expectations for the Orang Asli as it did for the indigenous Malays. There were some token Orang Asli headmen invited to the independence celebrations in Kuala Lumpur and other major centers. The *Malay Mail* reported that "The *Merdeka* Celebrations Central Committee has almost forgotten the aborigines of the country—Malaya's original inhabitants—in its programme of festivities." The paper went on to state that headmen from each state were invited to the handover of government ceremonies at *Merdeka* Stadium in Kuala Lumpur, but apart from that gesture and a few displays of Orang Asli dances in a hastily erected Temiar longhouse, the bulk of the tribespeople were practically ignored.[3]

It was announced in early August that the Perak Aborigines were to receive a treat from the state government on 31 August 1957. R.C. Corfield, the Protector of Aborigines, Northern Region, had been given three thousand Malayan dollars to buy food, supplies, and tobacco to be distributed to them with a request to perform exhibition dances. Field officers were told to explain the nexus between the gifts and the declaration of *Merdeka*.[4] There were other performances to be given by Orang Asli in other centers, mainly for their curiosity value and ability to attract sightseers rather than a genuine attempt to involve the tribespeople in the mainstream celebrations. In describing the ceremonies and festivities planned in Perak State, the *Straits Times* again reported: "The 11,000 aborigines in the State will have their own celebrations," then explained how the allocated money was to be distributed.[5]

The presence of the Orang Asli was an embarrassment to some in the new Malayan nation. Chauvinistic indigenous Malays were declaring themselves as the *Bumiputera,*[5] "sons of the soil," as distinct from the Chinese, Indian, or other social groups who lived permanently in Malaya. Despite their grandiose posturing that they alone were the original occupiers of the Peninsula, the presence of the Orang Asli was a constant reminder that the Malays, like the other ethnic inhabitants, had also been immigrants in a land that was already populated. An editorial in the *Straits Times* in July 1955 summed up the position of the Orang Asli in Malay society.

> The Emergency has had one salutary effect. It has focussed attention on a group of people toward whom the popular attitude has been one of indifference mixed with contempt. In the definition of Malay peoples the Aborigines were not included. They were part of the animal life around the fringes of the jungle. . . . All the people of Malaya have staked their claims and asserted their inalienable rights

> except our dispossessed hosts driven into the jungle fringes. . . . The old policy of treating them as interesting museum pieces to be protected and preserved could only mean the extinction of the real sons of the soil.[7]

In his maiden speech at the Federal Legislative Council, Tok Pangku Pandak, described in the press as the first Aborigine to be elected to that body, told the Council that his people were the "true sons of the soil." He demanded legislation that would provide protection for the Orang Asli "against further encroachment by immigrants."[8]

The 1954 *Aboriginal Peoples Ordinance* went some way toward giving the Orang Asli protection against exploitation and limited recognition to certain land rights. It also accepted the Aborigines as part of the Malay population.[9] Williams-Hunt had lobbied for its promulgation, as R. O. D. Noone did later, after it had been tabled for presentation to the Legislative Council in 1953. It was the Malay member for Home Affairs, Dato Sir Onn bin Jaafar, who pushed for its acceptance and who, as pointed out in a previous chapter, had supported Orang Asli rights through his official capacity in UMNO. As he said when presenting the Bill in late 1953, "Aborigines are human beings with human reactions . . . and the idea of the Bill is to provide for their protection as human beings and not as museum pieces or exhibits."[10]

By 1957 the shooting war had diminished to a series of sporadic clashes between the Security Forces and the MRLA. The declaration of *Merdeka* on 31 August 1957 removed any validity from the MCP's claim that it was fighting for an independent Malaya. Most of the country had been declared "white" apart from the main range areas and South Pahang and Johore.[11] The presence of Orang Asli in the main range area who were still ambivalent about which side they should support enabled the rapidly declining numbers of MRLA units to survive in those locations where they were difficult to find. The MRLA units were intent on survival rather than aggressive action and the initiative had passed completely over to the government forces. Neither the departing British nor the new

Malayan government were prepared to allow the remnants of the MRLA to remain hidden away in the jungle, possibly to emerge again at a more opportune time to attempt to disrupt government control. The pressure on both the Orang Asli and the MRLA continued unabated.

Opposition by Vested Interests

Pre- and post-*Merdeka* endeavours by both colonial and Malayan governments to win over the Orang Asli did not always receive the expected cooperation from all sectors of the bureaucracy. The introduction of the Aboriginal Ordinance Act was virulently opposed by the Forestry Department. This opposition commenced immediately after the Ordinance was promulgated in 1954 and continued after the declaration of *Merdeka.* The Acting Director of Forestry, J. S. Smith declared in July 1956 that

> We consider (and have often said) that the Aboriginal Peoples Ordinance is an ill-conceived piece of legislation to the extent that interested departments were not consulted before it was enacted.[12]

An acerbic correspondence continued between various officials of the Department of Forests and members of the Department of Aboriginal Affairs. The correspondents in both cases were not Malays but British. Senior positions in both services, particularly in specialist areas, remained in the hands of former colonial officials right up to the end of the Emergency in 1960 and beyond. Their example gave a precedent to their Malay successors in their attitude to the rights of the Orang Asli in their homelands. The issues are discussed in the following paragraphs.

State Forest Officer, Perak, Colin Marshall wrote long and bitter letters attacking the *Perak State Aborigines Ordinance.* He declared he could not comment in detail on the *Aboriginal Peoples Ordinance 1954* as it was a federal matter. There is no question, from the tone of his letters, that his real attack was directed at the Federal Ordinance. In a letter written to the Director of Forests in June

1956 he declared that "the Aborigines are to be given medical care, land, rights to destroy national forests and to foul jungle streams. They are to be given schools, houses in jungle forts, maintained by expensive helicopter ferry services, etc. etc. This is starry eyed idealism, but can we afford it and will the hard-headed electors agree to afford it in the future." In the same letter he continued to say that the Orang Asli should be taught to envy the higher Malay way of life and religion, and eventually rise to the level of the Malays.[13]

The same Colin Marshall, following his appointment as Conservator of Forests in Johore, renewed his attack on the Orang Asli in a letter to the State Secretary on 12 July 1959. It was a strange and ambivalent letter. In one paragraph he states the self-styled Sakai, now called Aborigines or "Abos," "like the more primitive Australian Aborigines," were intelligent and good forest workers. He also mentions a friend of his, a Sakai forester in Selangor. This follows an attack on the Aborigines in Perak, who, because of the official attitude of kindness and understanding and the exigencies of the Emergency, took advantage of both these situations to cause unnecessary and irreparable damage to the forests in that state. It left the "ignorant Sakais" only fit to be exhibited at agricultural shows. He recommended that they be converted to Islam: "The Aborigines Department should aim at its own eventual disappearance and not keep these people primitive worshipping jungle devils as an excuse for ethnographers. These are people, not animals."[14]

In March 1957 R.C. Corfield, the Protector of Aborigines in Perak, wrote to the Chairman, Perak State Aborigines Advisory Board, in answer to Marshall's first letter. He admitted that relocated Aborigines had had to be accommodated temporarily in a forest reserve, a location chosen by the SWEC and DWECS. They had cut ladangs in areas of workable forest reserve which damaged commercial timber stands. He stressed that this situation was a result of the Emergency, and if the Orang Asli had not been allowed to cut ladangs to feed themselves they would have had to be returned to their Communist-dominated homeland, or rationed by the government at a cost of several hundred thousand dollars. He pointed out that even if those Orang Asli were living in their normal locations, that those areas were inaccessible to forest workers despite some of their ladangs being in Forest reserves. The relocated people wanted to go home but it was an inopportune time to allow them to do so because they would be back in the control of the MCP. He considered that "the advantage gained by having control of the Aborigines is sufficient under the present Emergency situation to outweigh the loss of timber caused by their cutting ladangs." He also ridiculed the State Forest Officer's declaration that he would arrest any Aborigine felling or clearing land in a forest reserve. To do this he would have to arrest the greater proportion of Aborigines relocated under the Emergency requirements which would cause them to flee back into the arms of the CT.[15]

Assistant Federal Adviser on Aborigines Dr. Iskandar Yusof Carey[16] replied in June 1959 to the letter Marshall had written from Johore, requesting Marshall to show tolerance and understanding. He pointed out that the problem in Johore was fairly minor in comparison with Perak. In both states Aborigines had, for some thousands of years, lived in the areas now declared forest reserves. Many of the forest reserves had been declared long before there was a Department of Aborigines to advise about the hereditary rights of the aboriginal people.[17]

State Forest Officer Negri Sembilan, G.G.K. Setter, in an undated letter recommended that the government "should refuse to recognise the right of Aborigines to practise shifting cultivation." A policy of weaning the Aborigines from their old ways of cultivation should be instituted and they should be settled in the ways of permanent agriculture. Their reserves should be sited in such a way that would enable correct land utilization such as drainage, irrigation agriculture, forestry, mining, etc. The economies of the land use by Aborigines should be looked at, not only for their benefit, but for the state's as a whole.[18]

In June 1956 State Forest Officer, Pahang, F.S. Walker gave a less emotional and contrary view to that of his colleagues on the damage caused to the jungle by Orang Asli. He had been asked to comment on the *Aboriginal Peoples Ordinance* and referred to his different conclusions from those of his predecessor. Using diary entries from 28 to 31 October 1952, when he had examined the erosion of an area in the Ulu Tembeling on the Pahang River allegedly caused by Orang Asli, he concluded,

> Sakai need take little blame for the slow recovery of the Pahang River. The Malays of the Ulu, on the contrary, could be justly blamed. The position may be different now; but certainly in 1952 river bank cultivation in the Ulu Tembeling was shocking: not by Sakais.[19]

The forest industry had a vested interest in retaining sole control of jungle reserves. It regarded the presence of the Orang Asli as a potential obstruction to exploiting the national resources of the as yet barely touched jungle. As the Emergency began to peter out, authorities such as the Ministry of National and Rural Development began to look at the sparsely populated areas of the Peninsula, often Orang Asli homelands, for development of hydroelectric schemes, and forestry and mineral exploration industries.[20] The new Malayan nation now had its own government after *Merdeka* and no longer had the restraining and often penurious hand of a colonial master to restrict its plans for industrial, agricultural, and entrepreneurial development.

The attitude of the Colonial Forestry Department's bureaucrats to the Orang Asli did not augur well for their future. In Bilut Settlement, in Pahang, which had been opened up for settlement by Malays, fifty Orang Asli were found in June 1959. This land was opened up by the Land Development Authority without consultation with the Department of Aboriginal Affairs. The official spokesman for the Land Development Authority declared, "Of course there could be no question of dispossessing these people of the land they have exploited in a primitive way." No indeed! It was alleged they were to share the benefits the other settlers would receive and live in their own communities. It was then intimated that they would not be swamped by the new settlers.[21]

Field Officers—Department of Aboriginal Affairs

Most of the predominantly Malay staff of the Department of Aboriginal Affairs gave dedicated and selfless service to the people for whom they had been employed to guide and care. This included administration, medical, and education personnel. Some like Puteh bin Awang had had dealings with the Orang Asli since before World War II. Puteh had been Pat Noone's personal servant but over the years had developed into a valued and senior member of the Department of Aboriginal Affairs.[22] Gouldsbury wrote of his invaluable assistance to her after the death of Peter Williams-Hunt. She was the Acting Adviser on Aborigines and he was a Senior Field Assistant. She called him, "a charming, diffident Malay, he knew the tribes like the palm of his hand and spoke at least two of their dialects."[23] Due to Puteh's shrewdness and knowledge of Orang Asli ways, in 1950 he and Williams-Hunt had located the widow of Pat Noone. She was dying of "bronchial septice[a]mia" and unfortunately they were unable to get medical help before she died, taking her knowledge of Pat's death with her.[24]

These Malay Field Assistants performed a lonely, dangerous job in the forts. Relations with the fort commanders were generally good. Although responsible to those fort officers for daily routine matters, their primary responsibility was to the Department of Aborigines. The police had at first supplied the medical orderlies but from 1954 onwards, when the Department started to expand services such as medical orderlies and teachers, these were provided by the Department of Aboriginal Affairs.[25] The Field Assistants had to tread a narrow line between keeping visiting Department of Aborigines' officials advised of what was happening with the Orang Asli in the fort areas and not antagonizing the police with whom they had to live for up to six months at a time.[26] Their role remained unchanged after *Merdeka,* up to, and beyond, the declaration of the end of the Emergency.

John Slimming described the work of the Field Assistants in his account of a journey through Temiar territory in 1956–57. He wrote about two Field Assistants who were based at Fort Chabai on the Sungei Yai in Kelantan. One, a dresser (medical orderly),was in charge of the dispensary. In addition to attending to the Orang Asli around the fort who came in for medical treatment, he had to make routine visits to the Temiar groups living near the fort. To do his medical rounds of the ladangs he needed to accompany a regular police patrol which was susceptible to ambush by MRLA in the area. The other assistant was responsible for the trading post in the fort where the Orang Asli bought salt, parangs (machetes), and cloth with money they earned working around the fort, or as porters with fighting patrols. He also acted as a school teacher teaching the "male children between seven and eleven years of age, who live close enough." Slimming said they were taught the three R's but he then remarked "we look forward to a day when people of all ages will come and be taught simple hygiene, the rotation of crops, and things which will be of value to them."[27] Slimming was accompanied on his journey by an Indian, Hari Singh, who was also a Field Assistant.

Many of the Field Assistants were mainly Malay speaking and had difficulty communicating with the people for whom they were responsible. Despite this they often came to be trusted by the Orang Asli. Using Malay (the lingua franca of many Orang Asli) plus a smattering of the local dialect and sign language, or working through interpreters, they were used for preliminary interrogations and as go-betweens with wavering Asal members wanting to surrender.[28] As Malayanization of the Malayan Civil Service continued after *Merdeka,* a number of former Field Assistants became senior members in the Department of Aborigines and the police. These included Tuan Syed Zainal Abidin Alsagoff who joined the Department in 1955 and eventually became Commanding Officer of Battalion 20 Senoi Pra'aq Police Field Force, and Haji Ahmad bin Khamis who joined in 1957 and became Director of Operations for the Department. There were no Orang Asli promoted to senior positions.[29]

Education

The Rotary Club of Ipoh, in 1958, presented $M850 towards the construction of a new school for the Orang Asli near Tanjong Rambutan in Perak.[30] This was indicative of the recognition by responsible private members of the Malay community and the Orang Asli of the latter group's need for education so that they would be able to cope with their changing circumstances in the new Malaya. The Orang Asli helped to build the school. There were two remarkable features about the building of it. It was a multi-ethnic effort and was privately sponsored, unlike most other Orang Asli schools which were erected by the government.

The states' and federal governments had been aware before *Merdeka* that education was a requirement for the Orang Asli if they hoped to compete in a world that was fast swamping them and liable to leave them impoverished in its wake if they could not hold their own against the interlopers. In 1956 Minister for Education Dato Abdul Razak bin Hussein announced that fourteen government schools had been opened for the Orang Asli. There were twenty-eight schools with seven hundred pupils by February 1957; this number increased to 1,162 pupils in thirty six schools in May.[31]

There was conflict between different organizations and within government departments as to the purpose of educating the Orang Asli. Dato Razak said, "It was generally agreed that the Aborigines' standard of living should be raised so that they would eventually be assimilated by the Malay population."[32] The Department of Aborigines in Selangor intimated that Orang Asli schools in that state, in addition to teaching modern education programs, would encourage the Aborigines to "cultivate their ancient arts . . . Folk-dancing and the art of self defence" as part of the curriculum. It planned to build another fourteen schools in Selangor. The teachers would first be taught the customs and way of living of their charges. "We do not want them to forget their traditional customs," said Assistant Protector of Aborigines in Selangor, Inche Mohamed Hoessein bin Emas, "we do not want the other races to look down upon the Aborigines."[33] The Orang Asli in the more settled areas showed their willingness to help themselves by building their own schools. At Tanjong Sepat and Bukit Bankong in Selangor the local tribespeople built a school at each center at no cost to the government. Books were provided by the government and the Adult Education Association provided teachers for the children in the day time and for adults at night.[34]

Despite its best intentions the Department of Aboriginal Affairs simply could not afford to run a separate school system. In 1958 R. O. D. Noone announced that schools, other than those in the jungle forts, would be run by the Education Department. His Department had thirty-six schools, twenty-four of which were to be transferred to State Education Boards. A further twenty-four were needed to cope with the influx of Orang Asli pupils. These were expected to cost a paltry $M9,600. There were 1,025 children in the state's Aboriginal schools and this was expected to double within a few years. The demand for schooling came from the Orang Asli. The schools taught up to the Education Department's "Standard Three" in Malay, hygiene, reading, writing and arithmetic.[35] A boarding school for Aborigine children was started near a jungle fort in Kelantan in November 1956. The Malay teacher taught his twenty pupils, ranging from five to eighteen years, the "three R's," but special emphasis was placed on practical subjects such as carpentry and plant husbandry. This was an exceptional effort by a dedicated and enthusiastic teacher.[36]

The benefits of education were restricted to those Orang Asli who were living in permanent settlements, or close to forts or were resettled. It was too difficult to reach the wandering Semang, and the more remote Senoi and Orang Melayu Asli. It was also too dangerous and physically impractical to try to take teachers to them, or build schools in jungle areas where the MRLA still had a presence. There was resistance from some older Orang Asli to schools in certain forts. Gouldsbury described the obstructive attitude of an elderly Temiar, Pah Ah, toward the education of the children and younger adults at Fort Shean: he claimed that his people were too old to learn new ways as he was too old also; he and the older people in his group were not going to learn and they were not prepared to allow the children to attend lest they should come to know too much; this would lead to poor discipline and insubordination and then to the breaking up of the tribal laws with the possibility of total disintegration of the group. Gouldsbury overcame the problem by showing the children how to paint and model with Plasticine and the young women to sew. This in turn got the young adult males to try their skill at painting and shaping the Plasticine. This forced Pah Ah to acknowledge that his young people wanted to learn. In a compromise solution it was agreed that the children would attend school in the morning and the older Orang Asli would have their own classes in the afternoon.[37] As the more remote groups and hard core Orang Asli Asal members came under control later in the Emergency, the new Malay government was faced with this problem of getting the children to school.

Meeting the needs of even settled Orang Asli by supplying a school and teacher was not as simple as it appeared. The following case history of a school in Kuala Kubu Bharu in Selangor between 1951 and 1958 will disclose some of the problems associated with educating a group of Orang Asli in that area. These kinds of problems would also cause difficulties for the new government after Merdeka. The people were resettled in and around the Kampong in 1949–50. District Officer Ulu Selangor P.A. Coates indicated to the State Secretary in May 1951 that he was anxious to use a former Malay school for Orang Asli children. The Education Department insisted that the Orang Asli children must go to the same school as Malay children. Coates found that the Sakai children resolutely refused to do so, "Not only are they a little shy of mixing with the other Malay children, but they are a little shy to go to the Malay school which is almost inside the Army Camp area." Despite his best endeavours they would not go. Their parents were prepared to build a little shed near their settlement and the children would go there if the government supplied a teacher. Senior Inspector for Schools, Selangor, F. C. W. Edge told Coates there was no money for a teacher but he thought it was a good idea. A Malay teacher had given lessons previously in his spare time but when the government refused to pay him, he stopped. Coates told the State Secretary that he felt it was in everybody's interest to get a teacher for the sixty children in the settlement.[38]

Edge proposed to recruit a new teacher to supervise the class. Tuition would have to be in the afternoon, in the Malay school, as that was the only time the Orang Asli children would attend.[39] Coates wrote again in July and October 1951 asking for information from the State Secretariat on when the school would be ready.[40] It does appear that the school had commenced. In January 1955 Gouldsbury wrote to the Senior School Inspector Selangor concerning her visit to the Aborigines at Kuala Kubu Bahru. The government provided rations for the resettled tribespeople until early 1954 and because of this, attendance at the school had been good. "Rationing of this group was stopped, as a result all the Aborigine children, except six who continued at the school, left in order to work or collect jungle produce to supplement their families' food." Malay children replaced them. Gouldsbury spoke to the headman and he agreed that thirty children in the group would attend the school if they were given rations. Gouldsbury acquiesced and said that her department would supply rations because the group had been resettled for security reasons and could not return to their ladang to grow food. She requested that the children start school a week later and that the Malay children be sent to the Malay school in Kuala Kubu Bahru to make room for the thirty Aborigine children. She arranged to send a Field Assistant to Kuala Kubu Bahru to look after the Aborigines and liase with the District Officer.[41]

In April 1955 Gouldsbury again wrote to the Senior Inspector of Schools following a visit to Kuala Kubu Bahru. The teacher at the school there complained that he was unable to cope with the thirty Aboriginal children and eighteen Malay children he was expected to teach. She agreed with the teacher. The District Officer indicated that he did not want to move the Malay children because he thought it was both good "from a racial point of view" and for the groups to compete. The District Officer also supported the need for a new teacher. Gouldsbury could not offer the services of the Field Assistant, even part time, because of his other commitments. She asked for a student teacher.[42] The following day she wrote to the

District Officer at Kuala Kubu Bahru asking how much it would cost to put in piped water and two latrines at the school. The school lacked even the basic sanitary amenities.

Later that month she wrote to Chief Education Officer Mr. P. G. Haig complaining about the poor condition of the school and requesting its urgent repair. This was followed up by a terse letter in June 1955 demanding to know what action was being taken on her request. She included the State Secretary, the British Adviser, the Executive Secretaries of the SWEC, the Member for Home Affairs, and the Chief Education Officer Selangor as addressees in the letter.[43] It did not appear to get any result. She advised the Chief Education Officer in July 1955 that two Orang Asli headmen, Batin Kesum and Batin Dollah, had agreed to repair the school walls and roof if the materials were supplied. She expressed her pleasure that two groups of adults from the Kuala Kubu Bahru Aborigines, totalling twenty people, were attending evening adult literacy classes.[44]

By September 1955 Mr. Haig, the Chief Education Officer, had been replaced by a Mr. Foo. Gouldsbury wrote a very fulsome letter to him on the 30th, outlining more problems with the Kuala Kubu Bahru Aborigine school. She had received advice from the Field Assistant that only three Aborigine children had returned to the school after the last holiday. After he spoke to the parents a further three returned, making a total of six. The school had not yet been repaired because the adult Aborigines had not finished their planting but repairs would be continued now that the planting was done. The reason they gave for their children not going to school was because the Malay schoolmaster, Che' Gu Haji Yahaya, had caned and abused them. The school teacher confirmed to the Field Assistant that he had caned the children for coming to school unwashed and in dirty clothes, but he strenuously denied abusing them. Gouldsbury felt it was a great pity that this incident had happened when the children and their parents had previously been so enthusiastic. She offered a number of suggestions, including the building of an Aboriginal type longhouse to be used as a school, but only manned by an untrained teacher supplied by her department. In that event the Malay children would be sent to a Malay school.

She also wrote to Che' Ali the Field Assistant asking him to approach the parents of the six Aboriginal children left in the school to ensure they washed and wore clean clothes to school. If no soap was available, her department would supply each child with a cake of soap each week.[45]

In October she wrote to the Chief Education Officer again thanking him for his offer (not documented) to do his best in solving the problems at the school. She continued,

> The parents of the Aborigine children who stopped attending have now been spoken to most severely and I am glad to say that twelve of them are back at school again, and I hope that next week they will total eighteen again.[46]

There was no further correspondence in the records on this matter. There was some evidence that the school did revive and even prosper after *Merdeka. The Malay Mail* in May 1958 had a photograph of the Mentri Besar of Selangor scrutinising the work of a smartly dressed Orang Asli student during a visit by the Minister to the school.[47] This example highlights the difficulties of bringing education to the Orang Asli even in settled areas. The tribespeople had accepted the need for education but at the same time the bureaucracy had to be sensitive to their particular needs. They did not want their children to go to a Malay school, neither did they like them to be caned. Hygiene was not a priority but if they were guided they could learn. It was a pity that it was thought necessary to bully them to get their children to attend.

The standard of education offered to many Orang Asli, particularly in the forts, was not very good because of the lack of qualified teachers willing to go into the deep jungle.[48] However, beginnings had been made to educate a previously illiterate people and these endeavours would continue after *Merdeka. The Aboriginal People Ordinance of 1954,* clause 17, had clearly stated that "no Aboriginal child shall be precluded from attending any school by reason only of his being an Aborigine."[49] As demonstrated, this well intentioned declaration was not easy to implement and after *Merdeka* it would continue to cause problems in execution for the new government.

Religion

One of the problems associated with labelling actions good or bad is the observer's personal objectivity and judgment as to what is a positive or negative action. Were the actions of Christian and Islamic missionaries and proselytizers among the Orang Asli in the interests of the Orang Asli, or were they an attempt to undermine an old and different culture for the benefit of those who wished to change the beliefs of their converts? The rivalry between the various religions was present before the Emergency and continued beyond *Merdeka*.

The missionary role of the major world religions had been very limited among the Orang Asli prior to and during the Emergency. Before the Emergency geographic restraints due to the inaccessibility of the remote tribes and the strong attachment of the groups in the deep jungle to their traditional beliefs had inhibited the proselytizing of the tribespeople. During the conflict it had been too dangerous to venture into the jungle. In the schools within the forts the authorities discouraged the teaching of any religion.[50]

The Methodist Home Missionary Society expressed its interest in working among the Aborigines in Malaya in January 1948. This immediately caused a reaction from Muslim circles in Singapore. They objected to the Christian missionary work among the Orang Asli on the grounds that if they were approached the next step could be toward the Malays of the Kampong.[51]

In Segamat, in Johore, in December 1948, two groups of Jakun refugees totalling eighty-one people embraced Islam. The Segamat branch of UMNO supported by other district branches contributed to an aid fund to assist the Islamisation and give aid to the converts.[52]

In January 1949, an anonymous writer under the pen name, "Pro Bono Abo" of the Cameron Highlands wrote to the editor of the *Straits Times* advocating the rescue "of the Sakai who rejoice to be called Darat" from their existing dangerous (due to the Emergency) and straitened circumstances. "Throughout the ages nothing practical has been done to benefit the Aborigine of the Peninsula, except discourse on who was to do it and the respective sectarian heavens to which the Sakai soul should be guided." The writer continued that they should be taught to help themselves, "show them how to make and maintain a permanent field, to irrigate, to till, to harvest and store. Why don't we colonize them, settle them on the land?"[53]

He was answered by "Pro Bono Mantra" of Negri Sembilan who stated that a sectarian (sic) not a dozen miles away from civilization had been holding discourse with the Mantra (Orang Melayu Asli) in Negri Sembilan for many years. In spite of the Japanese occupation and the present jungle conflict, the nucleus of a community village was appearing on a government reserve granted to the group. "This village in the making can boast a Malay school with a most efficient and energetic young teacher from the Education Department. It has a nominal roll of twenty-tight, girls and boys, a small Roman Catholic church and a club cum council house." All the structures were just attap and bamboo.[54] The inference of the letter was that the benign influence of the Christian missionary was bringing about the result sought by the first writer and that these benefactors to the Orang Asli should not be forgotten once the government recovered from its difficulties with the Emergency. It was assumed that the tribespeople were grateful recipients of this benevolence.

In February 1950 a meeting of delegates from Muslim religious associations met in Muar to discuss the matter of missionary work among the Sakai. Apart from discussing the issue there appeared to be no concrete results from this meeting concerning the conversion of the Orang Asli.[55]

As the Emergency began to wane missionary activity among the Orang Asli increased. The presence of a majority of Malays in the new Malay government after *Merdeka* encouraged the belief that there would be more success by the Muslim missionaries. Even prior to the official declaration of *Merdeka* there had been plans in 1956 to convert ten thousand Aborigines to Islam. Keeper of the Ruler's Seal Tuan Haji Mustapha Albakri of the Religious Advisory Commission of the Conference of Rulers, gave details of the scheme. Several states, he reported, had started their own mission and campaigns. The Department of Religious Affairs in Perak had converted forty-three Aborigines—twenty-three in 1956 using only three missionaries. Their success had been restricted to the Tanjong Rambutan and Gopeng areas. In Selangor six of the twenty-one converts were Ulu Langat Orang Asli. The converts were given financial assistance for the first three months to help settle them in Kampongs.[56]

In April 1957 a meeting of an unnamed group in Kuala Lumpur said "that since Malaya would have its own State religion, those aborigines who had no religion should be taught the State religion."

It was again reported from Perak in December 1957 that Orang Asli were being slowly converted to Islam. Two converted Orang Asli and Malay missionaries who spoke Orang Asli dialects were active in converting the Aborigines.[57] The Selangor Religious Affairs Department announced that there were eight Aborigines among the two hundred and twenty-one Muslims who had been converted in the year until April 1958.[58] These results were far from exceptional. Carey attributes the failure of the Islamic proselytizers to the poor quality of the missionaries and the lack of coordination between the various states' bodies. The religious departments in the states had very little money and could not offer the Orang Asli any incentives in the form of welfare, education, or medicine.

The poorly educated religious teachers had no knowledge of Orang Asli customs and did not know how to deal with them. There was also the problem of prohibitions on food such as pork, which was highly prized by the Orang Asli, and the tribespeoples' inherent difficulty in adhering to the strict time schedules for Islam's daily prayers. Even after *Merdeka* to the end of the Emergency there was no mass conversion of the Aborigines to Islam.[59]

The Christian missionaries did not have much success either. In 1956 the *Singapore Standard* gave a description of an unusual Orang Asli Christian village in South Perak. The Semai in the village had been converted by a Batak Christian, Napitoepooloe,[60] before World War II. He had gone back to Indonesia after the War and the converts practiced their own version of Christianity. There was no marriage ceremony. If the elders approved that a couple could live together, then they were considered to be married. Divorce among the group was common and the *Standard* published a photograph of Melt, a Christian woman, who had three ex-husbands, including a Malay and a Chinese. The only Christian commandment they apparently obeyed was "Remember to keep holy the Sabbath Day." They observed the Sabbath by taking a complete rest and confining themselves to their homes. Christmas was the one Christian festival they observed with fasting and Ronggeng.[61] Before the War some Methodists had lived and worked with them but now they were on their own. The person interviewed by the newspaper had the non-Orang Asli names of Stem Johannes and his wife was Wah (Mrs.) Hannah.[62]

There are few accounts of Christian church activities among the Orang Asli during the Emergency. They continued to minister to the converts they had but appeared to do little or no prosletizing in that time. The Salvation Army baptized a ten month old Orang Asli boy found beside his dead mother in the jungle by the Security Forces in May 1956. His natural father, Pandak bin Long, had agreed he should be brought up in the Salvation Army Home in Ipoh. The father had remarried and had a new family.[63] There was no shortage of Christian missionaries in Malaya. Templer had written to the Conference of Missionary Societies and the College of Propaganda in Rome to send out Chinese-trained missionaries to work in the new villages in a missionary or medical missionary role. He also recruited Methodists from the United States for the same purpose.[64] It did not occur to anybody to second some of these to Orang Asli resettlement villages. There were dedicated medical people, doctors and nurses, who did work among Orang Asli but perhaps it was fortunate that they were spared the attentions of zealous missionaries for a while at least.[65]

Merdeka *No* Panacea

Merdeka was no more an instant answer to the Orang Asli's problems than it was to the problems of the ordinary Malays. While most of the inhabitants of Malaya were having the strictures of living under the Emergency regulations removed, pressure remained on the Orang Asli in particular areas. The Semalai around the Tasik Bera on the Pahang-Negri Sembilan border, and the Senoi on the main range were the subjects of operations by the Security Forces to clear their areas of the remnants of the MRLA. Both Orang Asli groups had also to endure the attempts by the hard-pressed MRLA to use them for their supplies and as scouts against the Government Forces. The Orang Asli just wanted to survive and return to their previous existence. This return was becoming less likely as the development needs of the newly emerging nation were added to the existing security problems facing the Malayan government. The Orang Asli were facing new threats to their homelands from developers and to their culture from an education system geared to a different set of values. The possible increase in various religious sects' efforts to wean them away from their old ways was also an increasingly worrysome issue.

The concept of Malaya, colonial or free, had meant nothing to the Orang Asli. Neither did the ideological pretensions of the MCP. It was not the prospect of political freedom that won them over to the government's side but their recognition of the technological superiority of the Security Forces who had the ability to provide better welfare services, medical attention, and cash income. They had survived the physical violence of the Emergency but their new struggle after *Merdeka* would be to preserve their religion, their homelands and their culture.

Notes

1. *Merdeka*, Malay, meaning independent, self governing. It was the word used to signify the advent of Malay independence from British colonial rule in 1957.

2. By June 1954 there were 161 British and 104 Malays at the highest level in the Malayan Civil Service. See J. B. Perry Robinson, *Transformation in Malaya* (London, 1956), 64. In 1957 most district police officers, company commanders, and middle level civil servants were Malays. See Clutterbuck, 148.

3. *M. M.*, 19 July 1957.

4. *S. T.*, 3 August 1957.

5. Ibid., 21 August 1957

6. *Bumiputera,* Malay, meaning indigenous people.

7. *S. T*, 1 July 1955.

8. *S. S.*, 13 December 1957. Even though he had been elected to represent them, some Orang Asli I met during my research visits to Malaya in 1988 and 1990 question the veracity of the statement that Tok Pangku was a genuine Orang Asli. He was the descendant of the To'Panku of Lasah who was of Malay Siamese, Senoi, origin. Chapter One.

9. See appendix for full text of the 1954 Ordinance.

10. *Federal Legislative Council Proceedings, March 1953–January 1954.*

11. *Federation of Malaya Annual Reports 1953–56.* In September 1953 the Government declared a part of Malacca as a "White Area." This meant that it was considered relatively free of MRLA activity. Areas declared "white" had most of the Emergency Regulations, such as food controls, curfews, and restrictions on movements, lifted. As the Security Forces gained the upper hand in other areas and the local populace proved cooperative, they in turn were declared "white." Johore proved recalcitrant to the end because of its hard core pro-Communist tradition.

12. *Arkib Negara*, D F 787/54, minutes from NA854/54, 27 July 1956.

13. Ibid., D F 787/54–59, 2 June 1956.

14. Ibid., D F 787/54–115., 12 July 1959.

15. Ibid., D F 787/54–95A., 28 March 1957.

16. Dr. Carey was a Hungarian of Jewish extraction who had served with the British Army in India in World War II. He joined the Department of Aboriginal Affairs in the 1950s and eventually became Commissioner of Aboriginal Affairs between 1961 and 1969. He was Associate Professor in the Department of Malay Studies of the University of Malaya in the 1970s.

17. *Arkib Negara*, D F 787/54–115B., 16 June 1959.

18. *Arkib Negara*, D F 787/54, undated letter.

19. Ibid., D F 787/54–62, 29 June 1956.

20. *S. S.*, 1 January 1959. The King of Malaya's message to the country highlighted the development of a hydro-electric scheme in the Cameron Highlands. *S. S.*, 5 January 1959, Jungle was expected to attract tourists. *S. S.*, 8 January 1959, The Minister for Lands in Kelantan state, announced the opening up of twenty thousand acres of land in that State under a five year plan.

21. *S. S.*, 6 June 1959.

22. R. O. D. Noone, 13–14 passim.

23. Gouldsbury, 111.

24. R. O. D. Noone, 144–45.

25. Gouldsbury, 107, and *S. T.,* 19 July 1954.

26. Interview with Ray Walker.

27. J. Slimming, *Temiar Jungle* (London, 1958), 102–103.

28. Carey, 317, 320. Carey remarked, "As is the case with all intelligence networks, about 90 per cent of the information obtained was probably fictitious. However, some measure of reality was achieved."

29. Carey, 298, also remarked that the standard of Field Assistants was not uniformly good due to the need to recruit rapidly and the difficulty in getting rid of deadwood in the public service.

30. *Berita Harian,* 20 January 1958.

31. *S. T.,* 16 November 1956. *M. M.,* 22 February 1957. *M. M.,* 29 May 1957.

32. Ibid., 16 November 1956.

33. *M. M.,* 25 October 1956.

34. Ibid., 17 October 1956.

35. *S. S.,* 20 June 1958.

36. *S. T.,* 21 November 1956.

37. Gouldsbury, 146–48.

38. Sel. Sec., 1148/1951. 11 May 1951-1.

39. Ibid., 15 May 1951,-2. Presumably because they had to help their parents sow or gather crops, or hunt or fish in the morning.

40. Ibid., 5 July 1951 and 5 October 1951,-3 and 4.

41. Ibid., 31 January 1955,-5 and 6.

42. Ibid., 15 and 16 April 1955, 7 and 8.

43. Ibid., 28 April 1955 and 14 June 1955,-9 and 10.

44. Ibid., 7 July 1955,-11.

45. Ibid., 30 September 1955,-12 and 13.

46. Ibid., 25 October 1955,-15.

47. *M. M.,* 9 May 1958.

48. Carey, 301.

49. *Aborigine Peoples Ordinance 1954, No.3 of 1954.* 30. It was reported from Perak in April 1958 that the Mentri Besar (Chief Minister) of that state had to make a special journey to a Malay Kampong some two miles from Kuala Kangsar to advise the Malay inhabitants against any attempt to segregate Aborigine children in the government primary school. He warned that such action was against the law. Parents who had objected to their children mixing with Orang Asli children and had wanted a separate school for the Orang Asli children dropped their opposition on hearing his recommendation. There were only twelve Aborigines among the two hundred pupils. Two other schools in the state where Orang Asli and Malay children mixed together had no problems. (*S. T.,* 15 April 1958).

50. This was confirmed to me by both European and Malay former police officers and members of the Department of Aborigines. In one instance an over zealous schoolteacher who tried to convert his charges had been removed. Assistant Protector of Aborigines Negri Sembilan, Rufus Cole, told the *Straits Times* in November 1956 that children in an Aborigine school at Simpang Petang in that state would be taught Malay "but there would be no religious teaching" (*S. T.*, 5 November 1956).

51. *S. T.*, 7 January and 9 January 1948.

52. *Warta Negara*, 22 December 1948.

53. *S. T.*, 8 January 1949.

54. Ibid., 18 January 1949.

55. *S. T.*, 21 February 1950.

56. Ibid., 22 August 1957.

57. *M. M.*, 10 April 1957 and *S. T.*, 14 December 1957.

58. *S. S.*, 21 May 1958.

59. Carey, 326, 327.

60. Carey, 327 uses the Dutch spelling Napitoepoloe.

61. Malay dancing where the partners do not touch.

62. *S. S.*, 16 September 1956. Tony Williams-Hunt told me an unsubstantiated account of Napitoepoloe acting as an intermediary between the Orang Asli and the Japanese during World War II and protecting some of the Semai groups from Japanese repression. See Carey, 327 for more details of this individual's activities among Orang Asli. Also see Paul B. Means and N. Means, *And the Seed Grew* (Toronto, 1981), 15–20. They refer to him as Napitupulu.

63. *S. T.*, 14 March 1957.

64. Cloake, 280.

65. Carey, 327–330 gives details of missionary activity among the Orang Asli immediately after the Emergency.

CONCLUSION

Perpetuating the Myth

OVER THE TWELVE years of the Malayan Emergency hundreds of thousands of Commonwealth troops had served in rotating tours of duty in that conflict (See Appendix A). It is doubtful that many of those who had contact with the Orang Asli learned much about their history, culture, or social practices. Their closest contact would have been with the Orang Asli porters who carried their patrol's radio equipment and any spare rations or other items not normally carried by the soldiers. Those ex-servicemen I have spoken to usually remember little men dressed in a cawat (loin-cloth), sometimes with a cast-off military jacket, plodding along barefoot in the middle of the patrol and carrying loads nearly as big as themselves. If there was a contact with hostile forces the porters or Orang Asli guides were sent to the rear, usually protected by the wireless operator and the medical orderly, while the patrol engaged the enemy. This tactic in protecting the porters or guides could have added to the belief in the timidity and peacefulness of the jungle dwellers.

As the Emergency drew to a close, pictures and stories of Orang Asli groups being "rescued" by Security Forces from MCP/MRLA control were prominent in the local media.

A ceaseless campaign was instituted by the Protector of Aborigines

> Department, with the help of friendly aborigines to wean the "hostiles" away from terrorist domination.
>
> The first success came during "Operation Termite" three years ago when large groups of aborigines sought government protection against the Communists. Gradually other groups of the little hillmen were won over to the side of the Government, the latest being a batch of 56 Temiars who were "rescued" by Security Forces a week ago.[1]

The emphasis in the reports was on the Orang Asli as helpless victims. Groups were variously described as "lost tribe"[2] or "asking for protection"[3] or "terrorist dominated."[4] The Director of Operations, in his 1955–56 report to the Chief of the Imperial General Staff (CIGS) on the situation in Malaya wrote, "Those Aborigines remaining under CT domination will continue to be sought out and protected."[5]

These accounts helped to perpetuate the myth of the Orang Asli as non-combative, unaggressive pawns who had no control over their own destiny. The influence of the tribal people in the Asal Protection Corps was ignored or treated as an aberration where misguided, backward, and guileless tribespeople were misled by clever propaganda. R. O. D. Noone did admit "that as long as there were terrorists left in the jungle there would be Aborigines to help them."[6] He called them hard-core "hostiles" akin to hard-core terrorists.

People in contact with the Orang Asli appeared to have no difficulty in accepting that violence was committed against the tribespeople by both protagonists. Indeed many reports in the media and official accounts were aware of the propaganda value in recounting details of acts of brutality against the tribespeople committed by the MCP/MRLA. An instance was the accounts of the massacre of the thirty-four Semai in the Cameron Highlands in July 1949, which was repeated many times in the local press around the time it occurred,[7] and was revived again by the press in January 1955.[8]

Williams-Hunt, Dawson, R. O. D. Noone, Short, and Carey all

confirm that resettling many Orang Asli groups, between 1948 and 1952, was a mistake which resulted in the deaths by disease of substantial numbers of the jungle dwellers due to lack of medical care and the poor location of the resettlement areas.[9] Those acts of unthinking maltreatment were regarded as being due to lack of judgment and carelessness by the authorities rather than deliberately malicious and cruel behaviour.[10]

The policy of mass resettlement of the tribespeople outside the jungle, which had been abandoned in 1953, was replaced by the euphemistically named policy of tribal or group relocation for operational or security reasons. This allowed for the movement of Orang Asli to other areas in the jungle at the instigation of the Security Forces. Slimming wrote:

> The SAS are a law unto themselves. Whilst their officers are very pleasant, socially, they seem to be unfavourably disposed towards the Department of Aborigines. They have an annoying habit of rounding up groups of Temiar and temporarily resettling them while they operate in a particular area. When their operation is finished the aborigines remain, living on a bald hillside miles from their own clearings, to become someone else's responsibility.[11]

Fort commanders, at their discretion, encouraged the surrounding settlements to move closer to the forts where it was less likely that the MRLA/MCP Asal Corps would contact them. Some families moved closer to the forts to obtain the benefits of the amenities such as medical attention, schooling, the fort trade store, or possible opportunities of employment in and around the fort.[12]

The antithesis of this acceptance of brutality against the Orang Asli is the reluctance by administrators and Security Forces to come to terms with the homicidal acts perpetrated by members of the tribal groups. Even though many who had dealings with the Orang Asli related incidents of murderous violence by the Senoi and others, they then continued to describe the tribespeople as peaceful and non-aggressive.[13] The fiction of pacifity and non-aggression was continued right through to the end of the Emergency despite the atrocities attributed to Bah Pelankin and Chawog against others of their kin.[14] The successes of the Police Aborigine Guards against the MRLA were published in the media and were in situation reports from the Security Forces.[15] Major Peacock, a Royal Engineers officer attached to the SAS, wrote to me about the Orang Asli he encountered,

> In my dealings with the Aborigines during fort construction, I was impressed by their family attitude. I found it difficult to believe that these people were capable of killing humans. They were kind and caring for the offspring of animals they had killed for food. (I recall at one fort site, a baby monkey being suckled alongside a human baby. The baby monkey's mother had been blowpiped, cooked and eaten.) Appreciating the communication restrictions created in the jungle environment, one never heard of murder within the Aborigine community. But there were hostile Aborigine[s] with the CT who did, on occasions, kill, or were by association, implicated.[16]

This extract from Peacock's letter sums up the ambivalence of peoples' attitude to the Orang Asli. In discussions with some former SAS soldiers, police and members of the Department of Aboriginal Affairs, and in letters from others, similar sentiments were expressed about the tribal groups. I do not doubt the sincerity of those who communicated with me, but just to deal with Peacock's opinion: because the woman had suckled the offspring of the monkey which had been killed and eaten by that woman's friends and relatives, does not mean that these same people were not capable of killing humans. Peacock confirms in his last sentence, that they could kill, and the other interviewees and correspondents admit that Orang Asli killed soldiers, police, MRLA, or other tribespeople, or led MRLA or Security Forces to hostile encampments where killings took place. It is difficult to understand the strange refusal to accept that Orang Asli could be murderously aggressive and kill in cold blood or in the heat of a skirmish. The belief in Orang Asli pacifity was just a myth and the Emergency gave those of them who were aggressive the opportunities and the weapons to give vent to that aggression.

Changes to Orang Asli Culture

A further outcome of the Emergency for the Orang Asli was that it changed their lifestyle forever. Many of their cultural and social practices would remain, but the impact of the interlopers into the tribal lands was traumatic and abiding for those groups whose previous contacts with the outside world had been sporadic. It would be incorrect to assume that even before the Emergency the most remote and nomadic of Orang Asli did not have some communication with contiguous Malay or Chinese traders or prospectors. The more venturesome of the outside traders, prospectors, or tin poachers travelled into tribal homelands to trade or mine.[17]

Even though the MPAJA and the Japanese had had some presence in the Orang Asli areas during World War II the massive influx of Security Forces, and to a lesser extent the retreat of the MRLA into the hinterland in order to involve the inhabitants in their struggle, was unparalleled. The Orang Asli were conscious of and experienced the power of modern technology while still adhering to their traditional ways.

Many rode in helicopters before they had seen a car or a train. Those who were taken on Civics Courses to major centers saw displays of Security Forces firepower, the sights of the big city, and parties of them were taken to look at the sea for the first time.[18] Some who had managed to get money through work or rewards for eliminating MCP/MRLA personnel or fellow hostile Orang Asli, bought clothes, watches, clocks, and electronic goods such as portable battery gramophones which made them the envy of their friends. The consumer society was gradually infringing on the previously subsistence existence of the tribal society.[19] The more venturesome strayed into the towns and exploited their uniqueness by posing for tourists in full jungle regalia to be photographed for money. Their women exposed their breasts for the same purpose and others turned to prostitution.[20]

Not all the effects of the Emergency were negative. The children of the tribespeople were being educated to at least enable them to read and write Malay. Medical attention was available to groups who had not had access to modern medicine previously but had used the methods of their medicine men for treatment.[21] New and better roads and bridges were built or extended into Orang Asli homelands by the Security Forces to enable them to have quick access into those areas. This in turn allowed some formerly isolated groups to get to markets to sell their jungle produce. They did have limited representation on local councils and federal representation by the Tok Pangku.[22]

In an unprecedented action, which showed that at least one group of the Orang Asli was becoming more conscious of its worth and was prepared to take united action to preserve its income, the Semai in the lower Cameron Highlands in August 1957 refused to collect a jungle vegetable called *petai* (Parkia Speciosa), a bean-like food which grows on tall trees. The buyers cut the price offered from $2.50 to $1 for one hundred pods. Local State Councillor Inche Mohamed Shazilli bin Haji Jajuddin said he believed the "terrorists" were behind the strike. A Department of Aborigines spokesman ridiculed the accusation and claimed that it indicated that the Semai "now had a sounder business sense than before." Now that more Aborigines were being educated they were no longer prepared to be exploited any more.[23]

The terms of the Aboriginal Ordinance of 1954 did give some limited protection to land tenure for the tribespeople, but as shown in Chapter Six, it was a tenuous right. The Ordinance was in essence a statement of intent rather than of policy. On the negative side there was no statement of policy by the Malayan government on the Orang Asli between *Merdeka* and the end of the Emergency.[24] There were ominous signs that the Ministry of National and Local Development, under the dynamic Tun Abdul Razak[25] was pushing ahead with its rural development schemes with little regard to the rights of the Orang Asli.[26] This development was still inhibited by the Emergency but it boded ill for the future.

The jungle peoples' most immediate problems during the Emergency and beyond was the invasion of their homelands by outsiders seeking to further their own ends. The forts with their armed garrisons still remained after the declared end of the hostilities in

1960. Armed patrols still traversed the jungle areas and while the rest of Malaya was gradually relaxing as the struggle faded, the pressure remained in Orang Asli settlements and territories.

There was no let-up while the remnants of the MRLA in the deep jungle areas and over the border in Thailand were still a menace. The reminders of violence were still visible to the Orang Asli. They had their own armed units, in particular the Senoi Pra'aq, to keep them aware of the brutal times which they had gone through. In the new Malaya they were a tiny minority who would have to look to their own resources to help them resist the values and dictates of the religious and social mores of the predominantly Malay society which surrounded them. The Emergency had drawn the conflicting forces into the jungle; the victorious Government Forces had permanent locations within it and could multiply that presence at will. The Orang Asli could no longer retreat into their homeland fastnesses to escape outside influences and the pressures of the modern world. In that new environment, despite all the evidence to the contrary, the myth of Orang Asli pacifity persisted to become part of the folklore of the new nation.[27]

Notes

1. *M. M.*, 26 September 1956.
2. *S. S.*, 27 September 1956.
3. *S. T.*, 25 July 1957.
4. *Berita Harian,* 8 August 1958
5. PRO. Kew, WO216/885–55–6. Sit. in Malaya 53/73/7655.
6. *M. M.*, 3 July 1958.
7. Refer to Chapter Three and footnotes.
8. *S. S.*, 28 January 1955. Refers to an MCP document captured during Operation Termite in 1954 which details an MCP version of the killings in 1949. The explanation given in the document for the mass killing was that some Orang Asli resisted their detention by the MRLA resulting in the death of the others in the group.
9. See Chapter Two.
10. Carey, 307.
11. Slimming, 114.

12. Walker interview, also interviews with former members of the Department of Aborigines.

13. R. O. D. Noone, 2, wrote that he and his brother had established that the Temiar were "emotionally too well adjusted to be capable of committing any act that was violent or resulted in violence." In the same book, 175 he wrote, "I have heard the Aborigines accused of cowardice which is unfair. When sufficiently provoked and when they feel they have been wronged, their vengeance can be swift and terrible."

14. Slimming, 181, wrote: "This was the territory of Chawog, another Aborigine Asal organiser, whose record of murder and brutality was even worse than that of Bah Pelankin already eliminated in Perak."

15. *S. S.*, 8 January 1957, four Orang Asli Home Guards including Busu (see Chapter Five) were decorated for valour for killing one of five "terrorists" in Perak. This was the second time Busu had been decorated for valour.

16. Peacock to Leary, 25 January 1990.

17. Alberto G. Gomes, "Confrontation and Continuity: Simple Commodity Production among the Orang Asli," edited by Lim Teck Ghee and Alberto G. Gomes, *Tribal People and Developments in South East Asia* (Kuala Lumpur, 1990) 12–13.

18. R. O. D. Noone, 167, Cloake, 258.

19. Dawson, 211.

20. R. O. D. Noone, 181.

21. *Berita Harian,* 24 February 1958, reported that twenty two Orang Asli *Bomahs* (medicine men) had attended a course on basic modern medicine in Kuala Lipis. The course which covered hygiene and elementary medicine was sponsored by the Department of Aborigines. It followed a previous course for seventeen *Bomahs*. They were presented with first-aid kits containing anti-malarial pills, antiseptic lotion, and D.D.T. to take back to their settlements. They were also given badges identifying them as "doctors" assistants.

22. *M. M.,* 21 July 1953, Abdul Hamid bin Nagah Kandan was elected as local councillor for Sungei Durian New Village in July 1953. He was the only non-Chinese among the nine councillors elected. See footnote 8, Chapter Six re: the Tok Pangku.

23. *S. T.,* 20 and 21 August 1957.

24. PRO. Kew, CO1030–576–57/59–79/1/02. Letter 13 August 1959 from J. D. Hennings of the Colonial Office to R. N. Broome (or Brown) of the Foreign Office, stated that he was unable to produce any papers, "about the policies of the-Malayan Government towards its Aborigines in order to prevent them giving aid or being prevailed upon to give aid to the C.T. in the jungle." The letter went on to suggest that the enquirer

approach the federation government for assistance. A statement of policy was issued in 1961 by the federal government in which it was declared that it was the general intention (of the government) that the Aboriginal population should be ultimately integrated with the rest of the national community, but care must be taken that the process should conform with the different stages of development at present attained by the Aboriginal people themselves. To carry out this policy the government had approved the establishment of a permanent Department of Aborigines. See *Arkib Negara*, P/OA1-1961.

25. Stubbs, 264.

26. *S. S.,* 1 January 1959 and 6 June 1959.

27. *Suara Sam,* 1987, 2 and 3. Tok Batin Yan, a Semai chief in Sungei Cawang Hilir Perak, in reply to questions about the possibility of his people being moved from their homeland to make way for a plantation is quoted as saying, "The Mai [outsiders] will not force us to do anything but if they do we will not fight but instead be willing to be killed here." The article quotes extensively from Dentan's book *The Semai—A Non-violent People of Malaya.* It also quotes Anthony Williams-Hunt who said: "Violence in fact seems to frighten the Semai. They do not meet force with force but with passivity or flight." It is worth noting that there are many Semai in the Senoi Pra'aq and they are regarded by their Malay officers as good fighting men. Interviews with officers of Batt. 20 Senoi Pra'aq October-November 1988.

APPENDICES

Note:

Although copies of original documents are used in the Appendices with their original page numbers shown, these are also numbered in sequence with this book's page numbers.

APPENDIX A

Military units which served in the Malayan Emergency 16 June 1948–31 July 1960

Note: It is not practicable to record detailed dates as several units carried out more than one tour as well as moving in and out of the theatre of operations during a tour.

This list does not include Police, RAF, RAAF, RNZAF, or any Naval units.

United Kingdom

1st King's Dragoon Guards
4th Queen's Own Hussars
11th Hussars (Prince Albert's Own)
12th Royal Lancers (Prince of Wales)
13/18th Royal Hussars (Queen Mary's Own)
15th/19th The King's Royal Hussars
2nd Field Regiment RA
25th Field Regiment RA
26th Field Regiment RA
48th Field Regiment RA
11 Independent Field Squadron RE
50 Gurkha Field Engineer Regiment RE
51 Field Engineer Regiment RE
74 Field Park Squadron RE
410 Independent Plant Troop RE
17th (Gurkha) Signal Regiment
208 (Commonwealth) Signal Squadron

Malaya Command Signal Squadron
3rd Grenadier Guards
2nd Coldstream Guards
2nd Scots Guards
1st Bn The Queen's Royal Regiment (West Surrey)
1st Bn The Royal Lincolnshire Regiment
1st Bn The Devonshire Regiment
1st Bn The Somerset Light Infantry (Prince Albert's)
1st Bn The West Yorkshire Regiment (The Prince of Wales Own)
1st Bn The East Yorkshire Regiment (The Duke of York's Own)
1st Bn The Green Howards (Alexandra, Prince of Wales Own Yorkshire Regiment)
1st Bn The Royal Scots Fusiliers
1st Bn The Cheshire Regiment
2nd Bn The Royal Welsh Fusiliers
1st Bn The South Wales Borderers
1st Bn The Kings Own Scottish Borderers
1st Bn The Cameronians (Scottish Rifles)
1st Bn The Royal Inniskilling Fusiliers
1st Bn The Worcestershire Regiment
1st Bn The Royal Hampshire Regiment
1st Bn The Sherwood Foresters (Nottinghamshire and Derbyshire Regiment)
1st Bn The Loyal Regiment (North Lancashire)
1st Bn 3rd East Anglian Regiment (16th/44th Foot)
1st Bn The Queen's Own Royal West Kent Regiment
1st Bn The King's Own Yorkshire Light Infantry
1st Bn The Manchester Regiment
1st Bn Seaforth Highlanders (Ross-Shire Buffs, The Duke of Albany's)
1st Bn The Gordon Highlanders
1st/2nd King Edward VII's Own Gurkha Rifles (The Sirmoor Rifles)
2nd/2nd King Edward VII's Own Gurkha Rifles

1st/6th Queen Elizabeth's Own Gurkha Rifles
2nd/6th Queen Elizabeth's Own Gurkha Rifles
1st/7th Duke of Edinburgh's Own Gurkha Rifles
2nd/7th Duke of Edinburgh's Own Gurkha Rifles
1st/10th Princess Mary's Own Gurkha Rifles
2nd/10th Princess Mary's Own Gurkha Rifles
1st Bn The Rifle Brigade (Prince Consort's Own)
22 Special Air Service Regiment
The Independent Parachute Squadron
40 Commando Royal Marines
42 Commando Royal Marines
45 Commando Royal Marines

Commonwealth

The Royal Malay Regiment (six battalions formed before end of Emergency under two Brigade headquarters with supporting arms and services)
1st Singapore Infantry Regiment
1st Bn The King's African Rifles
2nd Bn The King's African Rifles
3rd Bn The King's African Rifles
1st Bn The Northern Rhodesia Regiment
1st Bn the Fiji Infantry Regiment
1st Bn The Royal Australian Regiment
2nd Bn The Royal Australian Regiment
3rd Bn The Royal Australian Regiment
1st Bn The New Zealand Regiment
2nd Bn The New Zealand Regiment
The Rhodesia Squadron (Special Air Service)
The New Zealand Squadron (Special Air Service)
1st Singapore Regiment RA
100 Field Battery RAA
101 Field Battery RAA
105 Field Battery RAA

Throughout the Emergency there were units, sub units, or individuals from all the normal supporting services:

Royal Army Chaplain's Department
Royal Army Service Corps
Royal Army Medical Corps
Royal Army Ordnance Corps
Corps of Royal Electrical and Mechanical Engineers
Corps of Royal Military Police
Royal Army Pay Corps
Royal Army Educational Corps
Army Catering Corps
Queen Alexandra's Royal Army Nursing Corps

E. D. Smith

APPENDIX B

Sakai Reserves and Sakai Head-men
Summary of Replies Received for Selangor

Sel. Sec. 675/1948. (12)

Sakai Reserves and Sakai Head-men

Summary of Replies Received.

Suggestion:

All Sakai Reserves in the Federation be surveyed and gazetted under the appropriate land laws.

The present system of ear-marking certain areas as Sakai Reserves without survey and publication in the Gazette as intended by law does not give the Sakais sufficient security. Cases had been known of such land being alienated to Non-Sakais.

Views:

K.Lumpur. (a) If Sakais prefer to remain and be treated as Sakais the request is fair and reasonable and a condition should be imposed prohibiting non-Sakais to enter, remain or occupy any land in such reserves.

(b) If they prefer to be Malays and profess the Moslem religion, they will come under the definition of "Malay" in the Malay Reservation Enactment (Cap.142). The areas may then be declared Malay Reservations without survey.

Klang.

There are 7 Sakai Reserves - 2 on the mainland and 5 on Carey Island. Considers it not necessary to gazette further areas. Those areas which are within Forest Reserves can remain as they are unless the Forest Department finds it difficult to control them. They are bound to clear part of the Forest Reserve to extend their holdings without permission. Not in favour of creating Sakai Reserves. Feels that they are being put away from civilization. Suggests that all Sakai Reserves be declared Malay Reservations. Does not mean to deprive them of their rights - such as free holdings - but to encourage them to come out and mix with the Malays and consider themselves as members of the Malay race. After all when any one of them is converted into Islam he becomes a Malay. There is no reason why a Sakai should not own land within Malay Reservation rent free even if he is not converted to Islam. It will, of course, be necessary to amend the Malay Reservation Enactment. In almost all Sakai Reserves there are Chinese who live and mix with the Sakais and some of them have married the Sakais. This sort of encroachment is difficult to detect in Sakai Reserves due to lack of contact, but when such reserves are declared as Malay Reservations, then there will be closer contact with the Land Office. When this is done a headman automatically becomes necessary.

K.Langat.

There are altogether 16 Sakai settlements of which 7 are gazetted Reserves with a total area of 675 acres. The remainder are not gazetted. The reserves were created before the war, and it appears that it was the intention of the Government to move all the Sakais in the district to these reserves, but from information received the Sakais were not keen to move into these reserves and preferred to remain where they were. Will however go into this question more fully and submit recommendations in due course as to the desirability and possibility of having all these settlements gazetted. No land within these Sakai settlements has been alienated. There may however be some unlawful occupations but in most cases they were made possible by the consent of these Sakais themselves, this is more particularly so in areas where they are rubber,

U.Langat.

Agrees.

U.Selangor.

It is highly desirable that all Sakai Reserves be clearly defined and gazetted and to effect this survey is necessary. The Sakais are of opinion, and no one can blame them for it that all the jungles are free to them and they can settle down wherever they please. They can never understand the use of a Forest Reserve or the evil of clearing the slopes of steep hills, and it is a well-known habit of the Sakais to abandon a clearing after a season or two of Hill Padi planting, to start again a new clearing at some remote parts of the jungle. When ample Reserves clearly defined are provided for them then they can be told that their activities should be confined to within that Reserves only. Survey of the Reserves will also help in checking possible encroachment by persons other than Sakais. There are now four areas earmarked on the Land Office plans as Sakai Reserves. Earmarking further Reserves for the Sakais is under consideration.

K.Selangor.

Agrees. Suggests that the dificulty of defining boundaries be overcome by dividing such reserves into two categories.

(i) Those near areas already alienated.

(ii) Those at some distance.

In the case of category (i) a detailed survey of the boundaries from which alienation to other interests is likely to advance, could be undertaken. On the boundaries which run through areas at present uninhabited and not alienated and in the cases falling within category (ii) the boundaries of reserves could follow rivers and mountain or hill ridges, which in most areas have been mapped. From what the late Mr. Noone wrote about these people before the war, and from the District Officer's and others' experience it is fairly certainly true to say that any group of Sakai has a country or area which it regards as its own and which follows land marks usually well defined on existing maps. Local knowledge should be quite sufficient for marking thesse areas on the map and they could then be gazetted. Applications for alienation for other interests have to be surveyed and plotted on plans, so that it would be quite clear whether or not such an application falls with a reserve

S. Bernam.

No reserves and no comments.

__Suggestion__:

All Sakai Head-men in Selangor be appointed after consultation with the Persatuan Kaum Darat Selangor.

__Kuala Lumpur__.

Present practice is that Head-men are appointed by their people and recognised by the Penghulu in whose Mukim they live.

__Klang__. See previous views.

__Kuala Langat__.

The Sakais elect their own Batin or headmen and there are altogether 11 of them for the whole 16 settlements. 2 of them viz. Batin Pa'Lepan and Batin Bolos were each paid a bonus as were other ketuas for 1947. This office has never taken any hand in the election of their headmen, but recognizes the appointments made by them. Whether or not their headmen should be appointed after consultation with the Persatuan Kaum Darat - Selangor is a matter for them to decide.

__Ulu Langat__.

Sakai headmen are appointed by their own people. No Government Official had a hand in the previous appointments.

__Ulu Selangor__.

Suggests officially appointing Ketuas of their choice for them, by giving the Ketuas "Kuasa" similar to the Kuasa given to Ketua Kampong. Through the Ketuas contacts can then be easily made to their "anak-buah" who are still too shy to see or speak to "outsiders". Appointing Ketuas after consultation with the Persatuan Kaum Darat Selangor may not be peaceable as some of them are still unaware of the existence of the Persatuan, and they are not known to the members of the "Persatuan". Where practicable this method of appointing Ketuas should be adopted.

__Kuala Selangor.__

From the late Mr. Noone's paper it is also clear that most groups have a traditional way of choosing their own leaders and I most strongly support their plea that they should be allowed to continue to do so. Government should only formally recognise the leaders so chosen.

__Sabak Bernam__. No comments.

APPENDIX C

Federation of Malaya

No. 3 of 1954

The Aboriginal Peoples Ordinance, 1954

FEDERATION OF MALAYA

No. 3 OF 1954

THE ABORIGINAL PEOPLES ORDINANCE, 1954

Their Highnesses the Rulers of the Malay States assent hereto

I assent

Witnesses to the affixing of the Rulers' Seal:

BADLISHAH
(IN MALAY)
Sultan of Kedah.

G. W. R. TEMPLER,
High Commissioner.

16th February, 1954.

PUTRA IBNI HASSAN JAMALULLAIL,
Raja of Perlis.

14th February, 1954.

An Ordinance to provide for the protection, well-being and advancement of the Aboriginal Peoples of the Federation of Malaya.

[25th February, 1954.]

IT IS HEREBY ENACTED by the High Commissioner of the Federation of Malaya and Their Highnesses the Rulers of the Malay States with the advice and consent of the Legislative Council as follows:

Short title. 1. This Ordinance may be cited as the Aboriginal Peoples Ordinance, 1954.

Interpretation. 2. In this Ordinance unless the context otherwise requires—

"aboriginal area" means an aboriginal area declared to be such under this Ordinance;

"aboriginal community" means the members of one aboriginal ethnic group living together in one place;

"aboriginal ethnic group" means a distinct tribal division of aborigines as characterised by culture, language or social organisation and includes any group which the Ruler in Council in a State or the High Commissioner in Nominated Council in a Settlement may, by order, declare to be an aboriginal ethnic group;

"aboriginal inhabited place" means any place inhabited by an aboriginal community but which has not been declared to be an aboriginal area or aboriginal reserve;

"aboriginal language" includes any language and such dialectal modifications or archaic forms of such language as any aborigines habitually use;

"aboriginal racial group" means one of the three main aboriginal groups in the Federation divided racially into Negrito, Senoi and Proto-Malay;

"aboriginal reserve" means an aboriginal reserve declared to be such under this Ordinance;

"aboriginal way of life" includes living in settled communities in kampongs either inland or along the coast;

"Adviser" means the Adviser on Aborigines and includes an Assistant Adviser on Aborigines appointed under sub-section (1) of section 5;

"alienated" in relation to land has the same meaning as it has in any written law relating to land for the time being in force in the Malay States;

"police officer" shall have the same meaning as in the Police Ordinance, 1952; No. 14 of 1952.

"Protector" means a Protector of Aborigines and includes an Assistant Protector of Aborigines appointed under sub-section (2) of section 5.

3. (1) In this Ordinance an aborigine is— Definition of aborigine.

(*a*) any person whose male parent is or was, a member of an aboriginal ethnic group, who speaks an aboriginal language and habitually follows an aboriginal way of life and aboriginal customs and beliefs, and includes a descendant through males of such persons;

(*b*) any person of any race adopted when an infant by aborigines who has been brought up as an aborigine, habitually speaks an aboriginal language, habitually follows an aboriginal way of life and aboriginal customs and beliefs and is a member of an aboriginal community;

(*c*) the child of any union between an aboriginal female and a male of another race, provided that such child habitually speaks an aboriginal language, habitually follows an aboriginal way of life and aboriginal customs and beliefs and remains a member of an aboriginal community.

(2) Any aborigine who by reason of conversion to any religion or for any other reason ceases to adhere to aboriginal beliefs but who continues to follow an aboriginal way of life and aboriginal customs or speaks an aboriginal language shall not be deemed to have ceased to be an aborigine by reason only of practising such religion.

(3) Any question whether any person is or is not an aborigine shall be decided by the Ruler in Council in a State or by the High Commissioner in Nominated Council in a Settlement (as the case may be).

Administration of aborigines.

4. An aborigine shall be administered by the Government of the State or Settlement in which he is permanently resident, or in the case of aborigines or aboriginal communities who wander from one State or Settlement to another State or Settlement by the Government of the State or Settlement in which he is residing for the time being:

Provided that nothing in this section shall preclude any aboriginal headman who has authority over aboriginal communities situated in two or more adjacent States or adjacent States and a Settlement from exercising his authority in matters of aboriginal custom and belief over all such aboriginal communities.

Appointment of Adviser on Aborigines and Protectors of Aborigines.

5. (1) The High Commissioner may appoint a fit and proper person to be Adviser on Aborigines, Federation of Malaya, charged with the responsibility for conducting research into all aspects of aboriginal life and for advising State and Settlement Governments on all matters pertaining to aboriginal administration, welfare and advancement and so many Assistant Advisers on Aborigines as he thinks fit.

(2) The Mentri Besar in a State and the Resident Commissioner in a Settlement may appoint a Protector of Aborigines and so many Assistant Protectors of Aborigines as may be necessary for carrying out the purposes of this Ordinance.

(3) Every person appointed under this section shall be deemed to be a public servant within the meaning of the Penal Code.

F.M.S. Cap. 45; F. of M. No. 32 of 1948.

Aboriginal areas.

6. (1) The Ruler in Council in a State or the High Commissioner in Nominated Council in a Settlement may, by notification in the *Gazette*, declare any area predominantly or exclusively inhabited by aborigines, which has not been declared an aboriginal reserve under section 7, to be an aboriginal area and may declare such area to be divided into one or more aboriginal cantons:

Provided that where there is more than one aboriginal ethnic group there shall be as many cantons as there are aboriginal ethnic groups.

(2) Within an aboriginal area—

(i) no land shall be declared a Malay Reservation in accordance with the provisions of any written law relating to Malay Reservations for the time being in force in the Federation or any part thereof;

(ii) no land shall be declared a sanctuary or reserve in accordance with the provisions of any written law relating to the protection of wild animals and birds for the time being in force in the Federation or any part thereof;

(iii) no land shall be alienated, granted, leased or otherwise disposed of to persons not being aborigines normally resident in that aboriginal area or to any commercial undertaking without consulting the Protector;

(iv) no licences for the collection of forest produce in accordance with the provisions of any written law relating to forests for the time being in force in the Federation or any part thereof shall be issued to persons not being aborigines normally resident in that aboriginal area or to any commercial undertaking without consulting the Protector and in granting any such licence it may be ordered that a specified proportion of aboriginal labour be employed.

(3) The Ruler in Council in a State or the High Commissioner in Nominated Council in a Settlement may in like manner revoke wholly or in part or vary any declaration of an aboriginal area made under sub-section (1).

Aboriginal reserves.

7. (1) The Ruler in Council in a State or the High Commissioner in Nominated Council in a Settlement may, by notification in the *Gazette*, declare any area exclusively inhabited by aborigines to be an aboriginal reserve:

Provided that when it appears unlikely that the aborigines will remain permanently in such place it shall not be declared an aboriginal reserve but shall form part of an aboriginal area:

Provided further that an aboriginal reserve may be constituted within an aboriginal area.

(2) Within an aboriginal reserve—

(i) no land shall be declared a Malay Reservation in accordance with the provisions of any written law relating to Malay Reservations for the time being in force in the Federation or any part thereof;

(ii) no land shall be declared a sanctuary or reserve in accordance with the provisions of any written law relating to the protection of wild animals and birds for the time being in force in the Federation or any part thereof;

(iii) no land shall be declared a reserved forest in accordance with the provisions of any written law relating to forests for the time being in force in the Federation or any part thereof;

(iv) no land shall be alienated, granted, leased or otherwise disposed of except to aborigines of the aboriginal communities normally resident within the reserve;

(v) no temporary occupation of any land shall be permitted under any written law relating to land for the time being in force in the Federation or any part thereof.

(3) The Ruler in Council in a State or the High Commissioner in Nominated Council in a Settlement may in like manner revoke wholly or in part or vary any declaration of an aboriginal reserve made under sub-section (1).

Rights of occupancy.

8. (1) The Ruler in Council in a State or the High Commissioner in Nominated Council in a Settlement may grant rights of occupancy of any land not being alienated land or land leased for any purpose within any aboriginal area or aboriginal reserve.

(2) Such rights may be granted to—

(*a*) any individual aborigine; or

(*b*) members of any family of aborigines; or

(*c*) members of any aboriginal community.

(3) Such rights may be granted free of rent or subject to such rents as may be imposed in the grant.

(4) Such rights may be granted subject to such conditions as may be imposed by the grant.

(5) Such rights shall be deemed not to confer on any person any better title than that of a tenant at will.

(6) Nothing in this section shall preclude the alienation or grant or lease of any land to any aborigine.

Dealings in land by aborigines.

9. No aborigine shall transfer, lease, charge, sell, convey, assign, mortgage or otherwise dispose of any land except with the consent of the Protector and any such transaction effected without such consent shall be void and of no effect.

Aboriginal communities not obliged to leave areas declared Malay Reservations, etc.

10. (1) An aboriginal community resident in any area declared to be a Malay Reservation, a reserved forest or a game reserve in accordance with the provisions of any written law for the time being in force in the Federation or any part thereof may, notwithstanding anything to the contrary contained in such written law, continue to reside therein upon such conditions as the Ruler in Council in a State or the High Commissioner in Nominated Council in a Settlement may by rules prescribe.

(2) Any rules made under this section may expressly provide that all or any of the provisions of such written law shall not have effect in respect of such aboriginal community or that any such provisions shall be modified in their application to such aboriginal community in such manner as shall be specified.

(3) The Ruler in Council in a State or the High Commissioner in Nominated Council in a Settlement may by order require any such aboriginal community to leave and remain out of any such area and may in such order make such consequential provisions, including the payment of compensation, as may be necessary.

(4) Any compensation paid in accordance with the provisions of sub-section (3) may be paid in accordance with the provisions of section 12.

Compensation on alienation of State or Crown land upon which fruit or rubber is growing.

11. (1) Where an aboriginal community establishes a claim to fruit or rubber trees on any State or Crown land which is alienated, granted, leased for any purpose, occupied temporarily under licence or otherwise disposed of, then such compensation shall be paid to such aboriginal community as shall

appear to the Ruler in Council in a State or the High Commissioner in Nominated Council in a Settlement to be just.

(2) Any compensation paid in accordance with the provisions of sub-section (1) may be paid in accordance with the provisions of section 12.

Compensation.

12. If any land is excised from any aboriginal area or aboriginal reserve or if any land in any aboriginal area is alienated, granted, leased for any purpose or otherwise disposed of, or if any right or privilege in any aboriginal area or aboriginal reserve granted to any aborigine or aboriginal community is revoked wholly or in part, the Ruler in Council in a State or the High Commissioner in Nominated Council in a Settlement may grant compensation therefor and may pay such compensation to the persons entitled in his opinion thereto or may, if he thinks fit, pay the same to the Adviser or to the Protector to be held by him as a common fund for such persons or for such aboriginal community as shall be directed, and to be administered in such manner as may be prescribed.

Compulsory acquisition of land for aboriginal areas or reserves.

13. When any immovable property, not being State or Crown land, is needed to be acquired in order to declare the same to be an aboriginal area or an aboriginal reserve, such property may be acquired in accordance with the provisions of any written law relating to the acquisition of land for the time being in force in the State or Settlement in which such property is situate and any declaration required by any such written law that such property is so needed shall have effect as if it were a declaration that such property is needed for a public purpose in accordance with such written law.

Exclusion of persons from aboriginal areas and aboriginal reserves.

14. (1) Whenever it shall appear to the Ruler in Council in a State or to the High Commissioner in Nominated Council in a Settlement upon the written information of the Adviser or of the Protector and after such enquiry as the Ruler in Council or the High Commissioner in Nominated Council shall deem necessary that it is desirable that any person or class of persons should be prohibited from entering or remaining in any aboriginal area or aboriginal reserve or aboriginal inhabited place, the Ruler in Council or the High Commissioner in Nominated Council, as the case may be, shall make an order to that effect in the form in the Schedule

(2) (*a*) Such order when addressed to an individual person, may be served on the person named therein by a police officer or by any person whom the Mentri Besar in a State or the Resident Commissioner in a Settlement (as the case may be) may direct to serve the same.

(*b*) The order shall if practicable be served personally on the person named therein by showing him the original order and by tendering or delivering to him a copy thereof signed by the Mentri Besar in a State or the Resident Commissioner in a Settlement (as the case may be).

(*c*) If service cannot conveniently be effected as aforesaid the serving officer shall affix a copy of the order to some conspicuous part of the house or other place where the person named in the order ordinarily resides and thereupon the order shall be deemed to have been duly served.

(*d*) A certificate signed by the Mentri Besar in a State or the Resident Commissioner in a Settlement (as the case may be) that an order has been duly served on the person named therein shall be admissible in evidence in any judicial proceeding and on the production of such certificate the Court shall presume until the contrary is proved that such order was duly served.

(3) Such order, when addressed to a class of persons, shall be published in the *Gazette* and shall be given such additional publicity in the press and otherwise as the Ruler in Council or the High Commissioner in Nominated Council, as the case may be, shall direct.

(4) Any person on whom an order has been served in accordance with the provisions of this section who is found within any aboriginal area mentioned in such order or within any aboriginal reserve mentioned in such order or within any aboriginal inhabited place mentioned in such order and any person who is a member of any class of persons which has been prohibited from entering or remaining in any aboriginal area, aboriginal reserve, or aboriginal inhabited place who is found within such area, reserve or place shall be liable to a fine of one thousand dollars.

(5) Any person found committing an offence under sub-section (4) may be arrested without warrant by the Adviser or any Protector or any police officer.

Removal of undesirable persons.

15. (1) The Adviser, any Protector and any police officer may detain any person found in any aboriginal area, aboriginal reserve or aboriginal inhabited place whose activities he has reason to believe are detrimental to the welfare of any aborigine or any aboriginal community and shall remove any such person from such area, reserve or place within seven days from the date of detaining him.

(2) The Adviser, any Protector or any police officer who detains and removes any person in accordance with the provisions of sub-section (1) shall as soon as possible report all the circumstances in writing to the Mentri Besar of the State or the Resident Commissioner of the Settlement in which the aboriginal area, aboriginal reserve or aboriginal inhabited place is situated in which the said person was found.

Headman.

16. (1) The hereditary headman of an aboriginal community shall be the headman thereof or, in the case of an aboriginal community in which the office of headman is not hereditary, a person selected to be headman by the members of such community shall be headman thereof, subject in each case to confirmation by the Ruler of a State or the High Commissioner in a Settlement.

(2) The Ruler in a State or the High Commissioner in a Settlement may remove any headman from his office.

Aborigines not to be excluded from any school.

17. (1) No aboriginal child shall be precluded from attending any school by reason only of his being an aborigine.

(2) No aboriginal child attending any school shall be obliged to attend any religious instruction unless the prior consent of his father or of his mother if his father is dead, or of his guardian should both parents be dead, is notified to a Protector, and is transmitted by the Protector in writing to the Headmaster of the school concerned.

(3) Any person who acts in contravention of this section shall be liable to a fine of five hundred dollars.

Aboriginal children not to be adopted, etc.

18. (1) No person who is not himself an aborigine of the same ethnic group shall adopt or assume the care, custody or control of any aboriginal child except with the consent of the Protector, and in giving such consent the Protector may impose such conditions as he thinks fit.

(2) Any person who acts in contravention of this section or commits a breach of any condition imposed by the Protector shall be liable to imprisonment for six months or to a fine of one thousand dollars or to both such imprisonment and such fine.

19. The Ruler in Council in a State or the High Commissioner in Nominated Council in a Settlement may make regulations for carrying into effect the purposes of this Ordinance and in particular for the following purposes— **Regulations.**

(*a*) the creation, nature and regulation of aboriginal settlements within aboriginal areas and aboriginal reserves;

(*b*) prohibiting either absolutely or conditionally and controlling the entry into aboriginal reserves, aboriginal areas, aboriginal inhabited places and aboriginal settlements of any person or any class of persons;

(*c*) providing for the appointment of, and prescribing the qualifications of and the method of appointing, any headman;

(*d*) providing for the registration of aborigines;

(*e*) the manner of evidencing and recording rights of occupancy granted to aborigines under this Ordinance;

(*f*) prohibiting the planting of any specified product on lands over which rights of occupancy have been granted;

(*g*) permitting and regulating the felling of jungle within aboriginal areas and aboriginal reserves;

(*h*) permitting aborigines to take forest produce in aboriginal areas;

(*i*) regulating the taking of wild birds and animals by aborigines;

(*j*) providing for the establishment of schools in aboriginal areas, aboriginal reserves and aboriginal inhabited places, prescribe the curricula of such schools and the qualifications of teachers in such schools;

(*k*) prescribing the terms and conditions upon which aborigines may be employed, and such regulations may provide for the recovery by a Protector on behalf of an aborigine of any wages or salary due to such aborigine in accordance with the said regulations;

(*l*) prohibiting either absolutely or conditionally the entry into or the circulation within any aboriginal area, aboriginal reserve or aboriginal inhabited places of any written or printed matter, any cinematograph film and everything whether of a nature similar to written or printed matter or not containing any visible representation or by its form, shape or in any other manner capable of suggesting words or ideas and every copy and reproduction or substantial reproduction thereof;

(*m*) prohibiting either absolutely or conditionally the sale or gift of any intoxicating liquor as defined in any written law relating to excise for the time being in force in the Federation or any part thereof to any specified aborigine or aboriginal community or within any aboriginal area, aboriginal reserve or aboriginal inhabited place;

(*n*) prescribing the terminology by which aborigines, aboriginal communities and aboriginal ethnic group shall be referred to;

(*o*) imposing penalties in respect of breaches of any regulations made under this Ordinance.

Repeal and saving. Pk. No. 3 of 1939.

20. The Aboriginal Tribes Enactment, 1939, of the State of Perak is hereby repealed:

Provided that—

(*a*) any officer appointed under the said Enactment shall be deemed to have been appointed under this Ordinance; and

(*b*) any areas of land declared under the said Enactment to be aboriginal areas or aboriginal reserves and any rights of occupancy granted under the said Enactment shall be deemed to have been declared or granted under this Ordinance; and

(*c*) any order made under the said Enactment shall continue in force as if it had been made under this Ordinance.

SCHEDULE.

[Section 14 (1).]

FEDERATION OF MALAYA.

State / *Settlement* *of*

THE ABORIGINAL PEOPLES ORDINANCE, 1954.

ORDER UNDER SECTION 14 (1).

To:

WHEREAS it appears to His Excellency the High Commissioner in Nominated Council/His Highness the Ruler in Council that it is desirable that you should be prohibited from entering/remaining in *.....................................being an aboriginal area/reserve/inhabited place so declared by Notification No........ published in the Federation of Malaya Government *Gazette* (.............................Section) dated.........................†:

IT IS HEREBY ORDERED by His Excellency the High Commissioner in Nominated Council/His Highness the Ruler in Council that you be, and you are hereby, prohibited from entering/remaining in the aforesaid aboriginal area/reserve/inhabited place.

Made this...........day of.........................., 19......

Clerk of Council.

---

* Here insert description of the aboriginal area, reserve or inhabited place.

† Strike out the unnecessary words.

APPENDIX D

Semai Senoi Resettled
at Bt. Betong Pahang
Deaths and Births by Months

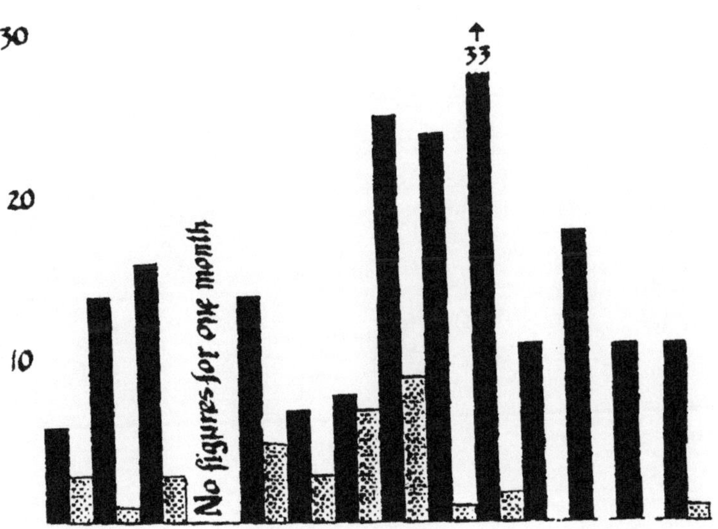

APPENDIX E

Evacuating Aboriginal Communities

P/P DMs Malayan Police Magazine
Vol II No 3 March 1950

Evacuating Aboriginal Communities.

by Major P.D.R. Williams-Hunt, FSA, FRAI.

Adviser on Aborigines, Federation of Malaya.

BEFORE the war very little attention was paid to the Malayan aborigines and usually their only contact with the Government was through the Malay Mukim Penghulus who seldom did anything for them. On the other hand there was considerable contact with the Chinese. Many Chinese took aboriginal wives, settled down in aboriginal communities and lived the same life earning the confidence and respect of the aborigines. Others placed their shops in aboriginal areas and did a great deal to aid the aborigines. The much publicised exploitation of the aborigines did not come from these people so much as from the Malay and Chinese shopkeepers in the towns and casual visitors. Naturally the aborigines came to look on these Chinese as their friends and when the Emergency came, knowing nothing of politics, turned to them rather than to the Government of which they had seen so little. Fortunately for us there has been a change in bandit policy and the aborigines are now being treated rather roughly. The aborigines only wish to be left alone but where they have no protection are bound to do what the bandits demand and deny information to us for fear of reprisals. Time and time again responsible aboriginal headmen tell me that they are heartily sick of the bandits and their demands and would like to help us but can not do so for fear of reprisals. The only alternative is to evacuate them for their own safety as a temporary measure.

It must be remembered that the aborigines are useful members of the Malayan community and are not the menace generally supposed by those who have not had practical experience of them in their own habitat. Not only do they support themselves in foodstuffs but they add materially to the economy of the country by their collection of jungle produce such as rotan, jelutong, bamboos and various gums. For example there would quite likely be a shortage of cane chairs if all the aboriginal groups were to be removed from the jungle. An evacuated aboriginal group suffers considerable hardship since it is denied its source of income from these products, fruit from jungle trees and its own orchards, wild game and raw materials for its own use. These items can not be made up by welfare grants.

Now there is a right and a wrong way to evacuate aboriginal communities and so far most of the cases which have come to my notice have been carried out in very much the wrong way. The result is that many groups now evacuated feel that they are far worse off under our direct administration than they might be with the bandits--the very situation we wish to avoid.

These aborigines are not easy people to deal with and evacuation needs to be carried out in a tactful and systematic way. A little thought will show efficient methods.

Where it is possible to do so it is better to put the aborigines in a position where they themselves ask to be evacuated rather than to rush in wholesale and evacuate them against their will. One way of actuating this is frequent visits by patrols who stay the night in the ladang, generally make friends, pass round tobacco and so on. This may lead to a situation where the aborigines are so threatened by the bandits that they ask to be taken out. Or air attack or shelling nearby may have the same effect. Circumstances will vary from group to group. The Negritos and the Senoi (Sakai) need more careful treatment than the Proto-Malay peoples in the southern part of the country. A false step may result in the whole group fleeing into the jungle as has happened more than once recently.

Now it is essential that before a group is evacuated that the local authorities know well in advance what is happening. The civil authorities are responsible for the welfare of the group once it is evacuated and in several recent cases the aborigines arrived without warning with resultant hardship. Naturally an aboriginal evacuation wants to be kept quiet but the local

District Officer wants to know at an early date —say a month before hand where this can be done—and if the office of the Adviser on Aborigines is contacted well in advance it may be possible to send out a trained member of the staff who has had experience in these evacuations At a later date the Mukim Penghulu of the area in which the aborigines will settle also wants to be told and he may accompany the party since it is his interest that the aborigines bring out everything of value. If an evacuation is out of one District or one State into another the authorities in both areas need to be informed to avoid subsequent friction.

The progress of an evacuation might be shown as a timetable:—

Day 1.	
Arrive in the ladang area and stop the night.	Even where the aborigines have asked to be evacuated they should not be told before hand It is essential to arrive the day before to ensure that people out in the jungle are collected. Nothing should be said about the evacuation the first night
Day 2.	
(a) Put out stops to prevent both the aborigines leaving and any interference by bandits.	
(b) Get the aboriginal headman to call the group together in one place and to count them to ensure that they are all there.	The group will need to be guarded if they are being evacuated against their will.
(c) Explain the reasons for the evacuation stressing that this is only a temporary move and that they will be allowed to return to their own area when circumstances permit Give details of the preparations made for their reception in the area they are going to.	This is best done by the Mukim Penghulu and translated by the headman.
(d) Visit each house with the headman and the head of the house and get an idea of what has to be removed.	The aborigines are very inclined to leave a lot of things behind and then claim they were not allowed to bring them. They must be forced to remove every object that can be shifted whether of apparent value or not.
(e) Get each household to pack up	House by house under guard if group is being evacuated against its will.
(f) Check that everything has been removed.	Make sure that all livestock chicken, dogs etc. are collected.

(g) Destroy the houses.

If this programme is carried out the evacuation should be fairly efficient and without undue hardship.

One or two points need to be amplified.

(a) It can be seen from previous visits if these people have a great deal of barang. If they have more than they can carry themselves an aboriginal carrying party from an already evacuated group should be taken along. They may also be required to carry out sick or old people who can not walk. This again can be found out beforehand. In such a case some form of stretcher may be needed.

(b) If the houses are well built of planks and are not too far from a road or river it will be a saving of funds if a certain quantity of useful material is brought along to build houses in the new areas. It will be only in rare cases that this can be done. Many groups burn their houses on a death. They may object to burning a house on the grounds that such action may cause a death in the near future. In such cases it may be possible to destroy a house another way—i.e. by pulling it down and throwing it in the local river—but where this can not be done the group's pawang might be consulted. He might be able to produce some spell to nullify the results of house burning. Let the aborigines destroy their own houses. They might as well get some fun out of the evacuation.

(c) If it is possible to do so as much foodstuff as can be carried for replanting should be brought along. It is not a practicable proposition to destroy a ladang but fences should be broken down. Usually it is quite impossible to set fire to the average aboriginal crop.

(d) Don't forget to remove any boats or rafts. If they are not used in the evacuation cast them loose down the river or destroy them in some other way.

(e) Finally make a list of anything which does have to be left behind so that proper claims can be submitted.

Circumstances will vary from place to place but if an evacuation is planned on the general lines given above there should be the minimum of hardship. What needs to be avoided is the type of evacuation so often reported to me where the aborigines are pulled out of their houses which are then burnt in front of their eyes without a chance to remove anything and then rushed to an area which is not ready to receive them.

BIBLIOGRAPHY

Primary Sources

Books and Monographs

Anderson, John. *Facsimile Reprint of Political and Commercial Considerations Relative to the Malayan Peninsula and British Settlements in the Straits of Malacca.* Introduction by Dr. J. S. Bastin (original 1824). Singapore: MBRAS, 1965.

Annandale, N. *Fasciculi Malayenses: Anthropological and Zoological Results of an Expedition to Perak and the Siamese Malay States, 1901–1902, Undertaken by N. Annandale and H. C. Robinson.* New York: Longmans, 1903.

Benjamin, J. "In the Long Term: Three Themes in Malayan Cultural Ecology." In *Cultural Values and Human Ecology in South East Asia.* Edited by Karl L. Hutterer, A. Terry Rambo, and George Lovelace. Michigan: Center for South and South East Asian Studies, The University of Michigan, November 27, 1985.

Carey, Iskandar. *Orang Asli The Aboriginal Tribes of Peninsular Malaysia.* Kuala Lumpur: Oxford University Press, 1976.

Cerutti, G. B. *My Friends the Savages. Amongst the Sakais in the Malay Peninsula: Notes and Observations of a Perak Settler (Malay Peninsula) richly illustrated with original photographs taken by the author..* Translated by I. Stone Sapietro. Comense: Tipografia Cooperative, 1908.

Chapman, F. Spencer. *The Jungle is Neutral.* London: Chatto and Windus, 1949.

Clifford, H. *In Court and Kampong.* London: The Richards Press, 1897.

Clutterbuck, R. *The Long Long War.* London: Cassell, 1967.

Dentan, Robert Knox. *The Semai:* A *Non-Violent People of Malaya.* New York: Holt, Rinehart and Winston, 1968.

———. "Notes on Childhood in a Non-violent Context," In *Learning Non-aggression: The Experience of a Non-Literate Society.* Edited by Ashley Montagu. New York: Oxford Press, 1978.

Evans, I. H. N. *The Negritos of Malaya.* Cambridge: Cambridge University Press, 1937.

Follows, R. with Popham, H. *The Jungle Beat: Fighting Terrorists in Malaya, 1952–1961.* London: Cassell, 1990.

Gomes, Alberto, G. "Confrontation and Continuity: Simple Commodity Production Among the Orang Asli." In *Tribal Peoples and Development in Southeast Asia.* Edited by Lim Teck Ghee and Alberto G. Gomes. Kuala Lumpur: University of Malaya, 1990.

Gouldsbury, P. *Jungle Nurse,* London: Jarrolds, 1960.

Henniker, Brig. M.C.A., CBE DSO MC. *Red Shadow over Malaya.* London: Blackwood, 1955.

Holman, Dennis. *Noone of the Ulu.* London: Heinemann, 1958.

Lyttleton, Oliver, Viscount Chandos PC DSO MC LLD. *Memoirs of Lord Chandos.* London: Bodley Head, 1962.

Miller, Harry. *Jungle War in Malaya: The Campaign Against Communism 1948–60.* London: A. Barker, 1972.

Miller, Harry. *Menace in Malaya.* London: Harrap, 1954.

Nicholas, Colin, Tiah Sabak, and Anthony Williams-Hunt. *Orang Asli in the News. The Emergency Years: 1950–1958.* Kuala Lumpur: (privately published), 1989.

Noone, Richard, O. D. *Rape of the Dream People.* London: Hutchinson, 1972.

Parsons, Claudia. *Vagabondage.* London: Chatto and Windus, 1941.

Rennie, F. *Regular Soldier A Life in the New Zealand Army.* Auckland: Endeavour Press, 1986.

Schebesta, Paul. *Among the Forest Dwarfs of Malaya,* 2d. ed. Kuala Lumpur: Oxford University Press, 1973. Orig. 1928.

Skeat, W. W. and Charles Otto Blagden. *Pagan Races of the Malay Peninsula.* London: Macmillan, 1906.

Slimming, John. *Temiar Jungle.* London: John Murray, 1958.

Smith, E. D. *Counter-Insurgency Operations: 1 Malaya and Borneo.* London: Ian Allan, 1985.

Thompson, Robert. *Defeating Communist Insurgency, Experiences from Malaya and Vietnam.* London: Chatto and Windus, 1966.

Trenowden, Ian. *OPS Most Secret, SOE The Malayan Theatre.* London: Kimber, 1978.

Wilkinson, R. J. *Papers on Malay Subjects: Supplement: The Aboriginal Tribes.* Kuala Lumpur: F. M. S. Government Press, 1910.

Williams-Hunt, P. D. R. *An Introduction to the Malayan Aborigines.* Kuala Lumpur: Government Press, 1952.

Newspapers, Magazines

Berita Harian (Malaya)
Malay Mail (Malaya)
Mars and Minerva—Journal of the SAS (London-UK)
Pernloi Gah (Orang Asli News) (Malaya)
Singapore Standard (Singapore)
Soldier—British Army Magazine (United Kingdom)
Straits Budget (Malaya/Singapore)
Straits Times (Malaya/Singapore)
Suara Sam (Malaya/Singapore)
Sunday Mail (Singapore)
Sunday Times (Singapore)
The Times (London-UK)
Time Magazine (USA)
Warta Negara (Malaya)

Theses

Dawson, J. M. A. "Aborigines and the Problem of their Administration." Unpublished manuscript, 1956. (Held privately by J. West, Surrey, UK.)

Nicholas, Colin G. "From Subsistence to Simple Commodity Production: Economic Relations in Two Semai Settlements." Master's thesis, Universiti Pertanian, Malaysia, 1985.

Robarcheck, C.A. "Semai Non-violence, a Systems Approach to Understanding." Ph.D. dissertation, University of California, 1977.

Working Papers

Benjamin, G. "Achievement and Gaps in Orang Asli Research." University of Singapore, 1988.

———. "Process and Structure in Temiar Social Organization." University of Singapore, 1988.

———. "Between Isthmus and Islands: Reflections on Malayan Palaeo-Sociology." University of Singapore, 1986.

Corfield, J. "A Comprehensive Bibliography of Literature Relating to the Orang Asli of West Malaysia, Working Paper 61." Centre of South East Asian Studies, Monash University, Clayton, 1990.

Articles

Benjamin, G. "Temiar Personal Names," *Bijdragen tot de taal-Land-en Volkenkunde* (Martinus Nijhoff) 124 (1968).

———. "The Ethnography of the Orang Asli of Peninsular Malaysia," *Federation Museums Journal, New Series* (Kuala Lumpur) 24 (1979).

———. "Headmanship and Leadership in Temiar Society," *Federation Museums Journal, New Series (* Kuala Lumpur) 13 (1968).

———. "Temiar Social Groupings," *Federation Museums Journal, New Series* (Kuala Lumpur) 11 (1966).

Couillard, Marie-Andree. "The Malays and the Sakai: Some Comments on their Social Relations in the Malaya Peninsula,", *Kajian Malaysia: Journal of Malaysian Studies* (Kuala Lumpur) 2 (1984).

Endicott, K., "The effects of slave raiding on the Aborigines of the Malay Peninsula," *Slavery Bondage and Dependency in South East Asia*. Edited by A. Reid with the assistance of J. Brewster (St. Lucia, 1983).

Hood Salleh, Ilmun Masyarakut: 6. "Orang Asli Perceptions of the Malayan World: A Historical Perspective." *Malaysian Social Science Association* (July–September, KDN1263/84).

Noone, H. D., "Report on the Settlement and Welfare of the Ple-Temian Senoi of the Perak-Kelantan Watershed," *Journal of the Federated States Museums* (Singapore) 19, Part I, (1936).

Ogilvie, C.S. "Che Wong." *Malayan Nature Journal* (Singapore) (1948).

Polunin, Dr. I. V., "The Medical Natural History of Malayan Aborigines." *The Medical Journal of Malaya* 8 (Singapore) 1 and 2 (1953).

Ranft, Captain D.D. "Parachuting in Malaya," *Army Quarterly* (July 1953).

Robarchek, C.A. "Frustration, aggression and the non-violent Semai," *American Ethnologist,* 4 (1977).

Stewart, K. R., "Mental Hygiene and World Peace," *Mental Hygiene,* 38 (New York, 1954).

Stewart, K. R., "The Dream Comes of Age," *Mental Hygiene,* 46 (New York, 1962).

The Senoi Pra'aq: A Brief History and Description, (author unknown) Senoi Pra'aq H.Q., Kuala Lumpur: 1966.

Williams-Hunt, P. D., "A Technique for Anthropology from the Air in Malaya," *Bulletin of The Raffles Museum* (Singapore) series B. No-4 (December 1949).

Williams-Hunt, P .D. "Evacuating Aboriginal Communities," *Malayan Police Magazine* (Kuala Lumpur) 2, no. 3 (1950).

Woodhouse, Captain J. M., MC. "Some Personal Observations on the Employment of Special Forces in Malaya," *Army Quarterly* (April 1955).

Reports

Del Tufo, M. V. *A Report on the 1947 Census of Population,* London: Crown Agents, 1949.

Department of Public Relations, Federation of Malaya. *Communist Banditry in Malaya,* Kuala Lumpur: 1950.

Director of Operations. *The Conduct of Anti-Terrorist Operations in Malaya. 1st Edition,* Kuala Lumpur: 1952.

Government of Malaya, *Weekly Press Summary,* 15 August 1953.

Malayan Union and Federation of Malaya Annual Reports, 1947–57, Kuala Lumpur: Government Press, 1948–58.

Williams-Hunt, P. D. *Notes on the Administration and Recording of Technical Data Relating to the Malayan Aborigine,* compiled by the Department of the Adviser on Aborigines, Federation of Malaya, Kuala Lumpur: 1951.

Documents Consulted

Aboriginal Peoples Ordinance 1954, No 3 of 1954.

Arkib Negara, Kuala Lumpur.

AP/66/6/55–56

DF 787/54

Fed Sec:	12354/50	12865/50
	12663/50	12948/50
	12072/50	13095/50
	12121/50	8916/52
	12198/50	F35400/54
	12029/50	14335/49
	12671/50	14453/49
	FS2203/48	12/21/50
MUS:	63/46	7/49
	24/47	13/54
	11/51	106/53
	118/53	1/49
	2/58	64/48

MU 10263/46

NA 854/54

PK/MU 1156

P/OA l–6l
P/PDM 8/56
P/PDM(PH1)/54
P/PDM/Al/50
P/H 13/48
POA/l/61
UMNO/SG48/47

Federal Legislative Council Proceedings, February 1951–February 1952.

Federal Legislative Council Proceedings, March 1953–January 1954

Federation of Malaya No. 3 of 1954. The Aboriginal Peoples Ordinance, 1954.

Hansard, British Parliamentary Debates, House of Commons, 5th Series, Vol. 499, 30 April 1950, H.M.S.O., 1952.

Hansard, Parliamentary Debates, House of Commons, 5th Series, Vol. 795, 4 February 1970. H.M.S.O. 1970.

Public Record Office, Kew, London—Document Files.
File Numbers DEFE 7–11.
WO. 203, 208, 216, 291, 874.
CO. 537, 820, 871, 873, 927, 928, 1022, 1030, 1033.
GO. 1380–2608.
These files were the sources of the despatches, intelligence reports, signals and situation reports from Malaya Command and FARELF; also of inter-departmental letters, which were quoted in this study.

Selangor Secretariat, Document Numbers:

R.C. Sel. 677/46
675/48
1726/48
1867/48
2907/49
1601/49
1988/50
2297/50
481/50
2079/50
1411/50
1148/51
1519/51
2597/51

Correspondence

Letters were exchanged with the following between 1986–1991 requesting contacts, information, and personal experiences. Copies of the letters are held by the author. The originals of the Blacking letters are held at the National Army Museum, Chelsea, London, UK.

Azizah Bt Kasah Mrs., *Arkib Negara*, Kuala Lumpur.
Blacking, Prof. John, (Deceased) formerly in the Department of Social Anthropology, The Queens University, Belfast.
Boyden, Dr. Peter B., The National Army Museum, Chelsea, London.
Burrows, I. Brig. (Retd.), OBE MC, formerly N.Z. SAS, Auckland, New Zealand.
Carey, Dr Iskandar, KMN, Kuala Lumpur, Malaysia.
Corfield, R. C., Major (Retd.), Shewsbury, England.
Dennis, Prof. Peter, Department of History, Australian Defence Force Academy, Canberra.
Jimin bin Idris, KMN, Director, Jabatan Hal Ehwal Orang Asli, Kuala Lumpur.
Charles-Jones, D. E. T., Lt. Col. (Retd.), (Deceased), formerly seconded from the British Army to Malayan Police Force in 1952 to assist plan and select fort sites—Kergunyah, Victoria.
Kratoska, Dr P., National University of Singapore.
Lim Teck Ghee, Professor, University of Malaya, Kuala Lumpur.
Lim Cheng Leng, KMN, AMN, Former ASP Royal Malaysian Police, Kuala Lumpur.
Levett, R., BEM, Peterborough, England.
Nichola.s, Colin G., Kuala Lumpur.
Tan Sri Hanif Omar, Ketua Polis Negara, Kuala Lumpur.
Paget, J. R. Lt. Col., formerly Australian Military Attache—Kuala Lumpur.
Peacock, E. C. V., Major (Retd.) Royal Engineers.
Haji Ahmad bin Khamis, AMN AMP BPN, Jabatan Hal Ehwal Orang Asli—Kuala Lumpur.
Rennie, F., Col. (Retd.) OBE, N.Z. SAS, Auckland, New Zealand.
Ruslin bin Abdullah, former C.O. Senoi Pra'aq, Kuala Lumpur.
Shaw, C. M. A., formerly Superintendent of Operations, Malayan Police in 1950s—Albury, N.S.W.
Short, A., Prof. University of Aberdeen—Aberdeen, Scotland.
The Viscount Slim, J., Colonel (Retd.) OBE, Chairman, SAS Association —Chelsea, London.
Smith, E. D., Brig. (Retd.), Devon, United Kingdom.
Smith, I. F., Lt. Col. (Qm), MBE, Chelsea, London.
Stockton, W. J., Lt. Col. (Retd.), OBE, Army Historical Branch, Ministry of Defense, Whitehall, London.
West, John, former ASP Malayan Police, Virginia Waters, United Kingdom.
Williams-Hunt, A., (Bah Toneh), Kuala Lumpur, Malaysia.
Woodhouse, J. M. Lt. Col. (Retd.), MBE MC, formerly 22 SAS, Dorset, United Kingdom.

Y. Bag Dato Zaliah Hanum Nor, Ketua Pengarah, Jabatan *Arkib Negara*, Kuala Lumpur.

Zubir Ali, Timbalan Pengarah, Ibu Pejabat Polisi Di Raja, Kuala Lumpur.

Former members of the 22 SAS and Malayan Police who do not wish to be named. Other serving members of the Royal Malaysian Police. Many of the above were also interviewed personally following the exchange of correspondence.

Transcript

Transcript of an interview with Sir Frederick Scherger, 20 January, 1975 by M. Platt, for the National Library, Canberra. Tape 2 track 2:2/1.

Interviews

Ah Soo Choi, former member of MRLA, personal interview by author at Betong and Yala, South Thailand, 14 September and 28 October 1994.

Tuan Syed Zainal Abidin Alsagoff, KMN PTS AMN PPT, C.O. Battalion 20, Senoi Pra'aq, Royal Malaysian POlice, personal interview by author at Bidor, Malaysia, 29 September 1988.

Bah Dek, former Asal Protection Corps member, personal interview by author at Cameron Highlands, Malaysia, 8 July 1990.

Chung Choon Soon, Superintendent, Royal Malaysian Police, Special Branch, personal interview by author at Ipoh, Malaysia, 6 and 7 July 1990.

Benjamin, Dr. Geoffrey, Associate Professor, Department of Sociology, National University of Singapore, personal interview by author at Singapore, 16 September 1988 and 20 June 1990.

Gomes, Dr. Alberto, Department of Sociology, University of Malaysia, now at La Trobe University, Melbourne, personal interview by author at Kuala Lumpur, 26 September 1988.

Bah Hoi, survivor of massacre of Orang Asli, at Cameron Highlands, in 1949, personal interview by Author at Tapah, Malaysia, 7 July 1990.

Lawrence, Desmond, former Special Branch, Royal Malaysian Police, personal interview by author at Ipoh, Malaysia, 30 September 1988 and 6 July 1990.

Lee Ang Sing, former member of MRLA, personal interview by author at Yala, South Thailand, 28 October 1994.

Lim Cheng Leng, KMN, AMN, former ASP, Special Branch, Royal

Malaysian Police, personal interview by author at Kuala Lumpur, 25 June 1990.

Bah Sepidi, former Asal Protection Corps senior member, personal interview by author at Cameron Highlands, Malaysia, 8 July 1990.

Walker, R., former Royal Malaysian Police, former police garrison and fort commander, former Director of Operations Police Field Force, personal interview by author at Kuala Lumpur, Malaysia, 27 September 1988.

Udah Mat bin Long Sor, Orang Asli from Kampar, personal interview by author at Ipoh, Malaysia, 7 July 1990.

Secondary Sources

Books and Monographs

Andaya, Barbara Watson and Leonard Y. *A History of Malaysia.* London: MacMillan, 1982.

Barber, Noel. *The War of the Running Dogs.*London: Collins, 1971.

Baker, W. D. *Dare to Win, The Story of the NZ SAS.* Melbourne: Lothian, 1981.

Blaxland, G. *The Regiments Depart, The British Army 1945–70.* London: William Kimber, 1971.

Cant, R.G. *An Historical Geography of Pahang.* Singapore: Monographs of the Malaysian Branch Royal Asiatic Society No.4, 1973.

Cheh Boon Kheng. *Red Star over Malaya, Resistance and Social Conflict During and After the Japanese Occupation 1941–1946.* Singapore: Singapore University Press, 1987.

Cloake, John. *Templer. Tiger of Malaya: The Life of Field Marshal Sir Gerald Templer.* London: Harrap, 1985. (See comment at end of Bibliography)

Clutterbuck, R. *Guerrillas and Terrorists.* London: Faber and Faber, 1977.

Domhoff, G. W. *The Mystique of Dreams, A Search for Utopia through Senoi Dream Theory.* Berkeley: University of California Press, 1985.

Faraday, Ann G. *Dream Power.* London: Hodder and Staughton, 1972.

Geraghty, Tony. *Who Dares Wins. The Story of the Special Air Service, 1950–1980.* London: Arms and Armour Press, 1980.

Kennedy, J. A. *A History of Malaya 1400–1959.* London: Macmillan, 1962.

Komer, R. W. *The Malayan Emergency in Retrospect: Organization of a Successful Counter Insurgency Effort,* Santa Monica: The Rand Corporation, 1972.

Loh, P. F. S. *The Malay States 1877–1895, Political Changes and Social Policy.* Kuala Lumpur: Oxford University Press, 1969.

Means, P. B. and N. *And the Seed Grew.* Toronto: University of Toronto 1981.

O'Ballance, Edgar. *Malaya: The Communist Insurgent War.* London: Faber and Faber, 1966.

Parkinson, C. Northcote. *Templer in Malaya.* Singapore: Donald Moore, 1954.

Pike, Douglas. *Viet Cong.* Massachusetts: M.I.T. Press, 1966.

Purcell, V. W. *Malaya Communist: or Free.* Stanford: Institute of Pacific Relations, 1954.

Pye, Dr. Lucian Wilmot. *Guerrilla Communism in Malaya: Its Social and Political Meaning.* Princeton: Princeton University Press, 1956.

Rayner, Harry. *Scherger. A Biography of Air Chief Marshal Sir Frederick Scherger.* Australian War Memorial, ACT, 1948.

Reed, A., and J. Brewster, editors. *Slavery, Bondage and Dependency in South East Asia.* St. Lucia: Queensland University Press, 1983.

Robinson, J. B. Perry. *Transformation in Malaya.* London: Secker and Warburg, 1956.

Short, Anthony. *The Communist Insurrection in Malaya 1948–60.* London: Frederick Muller, 1975.

Strawson, John. *A History of the SAS Regiment.* London: Secker and Warburg, 1984.

Stubbs, Richard. *Hearts and Minds in Guerrilla Warfare. The Malayan Emergency 1948–1960.* Singapore: Oxford University Press, 1989.

Warner, P. *The Special Air Service.* London: William Kimber, 1971.

Winstedt, Sir R. O. *Malaya and its History.* London: Hutchinson, 1966.

Winstedt, Sir R. O. *The Malays—A Cultural History.* London: Keegan Paul, 1958.

Winstedt, R. and R. J. Wilkinson. A *History of Perak.* Reprint Number 3. Kuala Lumpur: MBRAS, 1974.

It was necessary to use Cloake in quoting the letters of General Templer. Although the bulk of Field Marshal (his rank when he died) Templer's papers are in the National Army Museum, they are not its property. As explained by the Museum's Head of Archives, "They have been neither accessioned nor catalogued, but the Director is in the process of promoting discussions with the Templer family to see if the papers may enter the public domain."

INDEX